The Best Name for
Your Baby

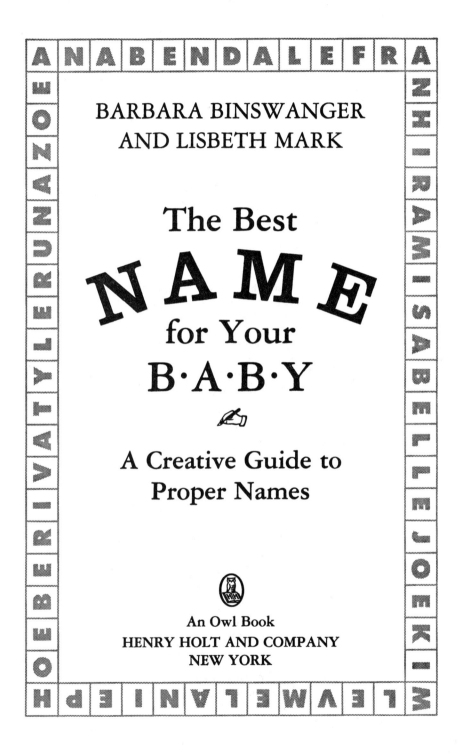

BARBARA BINSWANGER
AND LISBETH MARK

The Best

NAME

for Your

B·A·B·Y

A Creative Guide to
Proper Names

An Owl Book
HENRY HOLT AND COMPANY
NEW YORK

DEDICATED TO
SAMUEL McKENZIE AND MARGARET ROSE

Published by Henry Holt and Company, Inc.,
115 West 18th Street, New York, New York 10011.
Published in Canada by Fitzhenry & Whiteside Limited,
195 Allstate Parkway, Markham, Ontario L3R 4T8.

Library of Congress Cataloging-in-Publication Data
Binswanger, Barbara.
The best name for your baby : a creative guide to proper names /
Barbara Binswanger and Lisbeth Mark.
p.   cm.
"An Owl book."
Includes index.
ISBN 0-8050-0877-2 (pbk.)
1. Names, Personal—Dictionaries.   I. Mark, Lisbeth.   II. Title.
CS2377.B48   1990
929.4'03—dc20   89-32944
                                                          CIP

Henry Holt books are available at special discounts
for bulk purchases for sales promotions, premiums,
fund-raising, or educational use. Special editions
or book excerpts can also be created to specification.

For details contact:
Special Sales Director
Henry Holt and Company, Inc.
115 West 18th Street
New York, New York 10011

Designed by Kate Nichols
Printed in the United States of America
3   5   7   9   10   8   6   4   2

INTRODUCTION

How to Use This Book

For most parents deciding what to name the baby is much tougher than deciding to have a baby. Couples who share tastes in movies, books, and furniture are often horrified by their partner's penchant for names like Silas or Ethel. The name that one perceives as charming and old-fashioned the other sees fit only for a ninety-year-old. What one spouse considers classy, the other sees as horribly pretentious. Disagreements are inevitable.

We can't guarantee that this book will make the selection process any less difficult. In fact, it may become even more complicated as you read through choices you hadn't considered and opinions you haven't asked for. But rest assured, the book is packed with sound advice and a sense of humor that will make the process of selecting a name for your baby, at the very least, entertaining.

The first thing you may notice as you browse through *The Best Name for Your Baby* is that we have not divided them in the usual way, that is, into boys' names and girls' names. Since traditional masculine names are increasingly used as girls' names, and since so many families are interested in non-sex-specific names, we think it best to let everyone make their own decisions as to which names are appropriate to which sex. Accordingly we have combined boys' and girls' names into one alphabetized list.

To make it easier for you to try out variations on names, we have grouped the entries into clusters. These clusters are organized alphabetically by the "Source," or most basic, name; e.g., "John." Each "Source" name is followed by one or more "Relatives." As in real life, "Relative" carries a variety of meanings. A name might be included as a relative because it is related etymologically—that is, it comes from the same root. Or it might be a nickname, an alternate spelling, perhaps a foreign variation. So under "John" you will find "Jonathan, Johnny," and so on.

We have also provided an index to the "Relatives." If, for example, you are looking for the name "Georgina" and it hasn't occurred to you that you might find it under the "Source" name "Georgia," check the index. You will find a listing for it there that will refer you back to the proper "Source" name.

Another element included for each source name is its derivation, or derivations. We were surprised to discover how often our research turned up very different roots for the same name. "Farrah," for example, means both "wild ass" and "beautiful." Give that some thought the next time you see Ms. Fawcett.

Under the heading "Namesakes" you'll find a list of well-known people, fictional characters, or places that carry that particular name. Generally there will also be some additional comment or piece of information: a historical tidbit, a word about the name's current popularity, or simply our opinion of the name. Although our opinions have a considerable amount of thought and research behind them, you are, of course, free to ignore them.

The essays and lists found throughout the book offer advice, suggestions, sources, and names you won't find anywhere else. But we have not exhausted the possibilities. Ideas for names come from everywhere. Read movie and television credits, peruse the wedding announcements, check out racing forms, rediscover the Bible, consult your roadmap. And read the birth announcements or cradle roll in your local newspaper—this may give you some fresh ideas and will also help you discover (and perhaps avoid) the names popular in your area.

Once you've narrowed your choices, you might consider getting family and friends more closely involved. Barbara and Jim mailed out a ballot listing their top ten choices for a girl and the top ten for a boy (they open-mindedly left room for write-in suggestions) and asked everyone to vote. Not only did they have 100 percent participation, everyone made comments as well. The entire process was great fun, and they are sure that daughter Meg will someday enjoy looking over everyone's opinions and the "names she might have had."

The Ten Basic Rules of Name Selection

1. Check out the potential initials. A.C.E. is great; B.M. and P.P. will cause no end of trouble.

2. Avoid any combination of names that may be subject to scatological interpretation by eight-year-old boys. (See rule 1.)

3. We live in the computer age. Give your child a name that is short enough to fit into the allotted number of little blocks on the Social Security application.

4. Resist the temptation to be clever. Names like Jack Frost and Ima Hogg are really not funny.

5. Keep a sense of proportion. If your last name has more vowels than consonants or is otherwise complex, keep the first name simple.

6. Remember that children grow up. Consider how that adorable name will sound on a fifty-year-old.

7. Remember, too, that kids are kids for a long time. If you give your child a weighty name, make certain there is a lively nickname available.

8. Give your child the same last name as at least one of the parents. This sounds self-evident, but reports are in that some parents are picking totally new last names for their children. Whether this reflects dissatisfaction with their own surnames or is a misguided attempt to be nonsexist is unclear. Whatever the motivation, it is an awkward practice.

9. Ask your closest relatives how they feel about your favorite name. If your mother is going to wince every time you mention it, you might be better off picking something else.

10. Consider your roots. Combining first and last names that represent distinctly different ethnic backgrounds has been known to provoke a giggle. Irish names seem to be the exception to this rule; these days Irish names seem to go with everything.

But Can You Dance to It?

Names have a sound and a rhythm. And as much as you might like a name on its own, it just may sound awkward when paired with your last name. As you play with combinations of names, keep the following ideas in mind:

1. Alliteration within the name. Some people love it, some people don't, but you can certainly consider matching the first letter of the first name with the first letter of your last name.

2. Alliteration within the family. You can give all your children names beginning with the same letter. If you and your spouse have first names that begin with the same letter, you've already established a pattern that can be continued with your offspring. This can get complicated, and to some a little precious, if you're planning a large family. But it does make it possible to hand down monogrammed shirts.

3. Syllabic rhythm. The traditional rule is to match names of uneven syllables, that is, a multisyllabic name with a two-syllable or monosyllabic name. We don't necessarily agree with it. Elizabeth Montgomery sounds just as good to us as Elizabeth Dole.

4. Pronunciation. "*I*-van" or "I-*van*"? It's up to you, but remember if you choose the more unusual pronunciation, a certain amount of mispronunciation is inevitable. Throughout her life she'll be admonishing, "Yes, it's spelled 'Karen,' but it's pronounced 'Karn.' "

Diminutives

Diminutives are a fact of life. You cannot blithely name your child Robert or James and expect it to stick. Bobby or Jimmie—or Bob or Jim—is bound to come out the first time he ventures on a playground. No matter that your family and closest friends know to call the little tyke Thomas, somebody will be calling him Tommy before he's out of the crib. The more formal name *can* stick; it just takes hard work and constant correcting. If you already dislike the accepted diminutive, consider discarding the name. Pick something like Brook, Devin, Morgan, or Emory.

Remember, though, that people will still have an irresistible urge to make your child's name friendlier. What are his teammates going to call him? Her friends? And later on, his subordinates? Her partners at the firm?

The basic rule governing this situation is very simple. One-syllable names have a "y" or an "ie" tacked on to the end, whereas a multisyllabic name has one or more syllables lopped off. Thus Jim becomes Jimmy, and Darcy becomes Darce. There is some flexibility with this rule, and, as with manners, once you know the rule you are free to ignore it.

Giving Your Child a Family Name as a First Name

For generations bluebloods have been giving their offspring the mother's maiden name as a first name. There are many reasons for this. It is reassuring to a child to be given a sense of family; the use of the surname promotes a sense of continuity. The child soon realizes that he or she is someone out of the ordinary and performs that way. The cognomen is a reminder to all of just what the antecedents are—a person named Du Pont Smith is going to get a better table at Bookbinder's in Philadelphia than you are.

But remember, too, that many names that began as surnames have been taken over by the mainstream. In fact there is no reason not to name your child Binghamton Jones even if there is not a Binghamton to be found in your family tree. Who will ever know for sure? Of course many surnames don't lend themselves easily to use as a first name. Schwarzenegger and Heifetz are perfectly sturdy Middle European surnames, but life is hard enough without saddling a child with one of those as a first name.

The Question of Androgyny

Can you give a boy's name to a girl?

The answer, of course, is a resounding yes. Androgynous names are now in vogue. In fact, for this book, we have resisted the usual arrangement of boys' names in one section and girls' names in another for this very reason.

Sometimes the decision to give a girl a boy's name is accompanied by a change in spelling. Dylan becomes Dillon, Francis becomes Frances,

Sidney slides easily into Sydney. Other names are truly androgynous no matter how they are spelled. Jordan, Blair, and Brook are classics of the genre.

You should also be aware that giving a girl's name to a boy is extremely treacherous. Shirley Povich, the great Washington sportswriter, is forever explaining his name. So resist the temptation to name your boy Evelyn no matter how many times you've read Mr. Waugh's *Brideshead Revisited*.

Alternate Spellings

A very popular tactic these days is to take an ordinary name and give it an extraordinary spelling. To take an example, Nancy, Julie Anne, and Susanna are nice, simple names, but with just a twist of the alphabet they become Nansee, Julienne, and Siouxhannah. Double the consonants, change the vowels; there are endless ways to play this game, and we give many examples throughout this book. But remember that if you do opt for the unusual spelling, your child will undoubtedly endure a lifetime of saying "No, it's Leesa with a double 'e.' "

*The Best Name for
Your Baby*

A

In 1983, the Chinese government was faced with a multitude of citizens in northeastern China with identical names. An official guide for naming babies was printed and distributed introducing new choices.

Aaron: Hebrew for "shining light" or "high mountain" and Arabic for "messenger." Aaron was Moses's brother. This name has been the surprise hit of the 1980s.
Relatives: Aron, Ahron, Arron
Namesakes: Aaron Burr, Hank Aaron

Abbott: From the Arabic and Aramaic for "father." Especially popular in the nineteenth century.
Relatives: Abbot, Abba, Abbe
Namesakes: Abbott and Costello, Abba Eban

Abby: Latin for "head of a monastery." A nickname for Abigail, but also nice on its own terms.
Relatives: Abbey, Abbe, Abbie
Namesakes: "Dear Abby," Abbie Hoffman, Abbey Road, Abbe Lane

Abel: From the Hebrew for "breath." Adam and Eve's son, killed by his brother Cain. This name was very common in the Middle Ages.
Relatives: Able, Abell
Namesake: Elie Abel

Abelard: Old German for "resolute" and Middle English for "keeper of the abbey larder." He was the twelfth-century monk who seduced Heloise; their love letters are far better known than his theological writings.

Abigail: From the Hebrew for "a father's joy." Abigail has an Old World charm and has been consistently popular in the twentieth century.
> *Relatives:* Abagail, Abigayle, Abigale, Abby, Abbie, Gail
> *Namesakes:* Abigail Adams, Abigail Van Buren

Abner: From the Hebrew for "father of light." Popular in the nineteenth century.
> *Namesakes:* Abner Doubleday, "Li'l Abner"

Abraham: From the Hebrew for "father of a multitude." Almost a guarantee that your child will grow up to be very wise. Bram is a nice nickname that works well on its own.
> *Relatives:* Abram, Avraham, Avram, Avrom, Abe, Abie, Abra, Ibrahim, Braham, Bram
> *Namesakes:* Abraham Lincoln, Bram Stoker, F. Murray Abraham

Acadia: Origin unknown, but probably related to the Acadians of Canada (Nova Scotia). A nice melodic sound; this works well as a middle name.
> *Relatives:* Cadie, Caddie
> *Namesake:* Acadia National Park

Ackley: Old English for "meadow of oaks." This is one of those names that sounds as if it's been in the family for generations.

Acton: Old English for "town with many oaks." Anne Brontë picked this name for her pseudonym, "Acton Bell."

Ada: From the Hebrew for "adorned" and Latin for "of noble birth." A short, sweet palindromic name.
> *Relatives:* Adalia, Adalee, Adara, Adah, Eda, Etta
> *Namesake:* Ada Louise Huxtable

Adam: From the Hebrew for "earth." This is it, the original boy's name. Extremely popular in the nineteenth century; peaked again in the 1970s.
> *Relatives:* Adams, Adamson, Adie
> *Namesakes:* Adam Clayton Powell, Adam Smith, "Adam Cartwright"

Addison: Old English for "Adam's son."
> *Relatives:* Adison, Addisen
> *Namesakes:* Joseph Addison, "David Addison"

Adelaide: French variation of the German for "noble kind." Popular in nineteenth-century England, it was given a boost in the United States around the turn of the century by the popular song "Sweet Adeline." But that variation suffers today from its barbershop-quartet image. Try one of the others.
Relatives: Adalia, Adeline, Aline, Adele, Adell, Adelle, Della

Adena: From the Hebrew for "delicate."
Relatives: Adina, Adinna, Adenna
Namesake: Adena (Ohio)

Adie: Most often used as a nickname, but this occasionally stands on its own.
Relatives: Addie, Addy
Namesake: Addie Joss

Adlai: From the Hebrew for "refuge of God" and Arabic for "just." A strong but seldom-used name.
Namesake: Adlai Stevenson

Adler: German for "eagle." More common as a last name, it makes an impressive first name, too.
Namesake: Mortimer Adler

Adolph: German for "noble wolf." For obvious reasons, its post–World War II use has been limited. Adolphus is a possibility, with Dolph the preferred nickname.
Relatives: Adolf, Adolphe, Adolphus, Adolfus
Namesake: Adolphe Menjou

Adrian: A variation of "Hadrian," Greek for "rich" and Latin for "dark one." Very popular among popes. Sylvester Stallone gave it a seemingly permanent prefix with the line "Yo, Adrienne" in the *Rocky* movies.
Relatives: Adrien, Adrienne, Adria, Adrea, Adriana, Adrianna, Adrie, Hadrian
Namesake: Adrienne Rich

Agatha: Greek for "good." Agatha was a third-century saint. The French spelling, Agathe, livens this one up, but may present pronunciation problems.
Relatives: Agathe, Agace, Aggie, Aggy
Namesake: Agatha Christie

Agnes: Latin for "lamb." Agnes was an extremely popular saint in the third century. John Keats wrote a very sensual poem of the same name in the nineteenth century.

Relatives: Agnese, Agnesa, Aggie, Aggy, Agenta, Inez, Ines, Nessa, Neza, Ynes, Ynez

Namesakes: Saint Agnes, Agnes de Mille, Agnes Moorehead, *Agnes of God*

Ahab: From the Hebrew for "uncle." Both a king of Israel and the hunter of Moby Dick had this name.

Namesake: "Ahab the Arab"

Aida: Old English for "joyful." A grand opera by Verdi; the elephants come on stage for this one.

Namesake: princess of Ethiopia held captive in Egypt

Aidan: Middle English for "help."

Namesakes: Saint Aidan, Aidan Quinn

Aiken: Old English for "made of oak."

Namesakes: Conrad Aiken, William Aiken

Ainsley: Scottish for "my meadow." A delicate name.

Relatives: Aynsley, Ainsly, Ainslee, Ainsworth
Namesake: Aynsley china

Alan: Gaelic for "handsome." The feminine form, Alana, is currently in vogue. The "y" variations are also an interesting choice for a girl.

Relatives: Allen, Allan, Alana, Alain, Alaina, Alyn, Allyn, Alun
Namesakes: Alan Alda, Alan Shepard, Alana Davis, Alana Hamilton

Alastair: A Scottish version of Alexander. Conventionally a boy's name, occasionally used for a girl.

Relatives: Alistair, Alistaire, Alastaire, Alister, Alaster, Alasdair
Namesakes: Alistair Cooke, Alistair MacLean

Alban: From the Latin for "white," whence comes "albino." Albion was an early name for England, probably first used to describe the white cliffs of Dover.

Relatives: Alben, Albin, Albion
Namesakes: Saint Alban, Alben Barkley, Albany (N.Y.)

Albert: A German compound of "noble" and "bright." Extremely popular at the turn of the century both in this country and abroad, perhaps because of Queen Victoria's husband, Prince Albert.

Relatives: Alberta, Alberto, Albertina, Albertine, Albertus, Albrecht, Adelbert, Aubert, Elbert, Bertel, Berty, Bertie, Al, Alby, Albie

Namesakes: Albert Einstein, Albert Schweitzer, Alberto Salazar, Alberta Hunter

Alcander: Origin unknown.

Relatives: Alcindor, Alcandor

Namesake: Lew Alcindor

Alcina: A Greek enchantress who reigned over an island of sensual oblivion. She was celebrated in Handel's opera, *Alcina.*

Alcott: Old English for "old cottage," but its literary associations are what come to mind today.

Relatives: Alcot, Walcott, Walcot

Namesakes: Amos Bronson Alcott, Louisa May Alcott

Alden: From the Middle English for "antique." A real Plymouth Rock of a name.

Relatives: Aldan, Aldwin

Namesake: "Why don't you speak for yourself, John (Alden)?"

Alder: Middle English for a type of birch tree and Old English for "revered one."

Relatives: Elder, Aldus

Aldous: From the Old German for "old wealth."

Relatives: Aldus, Aldo

Namesakes: Aldous Huxley, Aldo Ray

Aldrich: Old English for "old king." This will look good on his prep-school diploma.

Relatives: Aldrych, Aldred, Aldren, Aldridge

Namesakes: Thomas Bailey Aldrich, "Henry Aldrich," Nelson Aldrich Rockefeller

Alexander: Greek for "protector of mankind." Extremely popular in all its forms, especially in royal circles. Take your pick.

Relatives: Alec, Alek, Aleks, Alex, Alesandro, Alessandro, **Alejo**, Alexei, Alysander, Alexandre, Alejandro, Aleksander, Alastair, Iksander, Ixsander, Sandro, Sander, Sanders, Sandor, Sandy, Sandie, Sacha, Sasha, Xander

Namesakes: Alexander the Great, Alexander Graham Bell, Alec Guinness

Alexandra: Feminine form of "Alexander." A favorite of models and soap opera divas, as well as princesses and empresses.

Relatives: Alexa, Alexia, Alexis, Alexandria, Alesandra, Alessandra, Allesandra, Aleksey, Alexine, Aleka, Alya, Aliki, Alejandra, Lexy, Lexie, Sandra, Zandra, Sanie, Sandy

Namesakes: Empress Alexandra of Russia, Alexis Smith, Sandra Day O'Connor, Zandra Rhodes

Alfred: Old English for "wise counsel." Seldom used these days despite some terrific antecedents.

Relatives: Alf, Alfric, Alfie, Alfrid, Allie, Elfred, Fred, Freddie

Namesakes: Alfred the Great, Alfred Hitchcock, "Alfred Doolittle," "Alf"

Alger: Old German for "noble warrior." Strongly associated with famous namesakes Horatio Alger and Alger Hiss.

Relatives: Elgar, Elger

Namesake: Sir Edward Elgar

Algernon: Old French for "mustachioed." "Algie" is the nickname, so be careful.

Namesakes: Algernon Swinburne, *Flowers for Algernon*

Algren: Origin unknown and more familiar as a surname, but it has a certain ring to it.

Namesake: Nelson Algren

Ali: A variation of "Allah" and American Indian for "little."

Namesakes: Ali Baba, Ali MacGraw, Muhammad Ali

Alice: From the Old German for "noble" and Greek for "truth." It was Lewis Carroll's "Alice" who journeyed through Wonderland and also stepped through the looking glass.

Relatives: Alicia, Alise, Alison, Allison, Alyse, Alix, Alyce, Alexis, Alika, Aliki, Ali, Allie, Ally

Namesakes: Alice Liddell, Alice B. Toklas, Alice Roosevelt Longworth, *Alice Adams,* Alison Lurie, "Kate and Allie"

Alida: Greek for "beautifully dressed." Perfect for the child of a compulsive shopper.
Relatives: Aleda, Aletta, Alette, Allida, Allidia, Alidia, Lida

Allard: Old English for "noble and brave."
Relative: Alard
Namesake: Allard K. Lowenstein

Allegra: Latin for "brisk and cheerful." This name has cultural overtones perhaps because Allegro is a musical notation for a composition that is to be played at a fast tempo.
Namesake: Allegra Kent

Allston: Old English for "Al's town."
Relatives: Alston, Alton
Namesakes: Alton Maddox, Walter Alston

Alma: Latin for "soul" or "nourishing."
Namesakes: Alma Schindler, alma mater, Alma College

Alphonse: Old German for "noble estate." Seldom used these days.
Relatives: Alfonse, Alfons, Alphonso, Alonso, Alonzo, Alonza
Namesake: Alphonse D'Amato

Althea: Greek for "healer."
Relatives: Allie, Alethea, Alithea, Thea
Namesake: Althea Gibson

Alvin: Old English for "elf wine." A favorite cartoon friend.
Relative: Alwyn
Namesakes: Alvin Ailey, "Alvin the Chipmunk"

Amadeus: Latin for "love of God." Strongly associated with the play and film about Mozart.
Relatives: Amado, Amadis
Namesake: Wolfgang Amadeus Mozart

Amanda: From the Latin for "love." Enormously popular. Singer Barry Manilow paid tribute to the nickname "Mandy."

Relatives: Mandy, Mandie
Namesakes: Amanda Blake, Amanda Plummer, Amanda Pays

Amber: Arabic for "yellow-brown." Making a deserved comeback, and a nice middle name, too.
Relative: Ambert
Namesake: Forever Amber

Ambrose: From the Greek for "immortal." Ambrosia was the mythical drink of the gods and was thought to bring immortality to anyone who tasted it.
Relative: Ambrosia
Namesakes: Saint Ambrose, Ambrose Bierce

Amelia: From the Latin for "flatterer." Similar feel to Amanda, but not as trendy. Yet.
Relatives: Amelie, Amalia, Amalie, Amela, Amala, Emelia
Namesakes: Amelia Earhart, "Amelia Bedelia"

Ames: From the Latin for "loves." Simple, clean, classy, not overused.
Namesakes: Ames Brothers, Ames (Iowa)

Amherst: Originally a British place name. A little pretentious, perhaps, even for the most devoted alumnus. Lord Jeffrey Amherst was a British general who refused a command in the Colonies during the American Revolution.
Namesake: Amherst College

Amon: Irish variation of Edmund. A nice name, the Irish "Eamon" spelling is particularly attractive.
Relatives: Eamon, Eammon
Namesake: Eamonn Coghlan

Amory: From the Latin for "loving." Terrific choice for boy or girl, whatever the spelling.
Relatives: Emory, Emery
Namesakes: Amory Houghton, Cleveland Amory, Emory University

Amos: Hebrew for "troubled." Pretty name, but reconsider if you already have a child named Andy.
Namesakes: Amos Otis, Amos Oz

Amy: Latin for "beloved." One of the great names, conventional but not plain, popular but not trendy.
Relatives: Aimee, Amia, Amity
Namesakes: "Amy March," Amy Alcott, Amy Irving, Anouk Aimee

Anabelle: A lacy name with a Victorian sensibility. But Queen Elizabeth deemed it too "yuppie" for the baby who is Princess Beatrice of York.
Relatives: Anabel, Annabel, Ann, Anna, Belle, Bella, Annabelle, Annabella
Namesake: "Annabel Lee"

Anais: Origin unknown, possibly a variation of Ann. However you pronounce this name ("*Ah*–na–ees," "Ah–*nay*–iss"), it's a beauty. And a lovely perfume as well.
Namesake: Anaïs Nin

Anastasia: Greek for "resurrection." A very rhythmic name that conjures up images of old Russia.
Relatives: Anastasio, Anastace, Anastasius, Anastice, Anastasie, Stacia, Stasa, Stacy, Stacey, Natasha, Tasia, Tasha
Namesake: Grand Duchess Anastasia

Anatole: Greek for "from the east." The kind of name that might be appreciated by an adult, but tough to live with for a kid.
Relative: Anatoly
Namesakes: Anatole Broyard, Anatoly Scharansky, Anatole France

Ancel: Old German for "deity." Underutilized, would work equally well for a future athlete or artist.
Relatives: Ansel, Ancell, Ancelot, Anselm
Namesakes: Saint Anselm, Ansel Adams

Anderson: "Son of Andrew." Most common as a surname, gaining popularity as a first name. You can get away with this one even if it's not a family name.
Relatives: Andersen, Anders, Andy
Namesakes: Hans Christian Andersen, Sherwood Anderson

André: French variation of "Andrew." An apropos choice if you have French antecedents, and becoming popular even among those who don't.
Namesakes: André Malraux, André the Giant, André Dawson

Andrew: From the Greek for "valiant, courageous." A classic. The feminine form, Andrea, has always been popular but never to the degree of the masculine version.

Relatives: Anders, Andres, André, Andrei, Andros, Andy, Andie, Andrews, Drew

Namesakes: Saint Andrew, Andrew Young, Andrew Jackson, Andrew Carnegie, Andrea Jeager, Andrea Mitchell, Andrea Martin, Drew Barrymore, *Andrea Doria,* "Andy Hardy"

Angela: From the Greek for "heavenly messenger."

Relatives: Angelica, Ange, Angel, Angell, Angelo, Angelico, Angie, Anjelica

Namesakes: Angela Davis, Anjelica Huston, Angel Cordero, Angie Dickinson

Angus: From the Gaelic for "superb" or "unique." According to Gaelic mythology, Angus was the god of love. Aonghus Turimleach is a legendary figure in Scottish history.

Namesakes: Angus Wilson, Black Angus cattle

Annabeth: A delightful compound name.

Relative: Anabeth

Annalynn: This compound name is sweetly euphonic.

Relatives: Annalynne, Analyn, Analynne

Namesake: Annalynn Swan

Anne: From the Hebrew for "gracious." Always in good taste, with or without the "e."

Relatives: Ann, Anna, Annis, Annys, Anya, Anika, Annie, Annice, Anita, Anca, Anneka

Namesakes: Princess Anne of England, Anne Boleyn, Ann Landers, Anne Archer, *Anne of Green Gables*

Annette: A French variation of "Ann." For many, this name will always conjure up images of beach blankets, Mouseketeers, and peanut butter.

Namesakes: Annette Funicello, Annette O'Toole

Anson: Anglo-Saxon for "son of a nobleman" or "son of Ann or Hans." A good, clear Celtic sound.

Relatives: Ansen, Ansonia, Hansen, Hanson

Namesake: Anson Williams

Anthony: From the Latin for "priceless" and Greek for "flourishing." The classic for an Italian-American boy; Antonia for a girl is much less common and quite nice.

Relatives: Antonius, Antoine, Anton, Antony, Antonia, Antonio, Antoinette, Antoinetta, Tony, Toni, Tonio, Tonia, Tonya, Toinette

Namesakes: Anthony Quayle, Mark Antony, Toni Morrison, *My Ántonia*

April: From the Latin for "blooming" and the spring month.

Relatives: Avril, Aprille, Ava

Namesakes: Jean Avril, Ava Gardner

Arabelle: German for "beautiful eagle." A unique turn on the more popular Anabelle.

Relatives: Arabel, Arrabelle, Arabella

Aram: Assyrian for "high place." An Old Testament name that doesn't get much mainstream use today. Aram was Noah's grandson.

Namesake: Aram Saroyan

Archibald: Anglo-Saxon for "bold prince." The nicknames take the starch out of this hefty moniker.

Relatives: Arch, Archie, Archy, Arkady, Arky

Namesakes: Archibald MacLeish, Archie Bell and the Drells, Archie Leach, "Archie"

Arden: From the Latin for "passionate" and an English place name. Lovely for a girl, chancy for a boy.

Relatives: Ardelia, Ardis, Ardon

Namesakes: Eve Arden, Elizabeth Arden, Forest of Arden

Argus: Greek for "bright." In Greek mythology the name of a creature with one hundred eyes, the builder of Jason's ship, and Odysseus's dog. But it still sounds Scottish to us.

Ariadne: In Greek mythology, Ariadne was the daughter of King Minos of Crete. She gave Theseus the thread that led him out of the labyrinth and was subsequently dumped for her trouble.

Relatives: Arianne, Arianna, Aria

Namesakes: Arianna Stassinopoulos, *Ariadne auf Naxos* (by Richard Strauss)

Ariel: From the Hebrew for "lion of God" and Shakespeare's sprite from *The Tempest*. Yours will not be the only Ariel in the playground.
    Relatives: Arial, Aryel, Ario, Ari, Ariella, Ariela
    Namesake: Ariel Durant

Arion: Arion was a Greek poet who was rescued by dolphins after being thrown into the sea.

Arland: Derived from Orlando. A poetic group of names.
    Relatives: Arles, Arleigh, Arlo, Arly, Arlie, Arlen, Arliss, Arlyss
    Namesake: Arlo Guthrie

Arlene: Origin unknown, possibly derived from Charles.
    Relatives: Arleen, Arline, Arlette, Arlynn, Arlyn, Arleine
    Namesake: Arlene Francis

Armand: A variation of Herman, but a stronger sound closer to its original meaning of warrior.
    Relatives: Armond, Herman, Hermann
    Namesakes: Armand Hammer, Armand Assante

Arnold: From the German for "eagle" and "powerful." Schwarzenegger is helping dispel a wimpy image.
    Relatives: Arnaud, Arnault, Arnie, Arnald, Arno, Arne, Arnell, Arnel, Arness, Arnot, Arnald
    Namesakes: Arnold Palmer, Benedict Arnold

Arnon: From the Hebrew for "rushing stream." Seldom-used name from the Old Testament.

Artemis: Originally the Greek goddess of hunting and childbirth but now considered masculine as well as feminine.
    Relatives: Artemus, Artie
    Namesake: Artemus Ward

Arthur: Welsh for "bear hero" and shrouded in the mists of British history. A name that deserves to be more popular than it is currently.
    Relatives: Artur, Art, Arta, Artie, Arty, Arturo, Arte, D'Artagnan
    Namesakes: King Arthur, Arturo Toscanini, Artie Shaw, Art Garfunkel

Asa: From the Hebrew for "healer."
    Namesakes: Asa Briggs, "Asa Buchanan"

Asher: From the Hebrew for "fortunate."
Relatives: Asser, Ashe, Ashbel, Anschel
Namesake: Arthur Ashe

Ashley: Old English for "ash-tree." Almost exclusively used for girls these days.
Relatives: Ashleigh, Ashford, Ash, Ashe, Ashby, Ashlie, Ashling
Namesakes: Ashley Putnam, Ashley Montagu, "Ashley Wilkes"

Astin: A variation of August. A nice name but probably confusing if your last name is Martin.
Relatives: Austin, Austen
Namesakes: Austin Dickinson (Emily's brother), Austin Pendleton, Jane Austen, John Astin, Aston Martin automobiles

Astrid: From the Greek for "star" and Old Norse for "super strength." A good choice for a New Age family.
Relatives: Astra, Astera, Astred, Asta, Astyr
Namesake: Astrid Gilberto

Athol: A Scottish place name. Lends itself to being deviously mispronounced.
Relative: Avery
Namesake: Athol Fugard

Aubrey: German for "elf rule." Interesting.
Namesakes: Aubrey Beardsley, John Aubrey

Auburn: Latin for "fair." A seldom-used color name.
Relatives: Alban, Aubin
Namesake: Auburn University

Audrey: Old English for "noble strength." Shakespeare's choice for the country wench in *As You Like It*.
Relatives: Audry, Audra, Audey, Audie
Namesakes: Audrey Hepburn, Audie Murphy

August: From the Latin for "exalted." This one gets better the more you hear it.
Relatives: Augustine, Augustina, Augie, Augustus, Augusta, Gus, Gussy, Gussie, Gusta
Namesakes: Augusta Wilson, August Busch, Augustus Caesar

Aurelia: From the Latin for "gold."
  Relatives: Aurora, Aurea, Aurore, Aurelie

Averill: Old English for "boar-warrior" and a variation of April.
  Relatives: Averil, Averell, Everill, Everil, Haverel, Haverhill
  Namesakes: Averell Harriman, Earl Averill

Aviva: From the Hebrew for "springtime." This lively name sounds like a stadium cheer.
  Relatives: Avital, Avi, Avia, Avivah

Axel: Swedish for "divine source of life."
  Relative: Axtel
  Namesakes: Axel Munthe, "Axel Foley"

Azura: Persian for "sky-blue." A name with a New Age quality to it. Give this child a crystal for a baby present.
  Relative: Azure

With a Bullet

Throughout the book you will find various "Top Ten" and "Top Twenty" name lists. For the United States we have included lists for only those states that could provide us with complete birth–name records; in fact, only a few states can do so. Be leery of "national" lists. These are generally based on small samples and are not always accurate reflections of naming trends.

And speaking of trends, let's first have a look at California.

CALIFORNIA TOP TWENTY
1986

Girls	*Boys*
Jessica	Michael
Ashley	Christopher
Jennifer	Daniel
Amanda	David

Sarah	Matthew
Stephanie	Andrew
Nicole	Robert
Melissa	Ryan
Elizabeth	Joshua
Christina	Anthony
Vanessa	James
Michelle	Jose
Brittany	Joseph
Heather	Jonathan
Lauren	John
Megan	Nicholas
Amber	Jason
Maria	Brandon
Danielle	Eric
Crystal	Steven

1981

Jennifer	Michael
Jessica	Christopher
Sarah	David
Melissa	Daniel
Michelle	Matthew
Nicole	Robert
Elizabeth	Jason
Maria	Joshua
Amanda	John
Christina	Ryan
Stephanie	Jose
Amber	Joseph
Lisa	James
Heather	Brian
Rebecca	Justin
Amy	Anthony
Tiffany	Jonathan
Crystal	Richard
Kimberly	Eric
Laura	Nicholas

1967

Lisa	Michael
Michelle	David
Kimberly	Robert
Christina	John
Jennifer	James
Julie	Richard
Cynthia	Mark
Mary	Steven
Karen	William
Patricia	Christopher
Elizabeth	Daniel
Susan	Jeffrey
Laura	Eric
Maria	Brian
Sandra	Timothy
Stephanie	Anthony
Deborah	Scott
Denise	Paul
Kelly	Thomas
Tina	Joseph

1960

Susan	Michael
Mary	David
Karen	Robert
Cynthia	John
Lisa	James
Linda	Mark
Debra	Richard
Patricia	Steven
Deborah	William
Sandra	Daniel
Laura	Thomas
Elizabeth	Jeffrey
Pamela	Timothy
Donna	Kenneth

Kathleen	Ronald
Lori	Kevin
Kimberly	Gregory
Teresa	Joseph
Julie	Charles
Cheryl	Donald

Information supplied by the State of California Department of Health Services.

B

Bailey: French for "bailiff," but originally Old English for "fortification."

Relatives: Baily, Bayley, Bailee

Namesakes: Pearl Bailey, "Beetle Bailey," "Rumpole of the Bailey," "Bill Bailey"

Baird: Scottish for "minstrel." A great name.

Relative: Bard

Namesakes: John Baird, Bard College

Baker: Occupational name. A female baker was a "baxter."

Relatives: Baxter, Baxley

Namesakes: Carlos Baker, Howard Baker, Anne Baxter

Baldwin: German for "bold friend."

Relatives: Baldwyn, Maldwyn, Win, Wyn

Namesake: Stanley Baldwin

Ballard: From the Old English and French for "a dancing song."

Namesakes: Kaye Ballard, J. G. Ballard

Bancroft: Old English for "bean field." Much classier sounding than its mundane origins.

Namesake: Anne Bancroft

Barbara: From the Latin for "foreign" and "strange." You won't find many Barbaras under age thirty.

Relatives: Barbra, Barbarella, Barbie, Barby, Barbs, Barb, Babette, Babs, Bobbie

Namesakes: Saint Barbara, Barbara Jordan, Barbra Streisand, Barbara Walters, "Barbie" doll

Barber: From the Latin for "beard."
Relative: Barbour
Namesake: Red Barber

Barclay: Old English for "birch meadow." Sounds rich even if you don't know it's a bank.
Relatives: Barklay, Barkley, Barksdale, Berkeley, Berkley
Namesakes: Catherine Barkley, Barclay's Bank

Barnabas: Hebrew for "son of prophecy." Depends on how you feel about the nickname Barney.
Relatives: Barnaby, Barney, Barnie, Barn
Namesakes: Barnaby Conrad, "Barnaby Jones," "Barney Rubble"

Barnett: Old English for "noble man." A preppier version of Bernard/ Barnard.
Relatives: Barnet, Barret, Barrett, Barr
Namesake: Elizabeth Barrett Browning

Baron: Derived from the title. Particularly effective if your last name is "von"-something.
Relative: Barron
Namesake: "The Red Baron"

Barry: Irish for "spear thrower" and Welsh for "son of Harry." Very solid.
Relatives: Barrie, Barris, Barie, Barrymore
Namesakes: Barry Gibb, Barry Goldwater, Barry Fitzgerald, John Barrymore

Bartholomew: From the Hebrew for "furrow." A terrific array of nicknames and variations.
Relatives: Barth, Bart, Barthol, Bartel, Bartlett, Bartley, Barton, Bertol, Bartold, Bat, Bart, Tholy, Tolly
Namesakes: Bartholomew Tucker, Bart Starr, John Barth, Clara Barton, A. Bartlett Giamatti, Bartlett pear

Baruch: From the Hebrew for "blessed." Generally a surname when it's not part of a Hebrew prayer.
Namesakes: Bernard Baruch, "Baruch Atah Adonai"

Basil: From the Greek for "royal." Veddy British.
Relatives: Basile, Basilio, Basilia, Basia, Vasilis, Vasily
Namesakes: Saint Basil, Basil Rathbone, basil plant

Bates: A surname probably derived from Bartholomew. Nice for a boy or girl.
Namesakes: Alan Bates, "Norman Bates," Bates College

Bathsheba: From the Hebrew for "daughter of the oath." King David's wife and Solomon's mother. A daring choice.
Relatives: Batsheva, Bathshua, Batya, Basia, Basya, Sheba
Namesakes: Basia Johnson, *Come Back, Little Sheba*

Bayard: Old French for "bay horse." A great name, no matter how you pronounce it.
Relatives: Baylor, Bayless, Baird
Namesakes: Bayard Dodge, Bayard Rustin

Beacher: Old English for "dweller by the beech tree." Unusual and interesting.
Relative: Beecher
Namesake: Harriet Beecher Stowe

Beardsley: Origin unclear. Seems to be an Old English compound for "beard" and "wood or glade," but "bearded wood" doesn't make much sense.
Namesake: Aubrey Beardsley

Beatrice: Latin for "happy." An old-fashioned name that had been ignored in the return to old-fashioned names until Fergie and Andy picked it for the Princess of York.
Relatives: Beatrix, Bea, Beah, Beattie, Beatirsa, Beatriz, Trixie
Namesakes: Beatrice Lillie, Beatrix Potter, Bea Arthur, Queen Beatrix of the Netherlands

Beau: French for "beautiful." Ashley and Melanie's little boy in *Gone with the Wind*.
Relatives: Beaumont, Beauregard, Bo, Bonita
Namesakes: Beau Bridges, Beau Brummell, Bo Hopkins, Bo Derek

Bede: Old English for "prayer."
Namesakes: the Venerable Bede, *Adam Bede*

Beldon: Old English for "beautiful pasture." More usual as a surname.
Relative: Belden
Namesake: "Trixie Beldon"

Belinda: From the Spanish for "beautiful." Making a comeback.
Relatives: Belynda, Belle, Linda
Namesakes: Belinda Carlisle, Belinda Lee

Bellamy: From the Old French for "handsome friend." For "Upstairs, Downstairs" devotees.
Namesakes: Ralph Bellamy, Carol Bellamy

Belle: French for "beautiful."
Relatives: Bella, Belva
Namesakes: "Belle Watling," Bella Abzug, Belva Plain

Bemus: Greek for "platform."

Benedict: Latin for "blessed." Used mainly by Roman Catholics; the liqueur was created by an order of Benedictine monks as an herbal medicine.
Namesake: Benedict Arnold

Benjamin: Hebrew for "son of my right hand." A perennial favorite.
Relatives: Benji, Benjie, Bennie, Benny, Ben
Namesakes: Benjamin Cardozo, Benjamin Britten, Benny Goodman, "Ben Cartwright," "Benji"

Bennett: An anglicized version of Benedict and much more popular.
Relatives: Benett, Bennet, Benoit, Benn, Bentley
Namesakes: Bennett Cerf, Joan Benoit, Constance Bennett, Bentley automobiles

Benson: "Ben's son." From the Department of Redundancy Department, the actual translation is "son son."
Relative: Bensen
Namesake: Benson and Hedges cigarettes

Bergen: German for "mountain dweller."
Relatives: Bergan, Bergin
Namesakes: Bergen Evans, Candice Bergen

Bernadette: Feminine version of "Bernard." This name is guaranteed to call to mind the classic song by the Four Tops.
Relatives: Bern, Bernie, Bernnadette, Bernadete
Namesakes: Bernadette Peters, *The Song of Bernadette*

Bernard: From the German for "bold as a bear." This entire group of names deserves a revival.
Relatives: Barnard, Barney, Barnie, Bernd, Berndt, Bern, Berne, Bernardo, Bernhard, Bernhardt, Bernie, Bjorn
Namesakes: Bernard Kalb, Barnard Hughes, Bjorn Borg, Sarah Bernhardt, Barnard College

Bernice: Greek for "bringer of victory."
Relatives: Berenice, Berry, Bunny

Bertram: German for "bright." An appealing group of names.
Relatives: Bertrem, Bertolt, Berthold, Bertil, Bertol, Berton, Bert, Bertha
Namesakes: Bertolt Brecht, Bertrand Russell, Bert Lahr

Beryl: Hebrew for "jewel."
Relative: Bijou
Namesake: Beryl Markham

Bethany: "Beth" is Hebrew for "house." A melodic alternative to Elizabeth if the nickname "Beth" is your goal.
Relatives: Bethany, Bethesda, Bethel
Namesake: Bethany Beach (Md.)

Beverly: Old English for "meadow of beavers." Sometimes used for boys, but it's a struggle.
Relatives: Beverley, Beverely, Bev
Namesakes: Beverly Sills, Beverly D'Angelo, Beverly Hills (Calif.)

Bevin: "Son of Evan."
Relatives: Bevan, Bevis

Bianca: Italian for "white." Jet-set image promulgated by Mick Jagger's ex-wife.
Relatives: Biancha, Blanche, Blancha, Blanca
Namesakes: Bianca Jagger, "Blanche DuBois"

Bingham: From the German for "kettle-shaped hollow." Classy; with any luck people will assume the child is related to the prominent Kentucky family.
Relatives: Bing, Binghamton, Binghampton
Namesakes: Bing Crosby, Binghamton (N.Y.)

Birch: From the Old English for "white." A beautiful tree.
Namesake: Birch Bayh

Blaine: Gaelic for "thin or lean" and Old English for "source of a river." A change of pace from Blake and Blair.
Relative: Blain

Blair: Gaelic for "from the plain." One of the earliest and still one of the most popular androgynous names.
Relative: Blaire
Namesakes: Blair Brown, Blair Hall

Blake: Old English for "fair-haired." You can't go wrong with this one.
Relatives: Blanchard, Blanco
Namesakes: Blake Edwards, William Blake

Blase: Latin for "one who stammers." A name from the soap operas.
Relatives: Blaise, Blaze, Bliss
Namesake: Blaise Pascal

Blossom: Old English for "lovely." It is rather lovely, if a little reminiscent of the sixties.
Namesake: Blossom Dearie

Blythe: Old English for "joyous." Hail to thee.
Relative: Blithe
Namesakes: Blythe Danner, *Blithe Spirit*

Bonnie: Scottish variation of French for "good."
Relatives: Bonny, Boni, Boniface, Bonita
Namesakes: Bonnie Bedelia, Bonnie Raitt

Booker: Old English for "beech tree." Parchment was made from beech trees; hence the derivation of the word "book."
Namesake: Booker T. Washington

Boone: Latin for "good." Has a "good old boy" quality.
Namesakes: T. Boone Pickens, Daniel Boone

Booth: Old English for "hut."
Relative: Boothe
Namesakes: Powers Boothe, Booth Tarkington, John Wilkes Booth

Borden: From the Old English for "near the boar's den" and Old French for "cottage." Slightly tarnished by the image of those contented cows, but still nice.
Relative: Bordan

Boris: Russian for "fight."
Relatives: Bors, Borys
Namesakes: Boris Karloff, Boris Pasternak

Boswell: Old French for "forested town." Definitely upper crust, perhaps a little too much so.
Relatives: Bosworth, Boz
Namesakes: Boz Scaggs, James Boswell, Brian Bosworth

Bowen: "Son of Owen."
Relative: Bowie
Namesakes: Bowie Kuhn, Jim Bowie

Boyce: From the French for "woodland."

Boyd: Irish for "blond" or "yellow."
Namesakes: Boyd Matson, Boyd Tarleton, William Boyd

Bradley: Old English for "broad meadow." A surname that has become quite common as a first name. The entire "Brad" ("broad") group is nice.
Relatives: Braden, Brad, Bradford, Brady
Namesakes: Bill Bradley, Omar Bradley, "The Brady Bunch"

Bramwell: English place name for "bramble well."
Relative: Branwell
Namesake: Patrick Branwell Brontë (brother of Charlotte)

Branch: From the Latin for "extension." The most basic of all tree names.
Namesakes: Branch Rickey, bourbon and branch water

Brandon: Old English for "fiery hill."
Relatives: Branden, Brand, Bran, Brenden, Brendan, Brant, Brent, Brennan, Brennen, Branford
Namesakes: Brandon Tartikoff, Brendan Gill, Branford Marsalis

Brenda: Feminine of "Brandon/Brenden." Its variant forms are more widely used today.
Relatives: Brenna, Brynna, Brynn
Namesakes: Brenda Vaccaro, "Brenda Starr"

Brent: A variation of Brandon.
Namesake: Brent Musburger

Brett: "A native of Brittany." Traditionally a boy's name, but Hemingway picked it for his female character in *The Sun Also Rises*.
Relatives: Bret, Bretton
Namesakes: "Lady Brett Ashley," Bret Easton Ellis

Brewster: Old English for "brewer." Has a *Mayflower* connotation and also makes for a great college nickname.
Relative: Brew
Namesakes: "Brewster McCloud," William Brewster

Brian: Celtic for "strong." Almost everyone likes this name.
Relatives: Brianne, Bryan, Bryant, Brianna, Briant, Briand
Namesakes: Brian Wilson, Bryant Gumbel, Bryan Brown

Brice: Celtic for "swift." Try it for a girl.
Relatives: Bryce, Brick
Namesake: Fanny Brice

Bridget: Irish for "resolute." A perennial favorite in Ireland.
Relatives: Brigitta, Brigitte, Brighid, Brigid, Britta, Brita, Britte, Brit, Biddy, Brie, Bree, Birgit, Birgitta, Brigada, Brigida, Brigita, Birget, Bridie, Bryde
Namesakes: Brigitte Bardot, Birgit Nelson

Brigham: From the Old English for "one who lives near a bridge" and Old French for "soldier." Handsome, even if you're not a Mormon.
Namesake: Brigham Young

Bristol: A variant form of Brice and a city in England.
Relative: Brystol
Namesakes: "The Bristol Stomp," Bristol-Myers

Brittany: An anglicized version of Bretagne, a section of France famous for its spectacular coastline. Extremely popular in California, which means it will drift inexorably eastward.

Relatives: Brita, Britta, Brittny
Namesake: Morgan Brittany

Brock: Old English for "badger." Very solid sound.
Relatives: Braxton, Brocton
Namesakes: Brock Peters, Brock Brower, Bill Brock

Broderick: "Son of Roderick."
Relatives: Rick, Brod, Roderick
Namesake: Broderick Crawford

Bromley: Old English for "brush-covered meadow." Sounds like an ancestral castle.
Relatives: Bromwell, Bromwood
Namesake: Mount Bromley

Bronson: Old English for "son of Brown."
Relatives: Bronwyn, Bronwen
Namesakes: Bronson Pinchot, Amos Bronson Alcott, Charles Bronson

Brook: Old English for "stream." Everyone's favorite Princeton graduate, Brooke Shields, has made this name even more popular. Works for boys and girls with the "e" or the "s" endings.
Relatives: Brooke, Brooks, Brookes
Namesakes: Brooke Astor, Brooks Atkinson, Brooks Brothers

Brown: Middle English for the color. A color name that is usually a surname.
Relatives: Broun, Bruno, Bruin, Bruins
Namesakes: Brown Meggs, Heywood Hale Broun, Brown University

Bruce: From the French for "thicket." Newly respectable.
Namesakes: Bruce Springsteen, Bruce Willis, Robert Bruce

Bryn: Welsh for "hill."
Namesake: Bryn Mawr College

Buckley: Old English for "meadow of deer." Won't do for a Democrat. An old-money name.
Relatives: Buckminster, Buck, Bucky, Buckner
Namesakes: Buckminster Fuller, William F. Buckley, Bill Buckner

Bud: Old English for "herald." Generally used as a nickname.
Relatives: Buddy, Buddie, Budd
Namesakes: Buddy Ebsen, Budd Schulberg, Zola Budd

Burdette: From the Middle English for "small bird."
Namesake: Lew Burdette

Burgess: Old English for "free citizen." Rarely used; you could start a trend.
Relatives: Burg, Bergess, Bergen
Namesakes: Burgess Meredith, Anthony Burgess

Burke: From the German for "castle." A rugged choice.
Relatives: Bourke, Burk, Birk, Birke
Namesakes: Edmund Burke, Robert Bork

Burle: Middle English for "knotted wood."
Relatives: Burl, Burleigh, Burley
Namesake: Burl Ives

Burne: Old English for "brook." Interesting choice.
Relatives: Burns, Byrne, Bourne
Namesakes: Robert Burns, Brendan Byrne, Jason Bourne

Burt: Old English for "fortress."
Relatives: Burton, Bert, Berton
Namesakes: Burton White, Burt Reynolds, Richard Burton, "Bert and Ernie"

Byron: From the French for "from the cottage." A name with haunting literary associations.
Relatives: Byram, Byran
Namesakes: Lord Byron, Byron James

Celebrity Baby Names

Do celebrity baby names set trends or reflect trends? "Max" *has* emerged as a popular choice since Amy Irving and Steven Spielberg chose it for their little boy, but it's doubtful that "Satchel" will ever make a Top Ten list.

Woody Allen and Mia Farrow—Satchel
Amy Irving and Steven Spielberg—Max
Frank Zappa—Moon Unit, Dweezil, Ahmet Emuukha Rodan, and Diva

Bette Midler—Sophie
Alice Cooper—Calico
Cybill Shepherd—Clementine and twins Ariel and Zachariah
The Prince and Princess of Wales—William Philip Arthur George and Henry Charles Albert David
The Duke and Duchess of York—Beatrice Elizabeth Mary
Mick Jagger and Jerry Hall—Elizabeth Scarlett and James Augustine
Mick Jagger and Bianca Jagger—Jade
Cheryl Ladd—Jordan
Pam Dawber and Mark Harmon—Sean
Billy Joel and Christie Brinkley—Alexa Rae
Diana Ross—Tracee, Chudney, and Rhonda
Roger Clemens—Kory
Dennis Rasmussen—Justin Casey
Anthony Perkins—Osgood and Elvis
Harrison Ford—Benjamin and Willard
Peter O'Toole—Lorcan, Kate, and Pat
Cher—Chastity and Elijah Blue
Meredith Baxter-Birney and David Birney—twins Mollie Elizabeth and Peter David Edwin
Loni Anderson and Burt Reynolds—Quinton
Patti Hansen and Keith Richards—Theodora and Alexandra
Darryl Strawberry—Diamond Nicole
Michelle Phillips—Chynna
John Lennon—Julian and Sean
Bruce Willis and Demi Moore—Rumer Glenn
Bill Cosby—Erika, Ensa, Evin, and Enna
Corbin Bernsen and Amanda Pays—Oliver
Chevy Chase—Cydney and Caley
Keith Carradine—Cade
David Bowie—Zowie
Christopher Reeve—Matthew and Alexandra
Sylvester Stallone—Sage Moonblood and Seargeoh
Robin Williams—Zachary
Melissa Gilbert—Dakota Paul

C

Cable: From the Old French for "rope."
   Relatives: Cabel, Cab
   Namesake: Cab Calloway

Caitlin: An Irish or Welsh variation of Catherine. One of the most popular names of the last few years. The "Jennifer" of the late 1980s. Sometimes pronounced *"Cat–lin."*
   Relatives: Caitlyn, Kaitlin, Kaitlyn, Katelyn, Catelyn
   Namesake: Caitlin Thomas (wife of Dylan)

Calandra: Greek for "lark." Very pretty, with strong nicknames.
   Relatives: Callie, Cally, Cal

Calder: Old English for "river of stones." An interesting choice, hip but not too trendy.
   Relatives: Caulder, Cal
   Namesake: Alexander Calder

Caldwell: Old English for "cold spring."
   Relatives: Cadwell, Cadmus
   Namesake: Erskine Caldwell

Caleb: From the Hebrew for "bold" or "dog." An Old Testament favorite. Caleb was one of twelve men sent by Moses to determine whether the Israelites could successfully invade Canaan.
   Relatives: Cale, Cal
   Namesake: Cale Yarborough

Calhoun: Old English for "warrior."
   Namesake: John Calhoun

Callis: Latin for "cup." Pretty and unusual.
Relatives: Callys, Calla
Namesake: Calla lily

Calvin: Latin for "bald." Think about it for a girl.
Relatives: Calvyn, Calvinnia
Namesakes: Calvin Coolidge, Calvin Klein, "Calvin and Hobbes"

Cameron: Old English for "bent nose." Don't be put off by its original meaning; this is a beautiful name.
Relatives: Camm, Cam, Cammie, Camyron
Namesakes: Cameron Mitchell, John Cameron Swayze, Richard Cameron

Camille: Latin for "attendant at a religious ceremony." The heroine of an Alexandre Dumas play, which was in turn the basis for Verdi's opera *La Traviata.* And we all remember Garbo's "I vant to be alone."
Relatives: Camilla, Camila, Camelia, Cammilla, Cammie, Cammy, Kamilla, Kamille, Mila
Namesake: "Camille"

Campbell: From the French for "beautiful field." A traditional Scottish name despite the French origins.
Relative: Camp
Namesakes: Glen Campbell, Campbell's soup

Candace: From the Greek for "white-hot." A favorite name of early Ethiopian queens.
Relatives: Candice, Candys, Candy, Candie, Candi
Namesakes: Candace Stevenson, Candice Bergen

Cara: Latin for "dear." Increasingly popular either with the "c" or with the "k."
Relatives: Kara, Carra, Karra
Namesakes: Kara Kennedy, "Cara Mia"

Carew: Latin for "run." Almost exclusively used as a surname but has real potential as a first name. Solid sound, good nickname possibilities.
Relatives: Carrie, Carry, Cary, Rew
Namesake: Rod Carew

Carey: From the Latin for "dear" and Welsh for "rocky island." Deservedly popular; truly androgynous.
Relatives: Cary, Carry, Carrie, Kerry, Kerrie
Namesakes: Cary Grant, Carrie Fisher, Hugh Carey

Carl: A variation of Charles. This name has dropped out of fashion, and it's hard to understand why. More popular in its feminine form, Carla.
Relatives: Karl, Karla, Carol, Caroll, Carlotta, Carlton, Carlisle, Carlyle, Carlie, Carly
Namesakes: Carl Bernstein, Karl Marx, Carroll O'Connor

Carleton: Old English for "Carl's town." A nice name. Only the most vehement antismoking activist will be put off by the fact that it is also the name of a cigarette.
Relatives: Carlton, Charlton
Namesakes: Carlton Fisk, Jim Charlton

Carly: Began as a nickname related to Carla and Carleen, but now stands on its own. "Carly, I love you, darlin', I do."
Relatives: Carla, Carleen, Karlie, Karly, Karleen, Karlene, Carlene
Namesake: Carly Simon

Carlyle: Old English for "Carl's island." A little pretentious perhaps, but nicknames are available from either syllable.
Relatives: Carlisle, Carl, Carlie, Carly, Lyle, Lisle
Namesakes: Thomas Carlyle, Hotel Carlyle

Carmen: From the Hebrew for "garden" or "field of fruit," but most popular in Spanish-speaking countries. The origin of this name offers a possible explanation for Ms. Miranda's fruited headgear.
Relatives: Carmel, Karmen, Karmel, Carmelita, Karmelita, Carmelle, Karmelle, Carmine, Carmita
Namesakes: Carmen Miranda, Carmen Cozza

Caroline: Feminine form of Charles. An old-fashioned charmer.
Relatives: Carolyne, Carolyn, Carolina, Cary, Carly, Carol, Karoline, Karolyne, Karolina, Karolyna, Caro, Karo, Carra, Cara, Carrie, Carry
Namesakes: Caroline Kennedy, Princess Caroline of Monaco

Carson: "Son of Carr," which is Scandinavian for "marshy land."
Namesakes: Carson McCullers, Johnny Carson, Kit Carson

Carter: Old English for "cart driver." Solid preppie sound, but not excessive.
Namesakes: Carter Burden, Carter Smith, Jimmy Carter

Case: From the Old French for "chest." You could make a case for this as a first name.
Namesake: Case Western Reserve University

Cassandra: The original prophet of doom, in classical mythology, but the name has a pleasant sound to it.
Relatives: Cassie, Cass, Sandra, Sandy
Namesake: "Mama" Cass Elliot

Catherine: From the Greek for "pure." Ever popular, always in good taste. A can't-miss name with endless variations.
Relatives: Cathryne, Kathryn, Katherine, Katharine, Cathy, Kathie, Catie, Cadie, Caddie, Katie, Kate, Katryn, Katrina, Catrina, Trina, Cathleen, Kitty, Cate, Cat, Catriana
Namesakes: Catherine the Great, Catherine Olim, Kathryn Harrold, Katharine Hepburn

Cecilia: From the Latin for "blind." A traditional upper-crust name.
Relatives: Cecil, Cecelia, Celia, Cecily, Cicely, Cissy, Sissy
Namesakes: Cecily Cardew, Cicely Tyson, Sissy Spacek, Cecil B. DeMille

Cedric: A combination of Welsh for "bounty" and "spectacle."
Relatives: Cedrick, Cedrych, Cerdric
Namesake: Sir Cedric Hardwick

Celeste: Latin for "heavenly." A beautiful name, but she may have to endure a few taunts about Babar's wife.
Namesakes: Celeste Holm, "Queen Celeste"

Chad: Old English for "warlike."
Relative: Chadwick
Namesakes: Chad Everett, Chad and Jeremy

Chaim: Hebrew for "life." People will always be drinking a toast to this child.
Relatives: Cahyim, Cahyyam, Haim, Haym, Cahya
Namesake: Chaim Potok

Chancellor: Old French for "secretary." A little highfalutin unless it really is a family name.
Relatives: Chance, Chauncey
Namesakes: Chauncey Howell, Chancellor Green, John Chancellor

Chandler: French for "candle maker." Surname used as a first name.
Relatives: Chan, Chaney
Namesake: Raymond Chandler

Channing: Old English for "knowing."
Namesakes: Stockard Channing, Carol Channing

Charity: From the Latin for "affection." One of the virtue names popular with the Puritans. The return to conservative values may bring these names back.
Namesakes: Charity Blackstock, *Sweet Charity*

Charles: Old English for "manly." Popularized by Charlemagne; a favorite ever since. Nicknames to suit every taste.
Relatives: Charlie, Charley, Charlton, Chuck, Chas, Chaz, Chip, Chuck, Carlos, Chico, Chick
Namesakes: Prince Charles, Charles Boyer, Charlton Heston, Chick Corea, Chuck Yeager, Charlie "Bird" Parker, Chico Marx, Carlos Baker

Charlotte: Feminine of Charles. A lovely old-fashioned name enjoying a deserved surge in popularity.
Relatives: Charlie, Carlotta, Lottie, Lotte, Charlene, Charmaine, Charmayne, Charlayne, Chatzie
Namesakes: Charlotte Brontë, Charlotte Russe, *Charlotte's Web*

Chase: From the Old French for "hunter."
Namesakes: Chase and Sanborn coffee, Chase Manhattan Bank

Chelsea: Old English for "river landing place." The Jane Fonda character in *On Golden Pond*. There are lots of little Chelseas around these days.
Relatives: Chelsie, Kelsie, Kelsey, Kelsy
Namesakes: Linda Kelsey, "Chelsea Morning"

Cheryl: From the French for "loved." A large group of names are available with the Cher prefix.

Relatives: Sherryl, Sherryll, Sherrill, Sheryl, Cheryle, Sheryle, Cher, Cherrie, Cherry

Namesakes: Cheryl Tiegs, Cher, Cheryl Ladd, Sherrill Milnes, "Cherry Ames"

Chester: From the Latin for "camp." A nice name, but unfortunately conjures up images of an Old West deputy with a limp and a squeaky voice.
Relatives: Chet, Ches, Chess
Namesakes: Chester Arthur, Chet Huntley, Chet Atkins

Chevy: From the French for "knight" and Old English for "chase" or "hunt."
Relatives: Chevie, Chevalier
Namesakes: Chevy Chase, Maurice Chevalier

Chilton: Old English for "farm by the spring." Unusual choice; yours will likely be the only one in his/her grade.
Relatives: Chill, Chil, Chilly

Chloë: A minor goddess and Greek for "blooming." A beautiful name; trendy but worth the risk.
Relatives: Cloe, Cloris, Chloris
Namesakes: Daphnis and Chloë, Cloris Leachman

Christian: Greek for "anointed." A tough name to handle if a bar mitzvah is in your child's future.
Relatives: Christiaan, Kristian, Chris, Chrestian, Karston, Karstan, Kristo, Cristo, Christo
Namesakes: Christiaan Barnard, Fletcher Christian

Christina: Feminine of Christian. Take your pick from the wide assortment.
Relatives: Christine, Kristen, Kristin, Kristine, Kirsten, Kristina, Chris, Christie, Kris, Christiana, Christa
Namesakes: Christine Lahti, Chris Evert, Christie Brinkley, Kirstie Alley

Christopher: Greek for "Christ-bearer." Adorable for a little boy; A. A. Milne was no fool. Matures nicely as well.

Relatives: Kristofer, Christof, Kristof, Chris, Kris, Kit, Christophe, Kester, Cristobel

Namesakes: Kris Kristofferson, Kit Carson, Kris Kringle, Christopher Columbus, "Christopher Robin"

Claiborne: Old English for "born of the earth." A group of names with a nice patrician ring.

Relatives: Clayborne, Claybourne, Claibourne, Clayton, Clay

Namesakes: Claiborne Pell, Henry Clay, Craig Claiborne, Liz Claiborne

Claire: Latin for "bright, shining." A terrific name.

Relatives: Clare, Clara, Clarice, Clarissa, Clarisse, Clarrie

Namesakes: Clara Barton, Clare Boothe Luce, "Clair de Lune"

Clancy: Irish for "offspring of red-headed soldier." A "faith and begorrah" kind of name.

Relatives: Clancey, Clan

Namesakes: John Clancy, Tom Clancy

Clarence: From the Latin for "clear, bright." A favorite from "Leave It to Beaver."

Relatives: Claron, Clarendon

Namesakes: Clarence Darrow, Clarence Birdseye

Clark: Old English for "cleric." A solid choice; unlikely to offend anyone.

Relatives: Clarke, Clarkson

Namesakes: Clark Gable, Ramsey Clark, Clarkson Potter, "Clark Kent"

Claude: Latin for "lame." A name that is much more popular in France than in the United States.

Relatives: Claud, Claudius, Claudell, Claudia, Claudette, Claudio

Namesakes: Claude Monet, Jean-Claude Killy, Claude Debussy, Claudell Washington, *I, Claudius*

Clay: From the German for "adhere." A good name for a child you intend to mold into your own image.

Relatives: Clayborne, Clayton

Namesakes: Clay Felker, Adam Clayton Powell, Henry Clay

Clement: Latin for "merciful." Classy and not often used.
Relatives: Clemente, Clemens, Clemmons, Clemon, Clem, Clementine, Clementyne
Namesakes: Clement Moore, Roberto Clemente

Cleveland: Old English for "land near the hill."
Relatives: Cleve, Clive, Cleavon
Namesakes: Cleveland Amory, Grover Cleveland, Clive Barnes, Clive Bell, Cleavon Little

Clifford: Old English for "hill." Very nice.
Relatives: Cliff, Clifton
Namesakes: Clifton Webb, Cliff Robertson, Tim Clifford

Clinton: Old English for "town near a hill."
Relative: Clint
Namesakes: Clint Eastwood, DeWitt Clinton

Clio: Greek for "praise." The muse of history. A good choice for the child of advertising execs.
Relatives: Clea, Cleo, Cleon, Cleopatra
Namesakes: Cleo Laine, Clio Awards

Clovis: Old English for "clover."
Relatives: Clothilde, Clotilde
Namesake: Clovis Ruffin

Clyde: Welsh for "heard from afar."
Namesake: Bonnie and Clyde

Cody: Irish for "assistant." Informal but catchy.
Relative: Codie
Namesake: Buffalo Bill Cody

Cole: Old English for "coal." Uncommon and very attractive.
Relatives: Colby, Coleman, Colemann
Namesakes: Cole Porter, Nat King Cole, Ornette Coleman

Colin: Irish for "youth." More widely used in Great Britain, but well worth considering.

Relatives: Collin, Collins
Namesake: Jesse Colin-Young

Colleen: Irish for "girl." You can't get much more Irish than this name.
Relatives: Colene, Coleen
Namesake: Colleen Dewhurst

Comfort: Latin for "strengthen." Another Puritan favorite.

Conan: Gaelic for "high."
Namesakes: Arthur Conan Doyle, *Conan the Barbarian*

Conner: Irish for "desire." Clean and crisp.
Relatives: Conners, Connor, O'Conner, O'Connor, Conor
Namesakes: Bart Conner, Jimmy Connors, Cardinal O'Connor

Conrad: Old German for "brave counsel."
Relatives: Connie, Rad, Konrad, Conroy, Cort
Namesakes: Conrad Aiken, Joseph Conrad

Constance: Latin for "faithful." A Puritan virtue name that has moved into the mainstream.
Relatives: Connie, Constantia, Constanza, Constantine, Constant
Namesakes: Constance Towers, Connie Chung

Conway: Welsh for "river."
Relative: Conwy
Namesakes: Conway Twitty, Tim Conway

Cooper: From the Latin for "cask." Not often used as a first name, but it works.
Relative: Coop
Namesakes: Gordon Gooper, Cooperstown (N.Y.)

Cora: Greek for "maiden."
Relatives: Coretta, Corita, Corin, Corina, Coralee, Coralie
Namesakes: Coretta King, Sister Corita

Coral: From the Latin for "rock."
Namesake: Coral Brown

Corbin: Old French for "raven."

Relatives: Corbett, Corbet, Corby, Corwin, Corwan, Corwyn
Namesake: Corbin Bernsen

Cordelia: Feminine of Cordell. King Lear's faithful daughter, and the one of the three with the best name.
Relatives: Delia, Cordy, Kordelia

Cordell: From the Latin for "rope." A little puffed up, but Cord is a nice nickname.
Relatives: Cord, Cordas, Cordie, Cordy
Namesake: Cordell Hull

Corey: Irish for "from the hollow."
Relatives: Cory, Corry, Corrie
Namesake: Corey Ames

Cornelia: Latin for "horn."
Relatives: Cornelius, Cornell, Cornel
Namesakes: Cornelia Guest, Cornel Wilde, Cornelius Vanderbilt, Cornell University

Courtland: Old English for "the king's land." People will think it's a family name.
Relatives: Cortland, Court, Cort
Namesakes: "Palmer Courtland," Cortland apple

Courtney: Old English for "from the court." This one conjures up images of prep schools in Connecticut and coming-out parties in Boston.
Relatives: Cortney, Cortie, Corey
Namesake: Courtney Kennedy

Craig: Irish for "crag." Always a popular choice.
Namesakes: Craig Claiborne, Jim Craig

Creighton: Old English for "town near a creek."
Relatives: Creigh, Cree, Crichton
Namesakes: Michael Crichton, Creighton University

Cressida: From the Greek for "gold." A pretty name, but keep in mind that she was a symbol of infidelity to the ancient Greeks. Having sworn eternal fealty to Troilus, she then betrayed him with Diomedes.
Namesake: Troilus and Cressida

Crispin: Latin for "curly." Crispin is the patron saint of shoemakers.
Relatives: Crispen, Crispus, Crispo, Krispen, Crisp
Namesakes: Crispus Attucks, Quentin Crisp

Crockett: Origin unknown. Generally used as a surname.
Namesakes: Davy Crockett, "Sonny Crockett"

Crystal: From the Latin for "clear." For "Dynasty" fans and New Age devotees.
Relatives: Chrystal, Christal, Krystal, Kristal, Cristal, Cristale, Cristol, Cristel
Namesakes: Billy Crystal, "Crystal Carrington," Crystal Light

Cullen: Irish for "handsome."
Relatives: Culley, Cullin
Namesake: William Cullen Bryant

Currier: Old English for "churn." Another surname used as a first name. "Currer Bell" was the pen name of Charlotte Brontë.
Relatives: Curran, Currie, Curry, Currey, Curren, Currer
Namesakes: John Curry, Currier and Ives

Curtis: From the Latin for "court" and Old French for "courteous."
Relatives: Curt, Curtys
Namesakes: Curtis Le May, Curtis Sliwa, Curt Flood

Cuyler: Irish for "chapel." Very nice.
Namesake: Ki Ki Cuyler

Cynthia: From the Greek for "moon." Traditional and melodic.
Relatives: Cindie, Cyndi, Cindy, Cinta, Cintia
Namesakes: Cynthia Gregory, Cyndi Lauper

Cyril: From the Greek for "lordly." This ninth-century saint catholicized Russia and invented its alphabet to boot.
Relatives: Cyrilla, Cyra, Kyril
Namesakes: Cyril Ritchard, Cyril Connolly, Cyra MacFadden

Cyrus: Persian for "the sun." Cyrus the Great was the founder of the Persian empire.
Relative: Cy
Namesakes: Cyrus Vance, Cy Young

Mom and Pop Organizations

The suffixes "–kin," "–son," "–sen," "–sohn," and "–datter" indicate that the name is based on a patronymic or matronymic root. For example, Harrison is "Harry's son," and Tompkin is "Tom's kin."

Such suffixes, as well as a variety of prefixes, usually appear in surnames. They may be added by creative parents searching for just the right appellation for their baby. If, for example, you want to name your baby Peter for his father and yet don't want a "junior," try Peterson.

The following is a guide to these family tags.

Prefixes

Ap or Up—Welsh for "son of"
Bar or bar—Aramaic for "son of"
Ben—Hebrew for "son of"
di or de—Italian and French for "of"
Fitz—Norman for "son of"
Mc or Mac—Celtic for "son of"
O'—Celtic for "descendant of"

Suffixes

-czyk, -wiak, -wicz—Polish for "son of"
-escu, -esco, -vici—Romanian for "like" or "akin to"
-ez—Spanish for "son of"
-ich, -vich—Russian for "son of"
-idas, -ides, -poulos—Greek for "son of"
-oglu—Turkish for "boy of"
-ov, -ev, -off, -eff—Eastern European and Russian for "of the (name)s"
-sky, -ski—Eastern European and Russian for "of the nature of"
-tze—Chinese for "son of"
-vna, -ova—Russian for "daughter of"
y—Spanish for "and"

D

Dag: Scandinavian for "day."
Relatives: Dagmar, Dagney, Dagny, Dagget, Dailey, Daily, Daley, Day, Dayton, Daymond
Namesakes: Dag Hammarskjöld, Daley Thompson, Doris Day

Daisy: Latin for "day's eye." Potential for a comeback; consider it.
Relative: Daisey
Namesakes: "Daisy Mae," *Princess Daisy*, "Daisy Buchanan"

Dakin: A variant form of "Danish." A wonderful line of plush toys; your child will probably receive one for a baby present.
Relatives: Dane, Daine
Namesake: Dane Iorg

Dale: Old English for "valley." A very nice name that has not been used much since the fifties.
Relatives: Dal, Dallan, Dallen, Dallas, Dallin, Dalton
Namesakes: Dale Evans, Dale Carnegie, "Chip and Dale"

Dalia: Hebrew for "branch." Pretty.
Relative: Dahlia

Dallas: Scottish place name. The city in Texas was named for George Dallas, U.S. vice president under James K. Polk.
Namesake: "Stella Dallas"

Damien: From the Greek for "tamer." A favorite among writers of horror stories.

Relatives: Damian, Damon, Daimen
Namesakes: Damon Runyon, Damon and Pythias, Father Damien, *Damien II*

Dana: Variation of Daniel, but also androgynous. In Greek mythology Danae was the daughter of King Acrisius of Argos and the mother of Perseus.
Relatives: Danna, Danae
Namesakes: Dana Ivey, Dana Andrews, Richard Henry Dana

Daniel: Hebrew for "God is my judge." Deservedly popular; a name with solid biblical roots and one that goes well with almost every surname.
Relatives: Dan, Danny, Danni, Daniels, Danilo, Danil, Dana, Danna
Namesakes: Daniel Boone, Danny Sullivan, Dan Rather, Jack Daniels

Danielle: Feminine form of Daniel. Hovering in or near the top ten for the past few years.
Relatives: Daniella, Daniele, Daniela, Danice, Dania, Danya
Namesake: Danielle Steele

Daphne: Greek for "laurel." According to Greek legend, she was the nymph who was changed into a laurel tree to escape the amorous attentions of Apollo. A lovely name.
Relative: Daphnis
Namesakes: Daphne du Maurier, Daphnis and Chloë

Dara: Semitic for "pearl of wisdom."
Namesake: Dara Nagel

Darby: Irish for "free man." Catchy. Darby and Joan are the archetype of the loving couple.
Relative: Derby
Namesake: Kentucky Derby

Darcy: Irish for "dark." If it was good enough for Jane Austen, it's good enough for us.
Relatives: D'Arcy, Darcie, Darcey, Darci
Namesakes: "Mr. Darcy," Darci Kistler

Darius: Persian for "king." Interesting choice.
Relatives: Daria, Darien, Darian
Namesakes: Darius Milhaud, Darien (Conn.)

Darrell: From Old French for "beloved."
Relatives: Darryl, Darryll, Daryl, Daryll, Darlin, Darlen, Darleen, Darlynn, Dare
Namesakes: Darryl Hannah, Darryl Strawberry, Darrell Evans

Darren: Old English for "rocky hill."
Relatives: Darrin, Darin, Dare, Dara, Darra, Darryn
Namesakes: Darren McGavin, Deron Johnson, Bobby Darin

Dartmouth: An English port and an Ivy League college. Seldom used as a first name, but it certainly has a classy sound.
Namesake: Dartmouth College

Darwin: Old English for "beloved friend."
Relative: Darwyn
Namesake: Charles Darwin

David: From the Hebrew for "beloved." On everyone's favorite name list.
Relatives: Davida, Davina, Davita, Dave, Davey, Davy, Davie, Davi, Davyd, Davis, Davidson, Dawes, Dawson, Dewi, Dewey, Devlin, Dabney
Namesakes: King David, David Letterman, David Bowie, Davey Johnson, Davy Jones

In 1955, then defense minister David Ben-Gurion ordered that no Israeli officer could represent Israel abroad unless he or she bore a Hebrew name.

Dawn: From the Scandinavian for "dawn." Peaked in the seventies, but continues to be popular.
Namesakes: Dawn Steel, Dawn Adams, "Delta Dawn"

Dayton: Old English for "bright town." Give this one a chance.
Relatives: Day, Daiton
Namesakes: Doris Day, Dayton (Ohio)

Deacon: From the Greek for "messenger."
Relative: Declan
Namesake: Deacon Jones

Dean: Old English for "valley." A popular name among U.S. secretaries of state.

Relatives: Deane, Deanna, Deana, Deanne, Deena
Namesakes: Dean Acheson, Dean Rusk, Deanna Durbin, John Dean

Deborah: Hebrew for "bee." A solid biblical name, but usage has fallen off somewhat.
Relatives: Debra, Debrah, Debbie, Debby, Deb, Debo, Devora, Devorah
Namesakes: Deborah Kerr, Debbie Allen, Debra Winger

Dee: A nickname for almost any "D" name that now stands on its own.
Relatives: Dee Dee, Didi
Namesakes: Dee Wallace, Dee Brown, Ruby Dee

Delia: From the Greek place name "Delos" and a pet form of Bedelia. Very pretty.
Namesake: Delia Ephron

Delilah: From the Hebrew for "amorous." Very melodic, but it carries a lot of baggage.
Relatives: Delila, Lila, Lilah
Namesake: Samson and Delilah

Della: Pet form of Adella.
Relatives: Dell, Adella, Adela
Namesakes: Della Reese, Adella Rogers St. Johns

Delmore: Latin for "sea." Del is a nice nickname.
Relatives: Delmar, Delmer
Namesake: Delmore Schwartz

Demelza: Old English for "fort on a hill." A romantic Cornish name and one for "Poldark" fans.
Relatives: Demie, Demi
Namesake: Demi Moore

Demetrius: Greek for "lover of the earth." Handsome; used regularly among those of Greek ancestry.
Relatives: Demitri, Dimitri, Dimitry, Dimity

Denholm: Scandinavian for "home of the Danes."
Relatives: Denholme, Denby, Denim
Namesakes: Denholm Elliot, Denby china

Denise: Feminine of Dennis. Creative spelling opportunities abound.

Relatives: Deniece, Deniese, Denice, Denyse, Denyce, Deneise, Dennice

Namesakes: Denise Williams, Denise Darcel

Dennis: From the Greek god Dionysus. Out of fashion, but why not try it for a girl.

Relatives: Denis, Dennys, Dennison, Denniston, Denzel, Denzil, Denzell, Denit, Dennit, Dion, Denny, Tennis, Tennyson

Namesakes: Dennis Hopper, Dennis Quaid, Denzel Washington, "Dennis the Menace"

Derek: Old German for "ruler." Never as popular here as in Britain.

Relatives: Derik, Dirk, Derick, Derrick, Derrik, Derych, Derry

Namesakes: Derek Jacobi, Dirk Bogarde, Bo Derek

Dermot: Irish for "free of envy." Underused.

Relative: Kermit

Desdemona: From the Greek for "misery." The wife of Othello, falsely accused of adultery and then murdered by him.

Desiree: From the Latin for "crave" and French for "desire."

Relatives: Desi, Desiderio

Namesakes: "Desiree Armfeldt," Desi Arnaz

Desmond: From the Latin for "society."

Relatives: Desi, Des

Namesake: Desmond Morris

Devon: English place name and Celtic for "poet." This name enjoyed a flurry of use in the seventies, but its popularity has dwindled of late. Pretty.

Relative: Devin

Namesakes: Devon White, Devon cream

Dewey: From a Welsh variation of David. Nice nickname.

Relatives: Dewy, Dewi

Namesakes: Thomas Dewey, Dewey Decimal System, "Dewey Duck"

Dexter: Latin for "right side" and the opposite of "sinister."

Namesake: Dexter Gordon

Diana: Latin for "divine." The Roman moon goddess; the British princess over whom we moon.

Relatives: Diane, Dyan, Dyanne, Dionne, Diahann, Di, Diandra, Diantha

Namesakes: Princess Di, Dyan Cannon, Dionne Warwick, Diana Rigg

Dickinson: American variation on a nickname for Richard.

Relatives: Dicken, Dickens, Dickenson, Dixon, Dix

Namesakes: Emily Dickinson, Dickinson College

Dierdre: Irish for "young girl." Enjoying a modest revival.

Relatives: Deirdre, Deirdra, Dierdra

Digby: Old English for "settlement near a ditch." Lowly origins, but upper-crust credentials.

Namesake: Digby Diehl

Dinah: From the Hebrew for "judgment." Fine name; give it a chance.

Relatives: Dina, Deena, Deanna

Namesakes: Dinah Shore, Dina Merrill

Dionne: A variation of Diana.

Relatives: Dion, Dione

Namesakes: Dionne Warwick, Dionne quintuplets, Dion and the Belmonts

Dixie: A variation of "Dixon" or "Dick's son." Apparently "Dixie-land" got its name as a mutation of "Dixon," as in the Mason-Dixon line.

Relatives: Dixon, Dixi

Namesakes: Dixie Carter, Dixie cup

Dolores: Latin for "lady of sorrows." Out of favor.

Relatives: Deloris, Dorrie, Dora

Dominick: Latin for "the Lord's." A Mediterranean favorite.

Relatives: Dominica, Dominique, Dominic, Dominik, Domingo, Dominy, Dom, Nick

Namesakes: Dominick Dunne, Dominique Wilkins, Dom DeLuise, Placido Domingo

Donald: Old English for "ruler of the world."

Relatives: Donn, Don, Donnie, Donny, Donaldson, Donne, Donghal, Donal

Namesakes: Donald Trump, Donny Osmond, Don Meredith, Sam Donaldson, "Donald Duck"

Donna: Latin for "lady."
Relatives: Dona, Domina, Madonna
Namesakes: Donna Reed, Madonna, "Dona Flor"

Donnelly: Irish for "dark man." A nice group of traditional Irish surnames that are beginning to see some use as first names.
Relatives: Donahue, Donnell, Donnel, Donner, Donovan, Donovon
Namesakes: Phil Donahue, Donner Pass, *Donovan's Reef*

Dooley: Origin unknown.
Relative: Dooly
Namesakes: Dooley Womack, Paul Dooley, Tom Dooley

Dora: Greek for "gift." A short form of Dorothy that has come to stand on its own. It is less popular now than before World War II.
Relatives: Dorene, Doreene, Dorine, Dore, Dorothy

Dorian: Derived from the Greek place name. Guaranteed to age well.
Relatives: Dorien, Dorie, Dorrien, Dorrian, Dory
Namesake: The Picture of Dorian Gray

Doris: Greek for "of the sea." Dory is a cute nickname.
Relatives: Dorris, Dorice, Dore, Dory, Dori
Namesakes: Doris Duke, Dore Schary

Dorothy: Greek for "gift of God." Immortalized in *The Wizard of Oz;* this child will always think there's no place like home.
Relatives: Dorothea, Dottie, Dot, Dotson, Dolly, Dolley
Namesakes: Dorothy Dandridge, Dolly Parton, "Little Dot," Dolly Madison

Dorset: Old English for "tribe near the sea."
Relative: Dorsey
Namesake: Tommy Dorsey

Douglas: Old English for "dark water." Very handsome; should be used more often.

Relatives: Douglass, Doug, Dougie, Dugan, Dougal, Dugald
Namesakes: Douglas MacArthur, Douglas Fairbanks, Michael Douglas

Dover: Old English for "water."
Namesakes: Dover sole, White Cliffs of Dover

Doyle: Old English for "dark stranger."
Relative: Doyl
Namesakes: Doyle Alexander, Arthur Conan Doyle, William Doyle

Drake: From the Latin for "dragon" and Old German for "male duck."
Namesakes: Sir Francis Drake, "Paul Drake"

Drew: A nickname for Andrew that now stands on its own.
Namesakes: Drew Barrymore, Drew Pearson, "Nancy Drew"

Duane: Old English for "dark."
Relatives: Dwayne, Dwane, Dwain, Dwaine, Duwayne
Namesakes: Duane McClain, Duane Eddy

Dudley: Old English for "people's meadow." A real sink-or-swim name, since the child will invariably be called "Dud."
Relatives: Dud, Duddy, Dudly
Namesakes: Dudley Moore, "Dudley Do-Right," "Duddy Kravitz"

Duke: From the Latin for "leader." Also pet name for Marmaduke.
Namesakes: Duke Ellington, Duke of Earl, Duke Snyder

Dulcie: Latin for "sweet." Don Quixote's lady love.
Relatives: Dulcinea, Dulce, Dulsie
Namesake: "Dulcinea del Toboso"

Duncan: Old English for "dark warrior." A great name, big with Scottish kings.
Relatives: Dunc, Dun
Namesakes: Duncan Phyfe, Duncan Hines

Durand: Latin for "enduring."
Relatives: Durandt, Durante, Durant, Duran
Namesakes: Duran Duran, William Durant, Jimmy Durante

Durward: Old English for "gatekeeper."
Relatives: Durwood, Durwald, Durwin, Derwood
Namesake: Durwood Kirby

Dustin: Old English for "dark stone." Consider it for a girl.
Relatives: Dusty, Dunstan, Dunston
Namesakes: Saint Dunstan, Dustin Hoffman, Dusty Baker

Dwight: Old English for "fair."
Namesakes: Dwight Gooden, Dwight D. Eisenhower

Dylan: Welsh for "sea god." According to Welsh legend, all the waves of the English and Irish seas wept when he died.
Relatives: Dillon, Dillan
Namesakes: Dylan Thomas, Bob Dylan, "Matt Dillon"

The Long and the Short of It

Is brevity the soul of naming or is it prolongation? Using multiple given names may strike you as silly. Looking down at your newborn, you may find it difficult to imagine he or she will ever "grow into" such a string of names. Then again, your family may have a tradition of using multiple names, so they seem perfectly appropriate to you. If you do decide to choose several names, your chances of finding one your child will approve of are greatly increased.

Maria Callas: Maria Anna Sofia Cecilia Kalogeropoulos
Prince Charles: Charles Philip Arthur George Windsor
Joseph Conrad: Jozef Teodor Konrad Walecz Korzeniowski
Charles de Gaulle: Charles Andre Marie Joseph de Gaulle
W. E. B. Du Bois: William Edward Burghardt Du Bois
John Le Carré: David John Moore Cornwell
Jelly Roll Morton: Ferdinand Joseph LaMenthe Morton
J. E. B. Stuart: James Ewell Brown Stuart
Kiefer Sutherland: Kiefer William Frederick Dempsey George
    Rufus Sutherland

But don't get bogged down with this question. Your child may grow up and decide to discard all but a single "signature" name.

Cappucine	Malcolm X
Cher	Pele
Colette	Prince
Erte	Sade
Fabian	Sting
Gallagher	Sukarno
Liberace	Twiggy
Madonna	Vanity

E

Eamon: Irish variation of Edmund. A good Irish name that has not been overused; a nice alternative to Sean, Ryan, and Kevin.
Relative: Amon
Namesakes: Eamonn Coghlan, Eamon De Valera

Earl: Old English for "a nobleman."
Relatives: Earle, Earland, Early, Erle, Errol, Erroll, Earleen, Erleen, Erlene
Namesakes: Earl Weaver, Earl Monroe, Erle Stanley Gardner, Errol Flynn, Early Wynn

Eartha: Old English for "earth." Well known, but seldom used. A good choice for a baby with both feet on the ground.
Namesake: Eartha Kitt

Eben: Hebrew for "stone."
Relatives: Ebenezer, Eban
Namesakes: Ebenezer Scrooge, Abba Eban

Ebony: Greek for "a hard wood."
Relatives: Ebonie, Ebonee
Namesake: "Ebony and Ivory"

Edda: Old English for "rich."
Relative: Eda

Eden: Hebrew for "delight." Provocative.
Relatives: Edie, Eddy, Eddie, Edan
Namesakes: Barbara Eden, Anthony Eden

Edgar: Old English for "properous warrior." Don't dismiss the "Ed" names; they are adorable for little boys and mature well.
 Relatives: Edgerton, Edger, Edgarton
 Namesakes: Edgar Allan Poe, Edgar Bergen

Edison: "Son of Ed." A nice selection from the "Ed" group.
 Relatives: Edyson, Edson
 Namesakes: Edison Armbrister, Thomas Edison, "Edison Carter"

Edith: Old English for "expensive gift." Extremely popular in the nineteenth century, but now completely out of fashion. Consider it.
 Relatives: Edithe, Edythe, Edie, Edyth, Edita, Edda, Editha
 Namesakes: Dame Edith Evans, Eydie Gorme, "Edith Bunker"

Edmund: Old English for "rich warrior." One of the children of *The Narnia Chronicles.* An excellent choice.
 Relatives: Edmond, Ed, Eddie, Ted, Teddy
 Namesake: Edmund Wilson

Edsel: Old English for "rich." American for "clunky car." Try another.
 Namesake: Edsel Ford

Edward: Old English for "rich guardian." A favorite of British kings and a reflection of your own good taste.
 Relatives: Eduard, Eduardo, Edwards, Edwardson, Eddy, Ted, Teddie, Ned, Neddie, Edvard, Edwardo
 Namesakes: Prince Edward, Edward Kennedy, Eddie Murphy, Ed Harris, Ted Williams

Edwin: Old English for "rich friend." Attractive choice from the "Ed" group.
 Relatives: Edina, Edwina, Edwyn, Edwyna, Edwynna, Edwinna
 Namesake: Edwin Newman

Egan: Irish for "little fire." Irish names are popular and this one is seldom used.
 Relatives: Egon, Egil
 Namesake: Egon Von Furstenberg

Egerton: Old English for "edge."
 Relative: Egmont

Eileen: An Irish variation of "Helen," it has never been as popular in this country as in England.
Relatives: Ilene, Evelyn, Alene
Namesakes: Eileen Brennan, "My Sister Eileen"

Elaine: French variation of Helen.
Relatives: Elaina, Elayne, Elana, Alaine, Alana, Laine, Laney
Namesakes: Elaine Stritch, Elaine May

Elder: Old English for "old." A Puritan favorite.
Relatives: Alder, Eldred
Namesakes: Elder White, Lee Elder

Eldon: Old English for "Ella's mound." A name that will sound at home in a law firm.
Relative: Elden

Eldridge: Old English for "old counsel."
Relatives: Eldred, Elbridge
Namesake: Eldridge Cleaver

Eleanor: From the Greek for "mercy." A royal name with many spelling possibilities.
Relatives: Eleanore, Eleanora, Elinor, Elinore, Ellie, Nell, Leonore, Leonora, Eliana
Namesakes: Eleanor of Aquitaine, Eleanor Roosevelt, Eleanor Donahue, "Little Nell"

Elias: Hebrew for "The Lord is God." Well worth considering.
Relatives: Elihu, Elyas, Ellis, Ellison, Ellsworth, Ellys, Elijah
Namesakes: Elias Howe, Ralph Ellison

Eliot: Hebrew for "high." The number of "l's" and "t's" are up to you.
Relatives: Eli, Ely, Elliot, Elliott, Eliott
Namesakes: Elliott Abrams, Elliott Gould, T. S. Eliot

Elise: Variation of Elizabeth.
Relatives: Lise, Elisa, Elissa, Elyssa, Elyse, Elysse, Alise, Alyse, Alysse, Alyssa, Alysa
Namesake: "Für Elise"

Elizabeth: Hebrew for "consecrated to God." Queens, saints, and actresses; how can you go wrong?

Relatives: Elisabeth, Lisbeth, Liz, Lizzie, Liza, Eliza, Ellie, Elsa, Beth, Bess, Betty, Bette, Bettie, Betsy, Elise, Aliza, Libby, Elspeth, Isabel, Isabelle, Isabella

Namesakes: Queen Elizabeth, Elizabeth McGovern, Elizabeth Taylor, Lisbeth Mark, Liza Minnelli, Bess Truman, "Eliza Doolittle"

Ella: Old German for "all." Elegant and simple.
Relative: Ellie
Namesake: Ella Fitzgerald

Ellen: A variation of Helen. A lovely name. Consistently popular but never trendy.
Relatives: Ellyn, Elen, Elyn, Ellin, Elin, Elena
Namesakes: Ellen Burstyn, Ellen Goodman

Ellery: From the Latin for "cheerful." Works well for boys and girls.
Relatives: Elery, Ellory, Elory, Ellary
Namesake: "Ellery Queen"

Ellis: A variation of Elias.
Relatives: Ellison, Elias, Elisha
Namesakes: Ellis Burks, Ellis Rabb, Ralph Ellison

Elmer: From the Old English for "famous nobleman."
Relatives: Elmo, Elman, Elmore
Namesakes: Elmore Leonard, Saint Elmo, "Elmer Fudd"

Elspeth: Scottish form of Elizabeth. A touch rarefied, but a nice alternative.
Relatives: Elsbeth, Elsbet, Elspet
Namesake: Elspeth Huxley

Elton: Old English for "Ella's town."
Relatives: Elten, Elroy
Namesake: Elton John

Elvira: Spanish variation of German for "close." The name of Noel Coward's *Blithe Spirit* and a song by the Oak Ridge Boys.
Relatives: Elvyra, Elvera, Elvie, Elva, Elvina
Namesake: *Elvira Madigan*

Elvis: Anglo-Saxon for "noble friend" and rock 'n' roll for "king." Nobody else even comes close.

Relatives: Elvin, Elva, Elwin, Elwyn
Namesakes: Elvis Presley, Elvin Hayes

Emanuel: Hebrew for "God is with us."
Relatives: Emmanuel, Emmanuella, Immanuel, Imanuel, Manuel, Manuella, Manny
Namesakes: Emanuel Lewis, Emmanuel Philbert, Manny Mota

Emiline: Old German for "labor." Sweet and old-fashioned; more popular overseas than in the United States.
Relatives: Emmeline, Emaline, Emmaline, Emlyn, Emelyn, Emylin, Emiline, Emmiline, Emmilyne

Emerson: Old English for "Emery's son." Classy.
Relatives: Emersen, Emmerson, Emmyrson, Emyrson
Namesakes: Emerson Boozer, Ralph Waldo Emerson

Emery: German for "powerful home."
Relatives: Emory, Emmery, Emmory
Namesake: Emory College

Emily: From the Latin for "eager." A traditional name with a lovely musical sound.
Relatives: Emilie, Emmilie, Emmily, Emil, Em, Emilia, Emilio, Emile, Emaline, Emeline, Emmaline
Namesakes: Emily Dickinson, Emilio Estevez

Emlyn: A Welsh place name. Very tony.
Relative: Emlin
Namesakes: Emlyn Williams, Emlyn Hughes

Emma: Old German for "all-embracing." Fashionable in the late nineteenth century and back again.
Relatives: Emmie, Emmy, Em, Emmot, Emmott
Namesakes: Emma Samms, Emmylou Harris, Lady Emma Hamilton, "Emma Peel"

Emmett: A variation of Emma.
Relatives: Emmott, Emmet
Namesake: Emmett Kelly

Emrick: Welsh variation on the Greek for "immortal." A good choice if you are looking for a little-used name.
Relatives: Emryk, Emrys, Emris

Enid: Welsh for "soul." A grandmother's name that has not returned to fashionability.
Namesake: Enid Haupt

Ephraim: Hebrew for "fruitful."
Relatives: Ephrem, Efrem
Namesake: Efrem Zimbalist, Jr.

Eric: Norse for "ruler of all." A name that has never gone out of vogue.
Relatives: Erik, Erica, Erika, Eryk, Eryka, Erikson
Namesakes: Eric the Red, Eric Clapton, "Erica Kane"

Erin: Gaelic for "western island." The Irish really come up with great names.
Relatives: Eryn, Erinn, Erinna, Erynn, Erynna
Namesakes: Erin Gray, "Erin Go Bragh"

Ernest: Old German for "vigorous." A resolute and purposeful name. There is an importance to being Ernest.
Relatives: Ernst, Earnest, Ernie, Ernestine, Earnestine, Ernesta
Namesakes: Ernest Hemingway, Ernie Pyle, Max Ernst

Errol: A variation of Earl. A swashbuckler, a pirate, or an outlaw, but always the romantic hero.
Relative: Erle
Namesakes: Errol Flynn, Erle Stanley Gardner

Erskine: Old English for "green heights." Several writers have carried this name.
Namesakes: Erskine Caldwell, Erskine Childers

Ervin: A variation of Irving.
Relatives: Irvin, Irving, Ervan, Erwin
Namesake: Ervin "Magic" Johnson

Esme: From the Latin for "esteem." Add an accent to the final "e" for a continental look.
Relatives: Esmee, Esma, Esmie

Esmerelda: Spanish for "emerald." The heroine of Victor Hugo's *The Hunchback of Notre Dame*.
Relatives: Esmeralda, Esmarelda, Esmaralda, Esmiralda, Esmirelda

Esmond: Old English for "protective grace."
  Relatives: Esmund, Desmond, Desmund
  Namesake: The History of Henry Esmond

Estelle: Latin for "star." One of the constellation names.
  Relatives: Estel, Estella, Stella, Estie, Estee
  Namesakes: Estelle Parsons, Stella Stevens, Estée Lauder

Estes: Latin for "estuary."
  Relative: Eston
  Namesake: Estes Kefauver

Esther: Persian for "star." The girl with this name will certainly be a star at the Purim carnival.
  Relatives: Ester, Esta, Essie, Ettie, Hester, Hesther, Hettie
  Namesakes: Queen Esther, Esther Williams, "Hester Prynne"

Ethan: From the Latin for "constant." A good choice; you'll be ahead of the crowd.
  Relatives: Ethen, Etan
  Namesakes: Ethan Allen, *Ethan Frome*

Ethel: Old English for "noble."
  Relatives: Adele, Ethelred, Ethelbert
  Namesakes: Ethel Merman, "Ethel Mertz," Ethelred the Unready

Etienne: French variation of Stephen. A fine line of leather goods; this child will always be able to find monogrammed shoes.
  Relatives: Estienne, Ettie, Etta
  Namesake: Etienne Aigner

Eudora: Greek for "good gift."
  Relative: Dora
  Namesake: Eudora Welty

Eugene: From the Greek for "well-born." And your child certainly will be.
  Relatives: Gene, Eugenia, Eugenie
  Namesakes: Eugene O'Neill, Empress Eugenie, Eugenia Falkenburg, Gene Kelly

Eunice: From the Greek for "victorious."

Relatives: Eunyce, Unice
Namesake: Eunice Shriver

Eustace: From the Greek for "fruitful." If you go with Eustace, call him Stacy.
Relatives: Stace, Stacie
Namesake: "Eustace Tilley"

Evan: Welsh variation of John. Like Ian, Ivan, and Sean, this is a popular alternative to John.
Relatives: Evans, Evanston
Namesakes: Evan Hunter, Walker Evans, Evanston (Ill.)

Evangeline: From the Greek for "messenger of good news." The heroine of the classic poem by Henry Wadsworth Longfellow.
Relatives: Evangelyne, Evangaline, Evangalyne

Eve: From the Hebrew for "life."
Relatives: Eva, Evy, Evie, Evita, Evander, Ev, Ava
Namesakes: Eve Arden, Evita Peron, Eva Marie Saint, "Little Eva," Ava Gardner

Evelyn: Variation of Eve. Generally a girl's name, though in the past it was a common choice for boys. Evelyn Waugh's first wife was named Evelyn. Friends called them he-Evelyn and she-Evelyn.
Relatives: Eveline, Evalyn, Aveline, Avaline, Avelina, Avalina, Evel, Evilio, Evalina, Evelina, Evette
Namesakes: Evelyn Anthony, Evel Knievel

Everett: Old German for "strong boar." That's "boar," not "bore."
Relatives: Everet, Everard, Eberhardt
Namesakes: Everett Dirksen, Edward Everett Horton, Chad Everett

Ewing: Origin uncertain, possibly Old English for "youth." A name made famous by the "Dallas" clan on TV.
Relatives: Ewan, Ewen, Ewart
Namesakes: Patrick Ewing, "J. R. Ewing"

Ezra: Hebrew for "salvation."
Relatives: Ezer, Ezri, Ezzret
Namesake: Ezra Pound

NEW YORK CITY TOP TEN

1987

Girls	*Boys*
Jessica	Michael
Jennifer	Christopher
Stephanie	Jonathan
Melissa	Daniel
Christina	David
Nicole	Anthony
Amanda	Joseph
Ashley	Matthew
Tiffany	John
Samantha	Andrew

1981

Jennifer	Michael
Jessica	Christopher
Melissa	David
Nicole	Jason
Michelle	Joseph
Elizabeth	Anthony
Lisa	John
Tiffany	Daniel
Christina	Robert
Danielle	James

1972

Jennifer	Michael
Michelle	David
Lisa	Christopher
Elizabeth	John
Christine	James
Maria	Joseph
Nicole	Robert
Kimberly	Anthony
Denise	Richard
Amy	Brian

1898

Mary	John
Catherine	William
Margaret	Charles
Annie	George
Rose	Joseph
Marie	Edward
Esther	James
Sarah	Louis
Frances	Francis
Ida	Samuel

Information supplied by the New York City Department of Health.

F

In 1974, National Fink Week was declared in Fink, Texas, in honor of the much-maligned name. Finks from all over the country attended the festivities.

Fabian: Latin for "bean." A beach-blanket heartthrob in the fifties, a society of intellectuals in the late nineteenth century.
Relatives: Fabius, Fab, Fabyan, Fabia, Fabya, Fabiana

Fairfax: Old English for "blond-haired." Oh, so classy.
Relative: Fairfield
Namesakes: Fairfield Osborn, Fairfax (Va.)

Faith: From the Latin for "trust." One of the prettiest and most enduring of the virtue names.
Relatives: Faithful, Faythe, Fayth, Fido, Fidel, Fidelity
Namesakes: Faith Daniels, Percy Faith, Marianne Faithfull

Farley: Old English for "distant meadow." In Scotland and Ireland a farl is a little muffin.
Relatives: Fairley, Fairleigh, Farland
Namesakes: Farley Granger, Fairleigh Dickinson University

Farrah: Old English for "beautiful" and Latin for "wild ass." Stick with the Old English.
Relatives: Farah, Farra
Namesake: Farrah Fawcett

Farrar: Latin for "blacksmith." Unusual and interesting.
Relatives: Farra, Farar, Farron, Faron, Farrier
Namesakes: "Brat Farrar," Faron Young

Farrell: Old English for "man of valor." This name screams Ivy League and a seat on the stock exchange.
Relatives: Farrel, Farrow
Namesakes: Mila Farrell, Mia Farrow

Fawn: From the Latin for "young deer." A.k.a. Bambi.
Relatives: Faun, Fauna, Fawne, Fawna
Namesake: Fawn Hall

Fay: Old French for "fairy." In Scotland, to be "fey" is to have a sixth sense or be especially prophetic.
Relatives: Faye, Fey
Namesakes: Fay Wray, Faye Dunaway

Felicia: Feminine of "Felix."
Relatives: Felice, Felicity, Felisse, Feliciana, Felyce, Phylice, Philicia, Phylicia
Namesake: Phylicia Rashad

Felix: Latin for "happiness." Four popes chose this name.
Relative: Felice
Namesakes: Felix Frankfurter, Felix Rohayton, "Felix the Cat"

Ferdinand: Old German for "courageous traveler." A royal name in the Spanish monarchy.
Relatives: Ferdie, Ferdy, Ferde, Ferd, Fernando, Fernandas
Namesakes: King Ferdinand, Ferde Grofé, "Ferdinand the Bull"

Fergus: Irish Gaelic for "strong man." This name sounds like it came directly from the Highlands. Buy this kid a kilt.
Relatives: Ferguson, Fergie, Fergy, Fergun
Namesakes: Ferguson Jenkins, Sarah Ferguson (Princess "Fergie"), James Fergus

Fern: Old English for "leafy plant." According to ancient lore, fern seeds were thought to make one invisible.
Relatives: Ferne, Fearn, Fearne, Fernly

Ferris: Latin for "iron."
Relatives: Ferrys, Ferrell, Ferrel
Namesake: "Ferris Bueller"

Fielding: Old English for "field." Strong and solid.
Relatives: Field, Fielder
Namesakes: Fielder Jones, Henry Fielding

Finnian: Irish for "fair-haired." Another choice from the Emerald Isle.
Relatives: Finn, Finnie, Finny, Finian, Finley, Fyn, Fynn
Namesake: Finian's Rainbow

Fiona: Old English for "white." Perfectly beautiful. This name has always been popular in the British Isles.
Relatives: Fione, Fionn
Namesake: Fiona St. Aubyn

Fitz: From the Latin for "son." Fitz names were commonly given to the illegitimate sons of royalty.
Relatives: Fitzgerald, Fitzroy, Fitzhugh, Fitzpatrick
Namesakes: John Fitzgerald Kennedy, Barry Fitzgerald

Flannery: From the Old French for "sheet of metal." A strong name for a boy or girl.
Relatives: Flan, Flann
Namesakes: Flannery O'Connor, Flann O'Brien

Fleming: A native of Flanders.
Relative: Flemming
Namesakes: Ian Fleming, Peggy Fleming

Fletcher: From the Old French for "seller of arrows." An ancient occupational name. Perfect for a little Sagittarian.
Namesakes: Fletcher Knebel, Fletcher's Castoria

Florence: Latin for "blooming flower" or "flourishing." An old-fashioned beauty that is just beginning to return to popularity.
Relatives: Flora, Floria, Florida, Florie, Floris, Florrie, Fleur, Flower, Florenz, Florentia, Flory, Floryn, Flossie, Flo
Namesakes: Florence Eiseman, Florence Henderson, Flo Ziegfeld

Flynn: Irish for "son of the red-haired man."
Relatives: Flinn, Flin, Flyn
Namesake: Errol Flynn

Ford: Old English for "river crossing." Better than Toyota.
Namesakes: Henry Ford, Harrison Ford

Forrest: Old French for "out of the woods." A good choice if you're having trouble deciding between Birch and Ash.
Relatives: Forest, Forestt, Forrestt, Forrester, Forster
Namesakes: Forrest Tucker, E. M. Forster, De Forest Kelly

Foster: From the Old French for "forest keeper." This also means "to cherish or sustain," as in "foster child."
Namesakes: Foster Grant, John Foster Dulles, Jodie Foster

Frances: From the Old French for "free." An androgynous name, though "Frances" is usually used for a girl and "Francis" for a boy.
Relatives: Francis, Fanchon, Francesca, Fran, Franny, Fanny, Frannie, Frank, Frankie, Francine, Franz, Franco
Namesakes: Frances Farmer, Fran Tarkenton, Sir Francis Drake, Francine du Plessix Gray, Franco Harris, Franz Kafka

Franklin: From the Old French for "free man."
Relatives: Frank, Frankie, Franklyn
Namesakes: Franklin D. Roosevelt, Benjamin Franklin

Fraser: Unknown, possibly Old French for "strawberry."
Relatives: Frazer, Fraiser, Frazier
Namesakes: Fraser Heston, Walt Frazier

Frederick: Old German for "peaceful ruler." A fine old name with a long tradition among European royalty.
Relatives: Frederic, Fredericka, Frederica, Frederika, Fred, Freddie, Freddy, Fritz, Fritzie, Fritzi
Namesakes: Frederick Forsyth, Frederick Douglass, Frederica von Stade, Fritz Weaver

Fremont: Old German for "guardian of freedom."
Namesake: Eliot Fremont-Smith

Frieda: Old German for "peace." Frieda is not particularly fashionable these days; try Frederica.
Relatives: Friede, Freida, Fredie, Freda, Winifred, Fritzi
Namesakes: Freida Payne, Frieda (Mrs. D. H.) Lawrence

Fuller: Old English for "one who works with cloth." A surname rarely used as a first.

Namesakes: Buckminster Fuller, Thomas Fuller, Fuller Brush man

Fulton: Old English for "town near the field."

Namesakes: Fulton Sheen, Samuel Fulton, Robert Fulton

Naming Your Baby Can Be a Daytime Drama

Is it inevitable that at some point during your pregnancy you will find yourself watching soaps? Probably; but you can put your viewing time to good use. Writers of soap operas are among the most creative namers around. They are particularly fond of giving their characters unusual and/or romantic names. Depending on your point of view, the remark that a name sounds like it's straight from the soaps could be a compliment or an insult. The following list includes some of our past and present favorites.

Cabot Alden	"Patch" Johnson
Seneca Beaulac	Silver Kane
Eden Capwell Castillo	Catsy Kirkland
Blaine Corey	Charmane L'Amour
Palmer Courtland	Duke Lavery
Elena dePoulignac	Egypt Masters
Harper Deveraux	Leanna Randolph
Echo Di Savoy	Olivia St. John
Shane Donovan	Reva Shayne
Adelaide Fitzgibbons	Holden Snyder
Ridge Forrester	Gunnar Stenbeck
Thorne Forrester	Crane Tolliver
Felicia Gallant	Cass Winthrop
Thomasina Harding	

G

Gabriel: From the Hebrew for "God is my strength." The archangel Gabriel has played important roles in the mythology of Christians, Jews, and Muslims. The name has a musical quality to it, perhaps because he heralds Judgment Day with his trumpet.

Relatives: Gabryel, Gabriello, Gavrila, Gabby, Gab, Gabe, Gable

Namesakes: Gabe Kaplan, Gabby Hayes, Clark Gable, Roman Gabriel

Gabriela: From the Hebrew for "God is my strength" and a feminine version of Gabriel. The exotic quality of this name makes it a winning choice.

Relatives: Gabriella, Gabrielle, Gavrila, Gavra, Galia, Galya, Gabby, Gabi

Namesake: Gabrielle Roy

Gage: Old French for "pledge." This is unusual and handsome.

Namesake: Thomas Gage

Gail: Irish for "stranger," Old Norse for "to sing," and an abbreviated form of Gaylord or Abigail. A short, sweet name that works for boys or girls, though it is usually assumed to be feminine.

Relatives: Gayle, Gale, Galatea

Namesakes: Gail Strickland, Gale Sayers, Gale Storm

Gaines: Middle English for "increase in wealth." You couldn't do better for a future stockbroker.

Relatives: Gaynes, Gainsborough, Gainor, Gaynor

Namesakes: Thomas Gainsborough, Rowdy Gaines, Gainesville (Fla.)

Galen: From the Greek for "tranquil." Galen was a second-century physician and philosopher who is called the grandfather of modern medicine.

Gallagher: Celtic for "eager aide."
   Relatives: Gallagher, Gahan
   Namesakes: "Gallagher," Gahan Wilson

Galloway: From the Latin for "from Gaul." Evokes distant times and faraway places.
   Relative: Galway
   Namesakes: Galway Kinnell, James Galway

Gamal: Arabic for "camel."
   Relatives: Jamal, Jammal, Gamali
   Namesake: Malcolm-Jamal Warner

Gardiner: From the Danish for "garden keeper." A noble profession and a vivid name.
   Relatives: Gardener, Gardenor, Gardner, Gardnard, Garden, Gar
   Namesakes: Erle Stanley Gardner, John Gardner

Gareth: Norse for "enclosure" and Old French for "watchful." Sir Gareth was the knight of the Round Table responsible for freeing Lady Lynette from the dreaded Sir Ironside.
   Relatives: Garth, Garret, Garrett, Garreth, Gareth, Garit, Gary, Garry, Gar
   Namesakes: Garrett Morris, Garrett Simmons

Garfield: Old English for "promontory." A name for fat cats.
   Relative: Gar
   Namesakes: James Garfield, "Garfield"

Garland: Old French for "wreath." Pretty name.
   Relatives: Garlan, Garlon, Garlyn, Gar
   Namesakes: Garland Jeffries, Judy Garland

Garner: From the Latin for "granary."
   Namesakes: James Garner, John Nance Garner

Garnet: Latin for "red seed." It is the birthstone for January babies.
   Relative: Garnett

Garrison: From the Old French for "fort." A slightly more formal twist on Gary.
Relative: Garson
Namesakes: Garrison Keillor, Garson Kanin, Greer Garson

Gary: From the Old German for "spear carrier."
Relatives: Garry, Garrie, Garvey, Garvie, Garvin, Gervis, Gervais, Gervase, Garrick
Namesakes: Garry Trudeau, Gary Larson, Gary Cooper, Steve Garvey

Gaspar: Persian for "treasure bearer." Gaspar was one of the three wise men; his gift to the Christ child was frankincense, representing divinity.
Relatives: Gasper, Jasper

Gavin: Welsh for "hawk." A proper name for a future pilot.
Relative: Gavan
Namesakes: Gavin McLeod, Gavin Maxwell, John Gavin

Gawain: Welsh for "courteous." Brave knight of the Round Table who tried to find and recover the Holy Grail.
Relatives: Gawaine, Gawen

Gay: From the Old French for "merry."
Relatives: Gaye, Gae, Gai, Gaea, Gaia (Greek for "the earth")
Namesakes: Gay Talese, Gae Exton, John Gay

Gaylord: From the Old French for "brave."
Relatives: Gaylard, Gayelord, Gay
Namesake: Gaylord Perry

Gelsey: A variety of jasmine (gelsemium). One of the more unusual floral names.
Relatives: Gelsi, Gelsy
Namesake: Gelsey Kirkland

Gemma: Latin for "precious stone." A lovely name more popular in Britain than in the United States. Try pronouncing it with a soft "g," as in "gemstone."
Relative: Jemma

Geneva: From the Old French for "juniper berry." An interesting change from Jennifer.
Relatives: Genevia, Genny
Namesake: Geneva (Switzerland)

Genevieve: Old Welsh for "white wave." Exquisite. A truly lovely-sounding name.
Relative: Genny
Namesake: Genevieve Bujold

George: Greek for "farmer." Saint George is the patron saint of England and is commonly depicted as the mighty dragon-slayer and damsel-saver.
Relatives: Georg, Georges, Georgio, Giorgio, Giorgis, Georgius, Georgie, Georgi, Georgy, Geordie, Goran, Jorge, Jorges, Jorgen, Jerzy, Jiri, Juro, Jurik, Jur, Jeorg, Juergen, Jurgen, Jurek, Jorrin, Jurgi, Yegor, Yura, Yurchik, Yurik, Yusha, Yurko, Yoyi, Yuri, Egor, Zhorka, Seiorse
Namesakes: King George III, George Washington, George Bernard Shaw, George M. Cohan, George Gershwin, George Balanchine, George Burns, McGeorge Bundy, Jorge Amado, "Curious George"

Georgia: Greek for "farmer" and a feminine version of George. The great southern state of Georgia was named in honor of England's King George II. It's a name always on one's mind.
Relatives: Georgea, Georgina, Georgianna, Georgine, Georgette, Georgeen, Georgeena, Georgeanne, Georgienne, Giorgia, Georgie, Georgy, Gina, Gerda, Gruzia, Jirka, Jirca, Jirina, Jorgina
Namesakes: Georgia Hampton, Georgia O'Keeffe, Georgette Klinger, "georgette" lace, *Georgy Girl*

Gerald: Old French for "spear warrior." You can see how popular this one is in Europe by the wealth of variations.
Relatives: Gerard, Geraud, Gerardo, Gerhard, Gerhardt, Gerhart, Geraldo, Garold, Gerek, Gerrit, Garrod, Garrard, Gerbert, Girard, Girauld, Girault, Giraut, Gerry, Jerry, Jerard, Jarett, Jarrett
Namesakes: Gerard Manley Hopkins, Geraldo Rivera

Geraldine: Old German for "hard spear" and a feminine version of Gerald.
Relatives: Geraldene, Gereldine, Geraldyne, Gerry, Geri, Gerrie
Namesakes: Geraldine Page, Geraldine Ferraro, Geraldine Chaplin

Germain: Middle English for "bud" and related to "German." A bit Teutonic perhaps, but pleasant sounding.

Relatives: German, Germaine, Jarman, Jermyn, Jermain, Jermayne, Jermaine, Jermana

Namesakes: Saint Germain, Germaine Greer, Jermaine Jackson

Gertrude: Old German for "adored warrior." Although the name sounds a bit dated, consider the charming variations.

Relatives: Gerta, Gerda, Gerte, Gertie, Gerty, Gert, Jera, Jerica, Trude, Truta, Trudy, Trudie, Trudi, True

Namesakes: Hamlet's mother, Gertrude Stein

Gideon: From the Hebrew for "mighty warrior." According to the Old Testament, Gideon tricked his enemy into thinking he led a massive army by breaking crockery and sounding the trumpets.

Relatives: Giddy, Gid

Namesakes: Gideon Putnam, Gideon Bible

Gifford: Middle English for "a worthy gift."

Relative: Giff

Namesake: Frank Gifford

Gig: Middle English for "horse-drawn carriage" and vaudevillian for "one-night stand."

Namesake: Gig Young

Gilbert: Old German for "bright desire." Gilberta is a feminine version.

Relatives: Gilberto, Guilbert, Gibbon, Gil, Gilly, Gip, Gipper, Gib, Gibby, Gibbs, Gibson, Gillett, Gillette, Wilbert, Wilbur, Bert

Namesakes: Gilbert Roland, John Gilbert, W. S. Gilbert, Astrid Gilberto

Gilda: Celtic for "servant of God" and Old English for "gold-coated." A variation on Golda.

Relative: Gylda

Namesakes: Gilda Radner, Rigoletto's daughter

Giles: From the Greek for "shield of hides" and French for "youth." Sounds like the name of a British butler. Saint Giles is the patron saint of the physically handicapped.

Relatives: Gyles, Gilles, Gilean, Gileon, Gil, Gillette, Gillian, Egedio, Egide, Egidius

Namesake: "Giles Goat Boy"

Gilford: Old English for "a ford near the wooded ravine."
Relatives: Guilford, Gilmore, Gilroy
Namesake: Jack Gilford

Gilia: Hebrew for "my joy is in the Lord."
Relatives: Giliah, Gilana, Gila, Gilah

Gillian: A variation of Juliana, popularized in Britain during the Middle Ages. May be pronounced with either a hard "g" (as in "glue") or a soft "g" (as in "gem").
Relatives: Gillianne, Gilliana, Gilly, Gill

Giselle: Anglo-Saxon for "sword pledge." Perfect for a future ballerina.
Relatives: Gisella, Gisela, Gizella, Gizelle
Namesake: Giselle

Gita: Hebrew for "good."
Relatives: Gitah, Gitel, Gittel

Gitana: Spanish for "gypsy." For the baby who responds to violins and tambourines.
Relatives: Gitane, Gypsy, Gipsy
Namesakes: Gypsy Rose Lee, Gitane bicycles, Gitane cigarettes

Gladys: A Welsh version of Claudia.
Relatives: Gladiss, Gladyce, Gleda
Namesake: Gladys Knight

Glen: Celtic for "secluded wooded valley." Thanks to actress Glenn Close, this name has found a new following among girl babies.
Relatives: Glenn, Glena, Glenda, Glyn, Glynn, Glynnis, Glynis, Glenard, Glenon, Glendon
Namesakes: Glenn Miller, Glenn Ford, Glenn Close, Glenda Jackson, Glynis Johns, John Glenn

Gloria: Latin for "glory." Gloriana was the fairy queen in Spenser's epic poem. The name was intended as a tribute to the dedicatee, Queen Elizabeth I.
Relatives: Glora, Glorya, Glory, Gloriana, Glorianne
Namesakes: Gloria Swanson, Gloria Steinem, Gloria Vanderbilt, morning glory

Godfrey: Old German for "God's peace."

Relatives: Goddard, Gottfried, Gotfrid, Goffredo, Giotto, Godofredo, Govert, Godrick, Godwin, Godin, Goddenn, Godding, Godard, Godhart, Gotthardt

Namesakes: Godfrey Cambridge, Arthur Godfrey, *My Man Godfrey*

Godiva: Old English for "gift of God." Sounds like an Aussie greeting. This name will be associated with the saucy lady who rode through town in nothing but a curtain of her own knee-length hair. Her husband had jokingly said he wouldn't levy taxes on the townspeople if she performed the stunt. Never joke with a Lady named Godiva.

Namesake: Godiva chocolates

Golda: Old English "to shine."

Relatives: Gold, Goldie, Golden, Goldman, Goldwin, Goldwyn

Namesakes: Golda Meir, Goldie Hawn, Golden Richards, Samuel Goldwyn

Gordon: Old English for "fertilized pasture." A Scottish clan name with a lovely tartan of navy blue, hunter green, yellow, and white.

Relatives: Gordan, Gordie, Gordy, Gordo, Gorton, Gore, Gorham, Gorrell

Namesakes: Gordon Cooper, Gordon Parks, Gordie Howe

Gower: Old English for "crooked coastline" or Old French for "harness maker."

Relatives: Gowell, Gowar

Namesake: Gower Champion

Grace: From the Latin for "grace." According to Roman mythology, the Graces personified truth, beauty, and charm. The Greeks called them Charities. Their individual names were Thalia (Flowering), Aglaia (Wisdom), and Euphrosyne (Joy). Grace is coming back into favor.

Relatives: Gracey, Gracie, Graza, Grazia, Grazina

Namesakes: Grace Kelly, Grace Slick, Grace Paley, Gracie Allen

Grady: From the Latin for "rank."

Namesake: Grady Tate

Graham: Latin for "grain" and Anglo-Saxon for "gray home." Graham flour (which is made from wheat kernels) is named for American physician Sylvester Graham.

Relatives: Gram, Grahame

Namesakes: Graham Kerr, Graham Greene, Graham Nash, Gram Parsons, Graham crackers

Granger: From the Old French for "farm steward."
Namesake: Stewart Granger

Grant: From the Old French for "to give." A refined name that suggests a certain elegance.
Namesakes: Grant Wood, Grant Tinker, Cary Grant, Ulysses S. Grant

Granville: Old French for "big town." An appropriate choice for a baby born in a major league town.
Relative: Grenville
Namesake: Granville Hicks

Gratia: From the Latin for "grateful." And let's not forget Gracias, Spaseba, Merci, Thanks, and Danke.
Relative: Gratiana

Gray: Old English for "to shine." For the baby who sees more than just black and white.
Relatives: Grey, Grayson, Graydon, Griswold, Greeley
Namesakes: Joel Grey, Horace Greeley

Greer: From the Greek for "watchful." Works well for a boy or girl.
Relatives: Grier, Gregoria
Namesakes: Greer Garson, Rosie Grier

Gregory: From the Greek for "watchman." This name has lent itself to the Gregorian chant and the Gregorian calendar in honor of Pope Gregory I and Pope Gregory XIII, respectively.
Relatives: Gregorius, Gregori, Gregoire, Gregor, Gregorio, Gregoor, Griogair, Grioghar, Gregus, Gragos, Greis, Grischa, Grigor, Grigori, Gries, Gero, Greg, Graig, Greig, Gregg, Gregson, Grig, Grigg, Grigson, McGregor
Namesakes: Pope Gregory, Gregory Peck, Dick Gregory

Griffin: A mythological beast—half lion and half eagle—that is charged with watching over golden treasures.
Relatives: Gryphon, Griffon, Griffith, Griff
Namesakes: Griffin Dunne, Griffon Bell, Merv Griffin, Andy Griffith

Griselda: Old German for "gray warrior." In Boccaccio's tale, "The Decameron," Griselda's husband doubted her love for him and put her through tests of anguish and heartbreak. Yet her love proved constant, and he was at last satisfied.

Relatives: Grizelda, Grishilda, Grishilde, Griseldis, Grisa, Gris, Chriselda, Selda, Zelda

Grover: Anglo-Saxon for "one who tends the groves." Akin to Farmer, Gardiner, and Forester.

Relative: Grove

Namesakes: Grover Cleveland, Grover Washington, "Sesame Street" character

Guinevere: Celtic for "white wave." King Arthur's lady and a jewel of a name. The French version, Genevieve, is also lovely.

Relatives: Guenevere, Gwendoline, Gwendolyn, Gwendaline, Gwendolen, Gwen, Gwenn, Gwenne, Gwenith, Gwenyth, Gwyneth, Gwyn, Guenn, Gwynne, Gwyndolyn, Jennifer

Namesakes: Lady Guinevere, Gwendolyn Brooks, Gwen Verdon, Gwyneth Jones

Gunnar: Old Norse for "war." A great name for a child with the proper Norse heritage.

Relatives: Gunn, Gunther, Gunter, Guntar

Namesakes: Gunnar Nelson, Günter Grass, "Peter Gunn"

Gustave: Swedish for "from the Goths."

Relatives: Gustavo, Gustavus, Gustav, Gustaf, Gus

Namesakes: Gustave Flaubert, Gustav Klimt, Gustav Mahler, Gustavus Adolphus

Guthrie: Celtic for "war hero" and American for "folk singer."

Namesakes: Woody Guthrie, Arlo Guthrie

Guy: From the Old French for "guide." Guy, like Bud and Mac, is a generic term for "hey, you."

Namesakes: Guy Burgess, Guy de Maupassant, Guy Fawkes

Invent-a-Name

There are many ways to create your own name for your bundle of joy. Try combining syllables from favorite names in your family; Cybill Shepherd got started that way. Or take the spin-art approach. Take first letters, syllables, and suffixes you like and print them on three sets of index cards. Herewith some suffixes to get you going.

-a/-ia/-e/-i/-y/-et/-el/-er/-ly/-ya/-ette/-etta/-elle/-ella/
-ine/-ina/-een/-ene/-ice/-ica/-ika/-ille/-issa/-ita/-lyn/
-lin/-an/-son/-san/-sin/-aziz/-aria/-ala/-alia/-ila/-ana/
-anna/-anya

Shuffle thoroughly, lay them out, and let the fun begin.

Hadden: Old English for "heath."
Relatives: Haddon, Hadley
Namesakes: Hadley Hemingway (Ernest's first wife), Hadley (Mass.)

Hadrian: From the Greek for "wealthy" and a form of Adrian. The Roman emperor Hadrian built a wall in England during the second century to keep the warrior Scots at bay.

Haley: Norse for "hero" and Gaelic for "wise one."
Relatives: Hailey, Hayley, Haylee, Haile, Hally, Halley, Halli, Hallie, Hale
Namesakes: Hayley Mills, Hallie Foote, Alex Haley, Nathan Hale, Arthur Hailey, Haley's Comet

Hall: From the Old English for "meeting room."
Namesake: Monty Hall

Halley: Old English for "oneness." This nifty choice has a nineteenth-century ring to it. Calico, braids, and Mary Janes.
Relatives: Haley, Haleigh, Hallie, Hollis

Hamlet: Old German for "home." This name will forever be linked with Shakespeare's tragedy about the Prince of Denmark. Still, the variations offer a chance to be or not to be Hamlet.
Relatives: Hamlit, Hamlin, Hamilton, Hammond, Hampton, Ham
Namesakes: Harry Hamlin, Alexander Hamilton, "The Pied Piper of Hamlin," *Hammond Atlas,* the Hamptons (N.Y.)

Hannah: From the Hebrew for "God is merciful" or "graceful one." Hannah is a palindromic name. Hana means "young flower" in Japanese.
Relatives: Hanna, Hana, Hannia, Hannya, Hanniah, Hania, Hanita, Hanka, Hannicka, Hannele, Channa
Namesakes: Hannah Arendt, Hana Mandlikova, Daryl Hannah

Hannibal: Old English for "steep incline." It was Hannibal who, in 200 B.C., invaded Italy from Spain by crossing the Alps with his army and his elephants.
Relatives: Han, Hanley
Namesakes: "Hannibal Smith," Hannibal (Mo.)

Hardy: Old English for "good health." For the stalwart, robust, sturdy, intrepid baby.
Relatives: Hardin, Harden, Harding, Hardley
Namesakes: Thomas Hardy, Warren G. Harding, "The Hardy Boys"

Harlan: German for "flax" and Old English for "rabbit archer." The names in this group have a sense of geniality about them.
Relatives: Harlin, Harley, Harlow, Harford
Namesakes: Harlan Ellison, Harley Davison, Jean Harlow

Harmon: From the Greek for "harmony" and Old English for "soldier."
Relatives: Harmony, Harman, Harmonie
Namesakes: Harmon Killebrew, Mark Harmon, Harmony (Md.)

Harold: From the Old German for "commander." A distinguished, traditional name with a powerful meaning.
Relatives: Hereld, Harry, Hal, Hiraldo
Namesakes: Harold Washington, Hal Linden

Harper: From the Old Norse for "whaler." Calls to mind the musical harp, ancient symbol of Ireland.
Relatives: Harpo, Harp
Namesakes: Harper Lee, Harpo Marx, Harper's Ferry, *Harper's*

Harriet: A feminine variation of Harry.
Relatives: Harriette, Hariot, Harriott, Hattie, Hatty, Hetty, Happy, Etta, Etty
Namesakes: Harriet Tubman, Hattie McDaniel

Harry: An Old English form of Henry. We're just wild about this name. Although Charles and Di named their second princeling Henry, he is known as Harry.

Relatives: Harris, Harrison

Namesakes: Harry Houdini, Harry S Truman, Harrison Ford

Hart: Middle English for "stag." And we all know you've gotta have Hart.

Relatives: Harte, Hartley, Hartman, Hartwell, Hartwig

Namesakes: Hart Crane, Gary Hart, Moss Hart, Bret Harte, "Mary Hartman"

Harvey: From the Old German for "battle." For movie buffs, Harvey will forever be a large invisible rabbit.

Relatives: Harve, Herve, Harv, Harvard

Namesakes: Harvey Korman, Laurence Harvey, Harvard University

In 1965, an organization was formed to defend the name "Harvey" from being used demeaningly in advertisements or in the media in general.

Haskel: Anglo-Saxon for "ash tree."

Relative: Haskell

Namesake: "Eddie Haskell"

Haven: From the Dutch for "harbor." A comforting name for a girl or boy.

Relatives: Hagen, Hagan, Hogan, Hazen, Havis

Namesake: Richie Havens

Hayden: Old English for "hay field." Get this baby pinstripe diapers and a subscription to the *Wall Street Journal.*

Relative: Haydn

Namesakes: Franz Joseph Haydn, Tom Hayden

Hayes: From the Old English for "hay farmer."

Relatives: Hays, Haze, Haywood, Hayward, Heywood

Namesakes: Rutherford B. Hayes, Susan Hayward

Hazel: Old English for "hazel tree."

Relatives: Hazella, Hazela, Hazlit, Hazlet, Haslett

Namesakes: William Hazlitt, Hazel Scott, "Hazel"

Heather: From the Middle English for "a heath or a shrub." Heather is used regularly for girls. Heath is much less common, quite romantic, and will work for either sex.
Relatives: Heath, Heathcliff
Namesakes: Heather Locklear, "Heath Barkley," Heath candy bar

Hector: From the Greek for "anchor." A hero of the Trojan War.
Relative: Hektor
Namesake: Hector Berlioz

Hedia: Hebrew for "God's voice."
Relatives: Hediah, Hedya, Hedley

Hedwig: Old English for "hidden weapon."
Relatives: Hedvig, Heddy, Hedy, Hedda, Havoise, Hedvick, Hedvicka
Namesakes: Hedda Hopper, *Hedda Gabler*

Heidi: A shortened version of Adelheid or Hedwig. The heroine of a favorite story for children written by Johanna Spyri.
Relatives: Heidy, Haidee

Helen: From the Greek for "torch." It was Helen's abduction, according to the Greek myth, that brought about the Trojan War.
Relatives: Helene, Helena, Helina, Helaine, Elaine, Elayne, Eleanor, Elinor, Eileen, Elena, Elene, Galina, Lenora, Lena, Lenny, Nelly, Jelena, Jelika
Namesakes: Helen of Troy, Helen Keller

Helmut: Anglo-Saxon for "helmet." Has a definite Teutonic shadow.
Relatives: Hellmut, Helmaer
Namesakes: Helmut Schmidt, Helmut Newton

Hendrick: Old English for "lord's manor." A classy choice.
Relatives: Hendric, Hedric, Hedrick, Hendrik, Henric
Namesake: Hendrick Smith

Henrietta: From the Old German for "house ruler" and a feminine variation of Henry.
Relatives: Henriette, Hendrike, Henrika, Henriot, Henriqueta, Hetty, Enrica, Enriqueta

Henry: From the Old German for "house ruler." A favorite name of British kings for centuries. Charles and Diana chose it for their second son.

Relatives: Henri, Harry, Hal, Hawkin, Hawkins, Harrison, Harris, Henriot, Heinrich, Heinz, Henke, Henryk, Hank, Henny, Henderson, Hawke, Enrique, Enrico, Enzio, Parry, Perry

Namesakes: Prince Henry, Hank Aaron, Hal Holbrook, O. Henry, Patrick Henry

Hepziba: Hebrew for "my love is with her." Not for the faint-hearted.

Relatives: Hepzibah, Hephziba, Hephzibah

Herbert: From the Old English for "exalted ruler" and Old German for "shining army." This fine name has fallen out of favor. Consider it.

Relatives: Herbie, Herb

Namesakes: Herbert Hoover, Herbie Hancock, Herbie Mann

Herman: Old German for "soldier." The variation Armand is a stronger sound closer to the original meaning of the name.

Relatives: Hermann, Hermie, Hermy, Herm, Herrick, Armand, Armando, Ermanno

Namesakes: Herman Melville, Herman Badillo, Hermann Hesse, Armand Assante, Armand Hammer, Herman's Hermits

Hermione: A feminine variation of Hermes, the messenger of the gods. A grand choice that defies nicknames. Say it several times: "Her-*my*-unee."

Relative: Hermine

Namesake: Hermione Gingold

Hershel: From the German for "deer."

Relatives: Herschel, Hersh, Hersch, Hirsh, Hirsch, Hertz, Heshel, Hershey

Namesakes: Hershel Walker, Hershel Bernardi, Hershey bar, Hertz Rent-a-Car

Hester: A Latin variation of Esther. Perhaps not as popular as Hannah, Hester nevertheless has that same Old World charm.

Relatives: Hesther, Hetty, Hetti, Hettie, Hetta, Hestia

Namesakes: "Hester Prynne," *Hester Street*

Hezekiah: Hebrew for "God is my strength." Hezekiah appears in the Old Testament as a king of Judah who worked to stamp out idolatry.
Relatives: Hezekia, Hezekial, Hezeki, Hez

Hila: Hebrew for "praise."
Relatives: Hillah, Hilly, Hilla, Hillela, Hillel

Hilary: From the Greek for "cheer." Although used for either sex, it has emerged as a more popular choice for girls in recent decades. This is a very proper proper name.
Relatives: Hillary, Hilaire, Hilaria, Hilliard, Hilar, Hill, Hilly, Ilario, Laris
Namesakes: Saint Hillary, Hilaire Belloc, Sir Edmund Hillary

Hilda: From the Old German for "warrior." Hildy was the hero/heroine of *The Front Page.*
Relatives: Hilde, Hildy, Hildegard, Hildegarde
Namesake: Saint Hilda

Hildebrand: Old German for "battle sword." A character from a German legend, Hildebrand was a superior warrior known for his outstanding swordsmanship.
Relatives: Hildabrand, Hildreth, Hill

Hiram: Hebrew for "noble one."
Relatives: Hyram, Hi, Hy
Namesake: Hiram Walker

Hobart: From the Danish for "Bart's Hill."
Relatives: Hobert, Hobie, Bart
Namesakes: Hobie Baker, Hobart (Tasmania), Hobie Cat, Hobart College

Hodding: From the Dutch for "bricklayer."
Namesake: Hodding Carter

Hogarth: Old Norse for "hilltop garden." This name screams old family distinction. Virginia and Leonard Woolf chose it for their publishing company. Philadelphians reserve Hoagie for a submarine sandwich.
Relatives: Hogie, Hoagy
Namesakes: Hoagy Carmichael, William Hogarth

Holden: Old English for "valley." William Holden's real surname was Beedle. What a difference a name makes.

Relatives: Holdin, Holbrook
Namesake: "Holden Caulfield"

Holly: From the Old English for "holly bush." Traditional greenery associated with Christmas.
Relatives: Hollye, Holli
Namesakes: Holly Near, Holly Hunter

Holm: Old Norse for "island." Which only goes to prove that some men are islands.
Relatives: Holms, Holmes
Namesakes: Oliver Wendell Holmes, "Sherlock Holmes"

Homer: Greek and Latin for "shown the way" and baseball for "home run."
Namesakes: Homer, Winslow Homer

Honey: From the German. Perhaps too cloying, this name suffers as a familiar alternative to "darling" or "dear."
Relatives: Honig, Honeah

Honor: From the Latin for "dignified" and Old French for "nobleman." If this child becomes a judge, he or she would be known as your honor Honor or, if elected mayor, the honorable Honor.
Relatives: Honore, Honora, Honoria, Nora, Norah, Noria, Norry
Namesakes: Honoré de Balzac, Honor Blackman

Hope: From the Old English for "faith." An ever-popular virtue name for a baby who is, after all, "the hope of the future."
Namesakes: Hope Lange, Bob Hope

Horace: Greek for "behold." A seldom-used classic.
Relatives: Horacio, Horatio, Horatius
Namesakes: Horace, Horace Mann, Horace Greeley, "Horatio Hornblower"

Hortense: From the Latin for "gardener." A tiny bit old-fashioned but wears well.
Relative: Hortensia

Horton: From the Latin for "garden" or "from the gray land."
Namesakes: Willie Horton, Edward Everett Horton, *Horton Hears a Who*

Hosea: Hebrew for "salvation." This is a beauty; start a trend.
Relatives: Hosia, Hosiah

Houston: Anglo-Saxon for "town house" and Texan for "serious city."
Namesakes: Sam Houston, Whitney Houston

Howard: Anglo-Saxon for "protector of the home." The nickname Ward jazzes up this erstwhile favorite.
Relatives: Howie, Ward
Namesakes: Howard Johnson, Howard Hughes, Howard Baker

Howe: Anglo-Saxon for "hill."
Relatives: Hough, Houghton, Howell, Howel, Howells, Howden
Namesakes: Julia Ward Howe, Irving Howe, Gordie Howe, William Dean Howells, Howell Rains

Hoyt: Middle English for "small boat." This is distinguished.
Relatives: Hoyle, Hoit
Namesakes: Hoyt Wilhelm, Hoyt Axton

Hubert: From the Old German for "shining spirit." Perhaps the media knew of this definition when they dubbed Hubert H. Humphrey the Happy Warrior.
Relatives: Hubbard, Hubbell, Hub, Huberto, Hubie, Uberto
Namesake: "Old Mother Hubbard"

Hudson: Old English for "son of Hud." Hudd is a long-forgotten form of Richard now more closely associated with Paul Newman's movie role.
Relatives: Hudd, Hud, Hudde
Namesake: Henry Hudson

Hugh: From the Old German for "bright soul." This name whispers the soft, green hills of Wales. Give it a whirl.
Relatives: Hew, Huey, Hughie, Hughes, Huet, Hugi, Hugo, Ugo
Namesakes: Hugh Downs, Hugh Hefner, Huey Lewis, Huey Long, Langston Hughes, Victor Hugo

Hume: Norse for "lakeside hill." Careful. In England it's pronounced "home."
Relatives: Holm, Holmes
Namesakes: Hume Cronyn, David Hume

Humphrey: From the Old English for "peaceful force." That phrase sums up the screen presence of Humphrey Bogart, the most famous namesake.

Relatives: Humphry, Hunfrey, Humpty, Humph, Humpy, Humfrid, Humfried

Namesake: "Humpty-Dumpty"

Hunt: From the Old English for "search." One of those nifty monickers recently discovered by yuppy parents. Perfect for an investment banker, real estate tycoon, or simply lazing at the club.

Relatives: Hunter, Huntington, Huntley

Namesakes: Huntington Hartford, Hunter S. Thompson, Evan Hunter, Chet Huntley

Huxley: Anglo-Saxon for "ash tree field" and Old English for "from Hugh's meadow." Literary-minded friends might assume you are related to the Huxley dynasty.

Relatives: Huxly, Huxford

Namesakes: Aldous Huxley, Thomas Huxley

Hyacinth: Greek for "blue crystal," associated with the sapphire. According to Greek myth, Hyacinthus was a beautiful boy much admired by Apollo. He was accidentally killed, and on the spot where his blood seeped into the earth, flowers grew—called hyacinths.

Relatives: Hyacynth, Hyacinthia

Namesake: Saint Hyacinth

Hyman: From the Hebrew for "life." This name may suffer when the kids take health education.

Relatives: Hyland, Hyatt, Hy

Namesakes: Hyman Rickover, Hyland Park (N.J.), Brian Hyland

Blow Hards

Until recently, hurricanes were given women's names, purportedly borrowed from the wives and girlfriends of weather service personnel. Having your name used for a hurricane may be interpreted as flattery or an embarrassing insult.

Perhaps to avoid litigious-minded spouses, there now exists a permanent, international list for tropical storms, hurricanes, and typhoons in the Atlantic, Caribbean, and Gulf of Mexico. And male names are included. The list rotates every six years. There are separate lists for hurricanes in the Eastern North Pacific and Western North Pacific. Hurricanes in the Central North Pacific have exotic-sounding names to suit the locale (such as Keli, Iniki, Alika, Ulia, and Pali).

1983 & 1989	1984 & 1990	1985 & 1991	1986 & 1992	1987 & 1993	1988 & 1994
Alicia	Arthur	Ana	Allen	Arlene	Alberto
Barry	Bertha	Bob	Bonnie	Bret	Beryl
Chantal	Cesar	Claudette	Charley	Cindy	Chris
Dean	Diana	Danny	Danielle	Dennis	Debby
Erin	Edouard	Elena	Earl	Emily	Ernesto
Felix	Fran	Fabian	Frances	Floyd	Florence
Gabrielle	Gustav	Gloria	Georges	Gert	Gilbert
Hugo	Hortense	Henri	Hermine	Harvey	Helene
Iris	Isidore	Isabel	Ivan	Irene	Isaac
Jerry	Josephine	Juan	Jeanne	Jose	Joan
Karen	Klaus	Kate	Karl	Katrina	Keith
Luis	Lily	Larry	Lisa	Lenny	Leslie
Marilyn	Marco	Mindy	Mitch	Maria	Michael
Noel	Nana	Nicholas	Nicole	Nate	Nadine
Opal	Omar	Odette	Otto	Ophelia	Oscar
Pablo	Paloma	Peter	Paula	Philippe	Patty
Roxanne	Rene	Rose	Richard	Rita	Rafael
Sebastien	Sally	Sam	Shary	Stan	Sandy
Tanya	Teddy	Teresa	Tomas	Tammy	Tony
Van	Vicky	Victor	Virginie	Vince	Valerie
Wendy	Wilfred	Wanda	Walter	Wilma	William

I

In 1945, twins born in Washington, D.C., were named in honor of the site of a major battle in the Pacific. They were named Iwo and Jima.

Ian: Scottish version of John. Quite nice, and not as common in the United States as in other English-speaking countries.
Relatives: Ianna, Ianthe, Iantha, Iain, John
Namesake: Ian Fleming

Ida: Possibly Old German for "youthful." Seldom used these days, but a nice, old-fashioned choice worthy of revival.
Relatives: Idana, Idanna, Idena, Idette, Idalee, Ita
Namesakes: Princess Ida, Ida Lupino

Ignatius: Latin for "fiery."
Relatives: Iggy, Ignaze, Ignace, Ignatz
Namesake: Saint Ignatius

Ilana: Hebrew for "tree." A melodic and increasingly popular choice these days.
Relatives: Illana, Ilanna, Alana, Allana, Alanna

Ilsa: Derived from Elizabeth. This name was immortalized by Ingrid Bergman in *Casablanca*.
Relatives: Ilse, Ilise, Ilse, Ilisa

Ilya: A variation of Elijah.
Relative: Ilia
Namesake: "Ilya Kuriakin" (a man from U.N.C.L.E.)

Imelda: German for "battle." Build another closet.

Relative: Ymelda
Namesake: Imelda Marcos

Imogene: Latin for "image" or "last born."
Relative: Imogen
Namesake: Imogene Coca

Imre: Hebrew for "well-spoken." A good name for a future debater.
Relatives: Imray, Imrie

India: India has been a popular girl's name in Great Britain since the Victorian era.
Relatives: Indiana, Indianna, Indy, Indie
Namesakes: India Wilkes, Robert Indiana, Indy 500, "Indiana Jones"

Ingram: German for "raven." A handsome name.
Relatives: Ingraham, Ingham, Ingrem, Gram, Graham
Namesake: Dan Ingram

Ingrid: Derived from Ing, the Norse god of fertility.
Relatives: Inga, Inge, Inger, Ingmar, Igor
Namesakes: Ingrid Bergman, Igor Stravinsky, Inger Stevens

Innis: Gaelic for "island." For boys or girls; different and distinctive.
Relatives: Innes, Innes
Namesakes: Roy Innes, Michael Innes

Irene: Greek for "peace." Pretty and not used much these days.
Relatives: Irena, Ireene, Irina
Namesakes: Irene Cara, Irene Worth

Iris: Greek goddess of the rainbow. A flower name that is making a modest comeback.
Relative: Irys
Namesake: Iris Murdoch

Irma: Old German for "whole."
Relatives: Irmin, Erma, Ermingarde, Irmingarde
Namesakes: Erma Bombeck, "Irma la Douce"

Irving: From the Old English for "sea friend."
Relatives: Irvin, Irvine, Irwin, Irwyn
Namesakes: Irving Berlin, Irving Thalberg, Washington Irving

Isaac: From the Hebrew for "laughter." A good biblical name for the offspring of older parents; Abraham was over 100 when Isaac was born.
Relatives: Ike, Zach, Isaak, Yitzchak, Isak
Namesakes: Isaac Stern, Isaac Newton, Isak Denison, Isaac Bashevis Singer

Isabel: Another variation on Elizabeth. We like this name, but you are bound to have at least one relative who doesn't.
Relatives: Isabella, Isabelle
Namesakes: Queen Isabella, Isabella Rossellini, Isabelle Adjani

Isaiah: Hebrew for "salvation of the Lord."
Relatives: Isa, Isiah
Namesake: Isiah Thomas

Ishmael: Hebrew for "God will hear." Go ahead; call him Ishmael.
Namesake: Ishmael Reed

Isidore: Greek for "gift of Isis," the Egyptian moon goddess associated with fertility. Seldom used these days, though the feminine form has its devotees among the free-spirited.
Relatives: Isidor, Isidora, Isadora, Izzy, Dora, Dorie, Dory
Namesake: Isadora Duncan

Isolda: Old English for "fair."
Relatives: Isolde, Yseult

Israel: Hebrew for "wrestled with God." The Puritans were fond of this one.
Namesakes: Israel Horowitz, Israel Putnam

Ivan: Russian variation of John.
Relatives: Ivanna, John, Evan
Namesakes: Ivan Boesky, Ivan the Terrible, Ivanna Trump

Ivy: From the Old English for "vine." Very pretty, due for a comeback.
Relatives: Ive, Ives
Namesakes: Saint Ives, Judith Ivey, Charles Ives

"Tell Me the First Thing That Comes to Mind . . ."

Names often become metaphors, symbols, or standards through patterns of associations. Some associations are intensely private. If, for example, you knew a bully named Derek, chances are you will never warm to the name. Other associations are a part of our common language, as any Tom, Dick, or Harry will tell you. These built-in associations should not influence your decision but are interesting to note.

Honest Abe	Slim Jim
Smart Alec	Tin Lizzie
Little Alice	Sweet Lorraine
Big Ben	Bloody Mary
Good-time Charley	Holy Moses
Dapper Dan	Nervous Nelly
Tricky Dick	Jolly Roger
Dumb Dora	Baby Ruth
Fast Eddie	Great Scott
Curious George	Simple Simon
Giggling Gertie	Lazy Susan
Amazing Grace	Doubting Thomas
Plain Jane	Tiny Tim
Spinning Jenny	Wee Willy

Some names have come to represent a type of person or a set of characteristics. Many historical figures and literary creations have stepped into these ranks—their names becoming eponyms.

Horatio Alger	Mata Hari
Benedict Arnold	Don Juan
Babbitt	Jezebel
Beau Brummell	Caspar Milquetoast
Casanova	Florence Nightingale
Ichabod Crane	Pollyanna
Eliza Doolittle	Don Quixote
Rube Goldberg	Ebenezer Scrooge
John Hancock	Svengali

J

In 1939, it was noted that the daughters of Mr. and Mrs. Iglesias had been named Fraternity, Peace, Liberty, Equality, Justice, and Light.

Jacob: From the Hebrew for "the supplanter" or "held by the heel." Jacob was the patriarch of the founders of the twelve tribes of Israel.

Relatives: Jakob, Jacobo, Jacoba, Jacobson, Jacobi, Jacobine, Jacobina, Jayme, Jacques, Jacinto, Jascha, Jake, Jack, Jackson, Jeb, Cob, Cobb, Giacobo, Giacomo, Iago, Iacovo, Yago, Yaacov, Yacov, Yakov

Namesakes: son of Abraham, Jackson Browne, Jackson Pollock, Yakov Smirnoff, Max Jacob

Jacqueline: A feminine variation of Jacob or James. A timeless name with a hint of a distinguished pedigree.

Relatives: Jacquelyn, Jackelyn, Jacklin, Jaklyn, Jaclyn, Jackie, Jackey, Jackee, Jacqui, Jacquetta, Jacquith

Namesakes: Jacqueline Kennedy Onassis, Jacqueline Bisset, Jackie Collins

Jade: Spanish for "stone of the loins." A semiprecious stone prized in the Orient for its rich green color and as a good-luck charm.

Relatives: Ijada, Jada

Namesake: Jade Jagger

James: An English variation of Jacob and the patron saint of Spain. This ever-popular name is always in good taste.

Relatives: Jaymes, Jaime, Jamie, Jaymie, Jaimie, Jamsey, Jameson,

Jamey, Jan, Jay, Jim, Jimmy, Jimmie, Jimbo, Diego, Giacomo, Seamus, Sheamus, Shamus, Hamish, Santiago

Namesakes: King James, James Joyce, James Stewart, James Dean, Jimmy Carter, Jimmy Cagney, Jimi Hendrix, Diego Rivera

Jane: Hebrew for "God is gracious" and a feminine version of John. Jane is a true classic. The hefty list of variations belies the simplicity of "plain" Jane.

Relatives: Jayne, Jain, Jan, Janet, Janot, Jannette, Janina, Janine, Jean, Jeanne, Jeannie, Jeanine, Jeanie, Jeanette, Jennette, Janice, Janyce, Janis, Janith, Janna, Jina (Sanskrit for "victory"), Joan, Joanna, Jo Ann, Johanna, Joann, Joanne, Jovanna, Joni, Janie, Janey, Gianina, Giovanna, Juana, Juanita, Sinead, Shena, Sheena, Sine Seonaid

Namesakes: Jane Austen, Jane Fonda, Jane Seymour, Jane Pauley, Jayne Mansfield, Jan Stuart, Joan Crawford, Joan of Arc, Joan Sutherland, Joan Baez, Joanne Woodward, Janis Joplin, *Jane Eyre,* "Bonnie Jean"

Jared: From the Hebrew for "descending." This name is pronounced "*Jair*-ud"—not "jarred" and it is finding a niche on the popularity charts alongside Justin and Jason.

Relatives: Jarrod, Jarrett

Namesakes: Keith Jarrett, "Jared Barkley"

Jarvis: From the Old German for "true spear."

Relative: Jervis

Namesake: Port Jervis

Jasmine: From the Persian for a form of flowering olive. The jasmine flower is wonderfully fragrant.

Relatives: Jasmin, Yasmin, Yasmine, Jasmina, Jessamine, Jessamyn

Namesakes: Yasmin Khan, Jessamyn West

Jason: From the Greek for "healer" and possibly an early form of Joshua. Jason was a hero of Greek mythology. It seemed every other male child born in the 1970s was named Jason. Although it has slacked off a bit, this is still wildly popular.

Relatives: Jayson, Jase, Jace

Namesakes: Jason Robards, "Jason and the Argonauts"

Jasper: Origin unknown; possibly from the Persian for "treasure." This stone is a type of striped quartz which, when polished, reveals miniature "landscapes."

Relatives: Jaspar, Caspar, Casper, Cap, Kaspar, Kasper, Gaspar

Namesakes: Jasper Johns, Caspar Weinberger, Karl Jaspers, "Casper the Friendly Ghost," Jasper National Park

Jay: Old French for "jay bird." The term "jaywalker" evolved from a slang term for a gullible person new to the big city. If Jay strikes you as too informal for a proper name, use James or Jason on the birth certificate.

Relative: Jai

Namesakes: Jay Leno, Jay Rockefeller, "Jay Gatsby"

Jedediah: Hebrew for "beloved by God." A bit of a mouthful, but Jed simplifies things.

Relatives: Jedidiah, Jed, Yedidiyah

Namesake: "Jed Clampet"

Jeffrey: From the Old French for "peaceful." It's hard to go wrong with Jeffrey or the variations.

Relatives: Jeffrie, Jeffry, Jefferey, Geoffrey, Geoff, Godfrey, Jeff, Jefferson, Jeffers, Joffrey, Jeffries

Namesakes: Jeffrey Banks, Jeff Bridges, Geoffrey Chaucer, Thomas Jefferson, Robinson Jeffers, Joffrey Ballet

Jemima: Hebrew for "dove." If the unfortunate association with pancakes can be overlooked, this is a truly endearing name. Maybe Jemma instead?

Relatives: Yemimah, Jemma, Jemmie, Jem, Gemma, Mimi

Namesakes: "Jemima Puddleduck," "Aunt Jemima"

Jennifer: From the Old Welsh for "white wave," a modern variation of Guinevere. This was the most popular name for girls born in the late 1970s and early 1980s. Lately it has been eclipsed by Jessica.

Relatives: Jenifer, Jenyfer, Jenny, Jennie, Jinny, Jenni, Jen, Jennett, Jenet, Jenna

Namesakes: Jennifer Warren, Jennifer Beale, Jenny Lind

Jeremiah: From the Hebrew for "exalted of God." A terrific name if you can forget that "Jeremiah was a bullfrog."

Relatives: Jeremia, Yirmeyah, Jerry, Jerrie, Jerri, Jeri, Jere

Jeremy: Hebrew for "chosen by God." Jeremy has become a modern adaptation of the biblical Jeremiah.
Relatives: Jeremiah, Jeremias, Geremia, Jerry, Dermot
Namesakes: Jeremy Irons, "Jeremy Fisher," Chad and Jeremy

Jermyn: Latin for "German."
Relatives: German, Germain, Germaine
Namesakes: Germaine Greer, Jermaine Jackson, German Rivera

Jerolyn: A variation of Geraldine. Jerolyn may also be considered a convenient feminine version of Jerold, Gerald, or Jerome, if you care to pay tribute to some family member with one of those names.
Relatives: Jeralyn, Jerelyn, Jerylin, Jeryl

Jerome: From the Latin for "sacred name." Saint Jerome is often depicted as an old man, studying, with a lion at his feet. According to the legend, a lion entered his schoolroom and frightened everyone away. Saint Jerome noticed the lion had a thorn in its paw and removed it. The lion remained thereafter at the scholar's side.
Relatives: Jerrome, Gerome, Jerry
Namesakes: Jerome Kern, Jerome Robbins, Jerome K. Jerome

Jesse: Hebrew for "wealth." A Jesse tree is often depicted in stained glass windows in churches. It is a genealogical chart tracing the descendants of the house of David to Jesus Christ.
Relatives: Jessie, Jessye, Jess
Namesakes: father of David, Jesse James, Jesse Owens, Jesse Jackson

Jessica: From the Hebrew for "wealthy one." One of the ten most popular girls' names in the 1980s, outpacing Jennifer on the cradle roll.
Relatives: Jessyca, Jessika, Jessie, Jessye, Jessy, Jessi, Jessa, Jessalyn
Namesakes: Jessica Tandy, Jessye Norman, Jessica Lange

Jesus: Hebrew for "God will help." A popular first name in Spanish-speaking cultures.
Relative: Yesus
Namesakes: Jesus Christ, Jesus Alou

Jethro: From the Hebrew for "preeminence." This name has an unfortunate association with the bumpkin on "Beverly Hillbillies."
Relative: Jethroe

Namesakes: father-in-law of Moses, Jethro Tull, Sam Jethroe, "Homer and Jethro"

Jewel: From the Old French, a "priceless gem." If you are undecided about whether to name your child Pearl, Opal, or Jade, why not go to the source?
Relatives: Jewell, Jewelle, Bijoux

Joachim: From the Hebrew for "God will judge."
Relatives: Joaquin, Akim
Namesakes: Joaquin Andujar, San Joaquin Valley

Jocelyn: Old English for "just one." Chiefly a boy's name until this century. Too rarely heard these days.
Relatives: Jocelyne, Joceline, Joscelyne, Joseceline, Joscelin, Joslyn, Joslin, Josalin, Jossie, Jocie, Justine, Justina, Justa
Namesakes: Saint Justina, Justine Bateman

Jody: A variation of Joseph. This choice would serve a girl or boy well.
Relative: Jodie
Namesakes: Jody Powell, Jodie Foster

Joel: Hebrew for "the Lord is God." Joel and the variations work well for either sex. Although popular, Joel has never been overused.
Relatives: Yohel, Joelle, Joella, Joellen, Joela, Jolson
Namesakes: Joel Grey, Billy Joel

John: From the Hebrew for "God's grace." Whereas the expression was once "every Tom, Dick, and Harry," the more likely choice would be "every John, Bill, and Mike," at least in recent decades. The Celtic variations (such as Ian and Sean) have become especially popular in recent years.
Relatives: Jon, Johnny, Johnnie, Jack, Jock, Jocko, Johann, Johan, Jean, Jan, Jenner, Janos, Jovan, Juan, Johannes, Johnson, Jansen, Janson, Jones, Jackson, Jenkins, Hanson, Hansen, Jonnel, Hans, Ivan, Ian, Iaian, Eoin, Sean, Shawn, Shane, Seain, Zane
Namesakes: Saint John, John F. Kennedy, John Glenn, Johnny Carson, Johann Sebastian Bach, Johann Strauss, Jack London, Jackson Pollock, Ivan Lendl, Ian Fleming, Jill St. John, Zane Grey, Jean-Luc Godard

Jolie: French for "pretty." The "J" is pronounced as the French do, with the emphasis on the second syllable.
Relatives: Jolene, Joline
Namesake: Jolie Gabor

Jonas: Hebrew for "dove." Jonas connotes wisdom, whereas Jonah will forever be linked with the ride in the belly of a whale.
Relatives: Jonah, Yonas, Yonah
Namesake: Jonas Salk

Jonathan: Hebrew for "God's gift." Jonathan provides a more formal alternative to John and gives you the added nickname possibilities associated with Nathan.
Relatives: John, Johnny, Jon, Nathan, Nate, Nat
Namesakes: Jonathan Swift, Jonathan Winters

Jordan: Hebrew for "descender." There are the country Jordan and the river Jordan for geography enthusiasts. As a first name, it carries a sense of strength.
Relatives: Jordana, Jordanna, Jourdan, Jourdain, Giordano, Jordy, Jordie, Jory
Namesakes: Jordan Marsh, Barbara Jordan, Louis Jourdan, Jordan River

Joseph: From the Hebrew for "He shall add." Saint Joseph is the patron saint of carpenters.
Relatives: Josef, Yoseph, Yosayf, Jose, Joe, Joey, Josie, Josiah, Josias, Jessup, Giuseppe, Isoep, Iosef, Seosaidh, Osip, Pepe, Pepito
Namesakes: Saint Joseph, Joseph Heller, Joe DiMaggio, *Pal Joey*

Josephine: From the Hebrew for "He shall increase" and a feminine version of Joseph. The most famous Josephine was Napoleon's beloved empress.
Relatives: Josefine, Josefina, Josepha, Josephe, Josefa, Joette, Josette, Josetta, Josie, Josey, Jo, Guiseppina, Pepita, Fifi
Namesakes: Empress Josephine, Josephine Baker, "Jo March"

Joshua: Hebrew for "God of salvation." Joshua fought the battle of Jericho with such intensity that the sound of his trumpet flattened the city walls and the sun stood still in the sky. The name peaked in the 1970s but remains a steady contender in the name game.

Relatives: Yehosha, Josh, Josiah
Namesakes: Joshua Logan, Josiah Wedgwood, Joshua tree

Joy: From the Latin for "rejoice." How better to express your delight with your new daughter?
Relatives: Joi, Joia, Joice, Joyce, Joyous, Jovita, Joyeuse
Namesakes: Joy Philbin, Joyce Carol Oates, Joyce Brothers, James Joyce, "Joy to the World"

Judd: From the Hebrew for "praised." One of those choices that rules out nicknames.
Relatives: Jud, Juda, Judah, Judas, Jude, Juddson, Yehudah, Yehuda, Yehudi
Namesakes: Judd Hirsch, Judd Nelson, Yehudi Menuhin, The Judds, *Jude the Obscure*

Judith: From the Hebrew for "praised." The biblical Judith inspired the Jewish army to victory by sneaking into the enemy camp and killing the general.
Relatives: Judyth, Judy, Judi, Judie, Jude, Jody, Jodie, Jodi, Judit, Siobhan, Siubhan, Yehudith
Namesakes: Judith Ivey, Judy Garland, Judy Collins, Siobhan McKenna, "Punch and Judy"

Julia: From the Latin for "youthful" and a feminine version of Julius. A fetching choice, Julia has inspired a number of charming variations.
Relatives: Julya, Julie, Juliet, Juliette, Julietta, Juliana, Julina, Julianna, Juline, Joliette, Joletta, Jill, Jillian, Jules, Juli, Gillian, Gilly, Gillie, Giulia, Giulietta, Sile, Sileas
Namesakes: Julia Ward Howe, Julia Child, Julie Harris, Julie Andrews, Julianne Phillips, Juliet Mills, Jill Clayburgh, Jill Ireland, "Juliet Capulet"

Julian: Latin for "of Julius." Saint Julian is the patron saint of innkeepers.
Relatives: Julien, Julyan, Julius, Jules, Jule, Julio, Giulo
Namesakes: Julian Lennon, Julian Bond, Julius Caesar, Julio Iglesias, Jules Verne, Jules Feiffer, Julius Irving

June: From the Latin for "young." A name that recalls a kinder and gentler time.

Relatives: Juin, Junia, Juniata, Junette, Junine, Juney, Juno
Namesakes: June Havoc, June Allyson, "June Cleaver"

Justin: From the Old French for "justice." You couldn't do better for a future lawyer, judge, or attorney general.

Relatives: Justice, Justis, Justino, Justus, Justinian, Juste, Justine, Justyn

Namesakes: Saint Justine, Justin Morgan, Justine Bateman

COLORADO TOP TWENTY

1987

Girls	*Boys*
Jessica	Michael
Ashley	Christopher
Amanda	Matthew
Sarah	Joshua
Jennifer	Andrew
Brittany	Daniel
Nicole	David
Stephanie	Justin
Christine	Ryan
Megan	Nicholas
Rachel	Joseph
Heather	James
Danielle	Robert
Amber	Kyle
Elizabeth	John
Lauren	Anthony
Samantha	Brandon
Emily	Tyler
Amy	Zachary
Melissa	Benjamin

1983

Jennifer	Michael
Jessica	Christopher
Sarah	Matthew

Amanda	Joshua
Nicole	Daniel
Ashley	Ryan
Stephanie	David
Elizabeth	Justin
Amber	Jason
Melissa	John
Heather	James
Christine	Joseph
Crystal	Robert
Megan	Andrew
Michelle	Brian
Amy	Brandon
Erin	Adam
Rebecca	Nicholas
Rachel	William
Andrea	Eric

Information supplied by the State of Colorado Department of Health.

Kahlil: Arabic for "best friend."
Relatives: Kalil, Khalila, Kailil
Namesake: Kahlil Gibran

Kane: Irish Gaelic for "tribute," Welsh for "beautiful," and Japanese for "golden." Consider your child a beautiful, golden tribute.
Relatives: Kaine, Kain, Kayne, Keyne, Cane, Cain, Caine
Namesakes: Saint Keyne, Michael Caine, *Citizen Kane, The Caine Mutiny*

Karen: A variation of Catherine. An enduring favorite with a treasure trove of possibilities.
Relatives: Karin, Karyn, Karan, Karon, Kari, Karrie, Karry, Kara, Karina, Caren, Carin, Caryn, Cari, Carrie, Carry, Cara
Namesakes: Karen Horney, Karen Allen, Kara Kennedy, *Anna Karenina*

Kasmira: Old Slavic for "demands peace." As Old Country as borscht and blinis.
Relatives: Kasamira, Kasmir, Kazamira, Casmir, Casimir

Kay: Old Welsh for "rejoicer" and Old German for "fort." A succinct letter name.
Relatives: Kaye, Kai, MacKay
Namesakes: Sir Kay of the Round Table, Kaye Ballard, Kai Winding, Danny Kaye

Keane: Middle English for "sharp-witted." Can be pronounced "Kane" or "Kene."

Relatives: Kean, Keen, Keene
Namesakes: Tom Kean, Keene (N.H.)

Keefe: Irish Gaelic for "noble."
Relatives: Keefer, Kiefer, Keever
Namesakes: Kiefer Sutherland, Georgia O'Keeffe

Keegan: Irish Gaelic for "little fierce one." If you are looking for something like Megan but with a twist, try this for a girl.
Relative: Keagan

Keely: Irish Gaelic for "good-looking." A name that manages to sound both classy and casual.
Relatives: Keeley, Kealy, Keel, Keelan, Keeler
Namesakes: Keely Smith, Ruby Keeler

Keenan: Irish Gaelic for "little ancient one."
Relatives: Kienan, Keanan, Keen
Namesake: Keenan Wynn

Keith: Irish Gaelic for "battlefield" and Old Welsh for "forest." You can't go wrong with Keith.
Namesakes: Keith Richards, Keith Carradine, David Keith

Kelda: Old Norse for "spring." This is as rare as hen's teeth but sweet.
Relatives: Kelley, Kelly, Kel, Kell

Kelilah: Hebrew for "laurel wreath." Suggests an air of mystery.
Relatives: Kelila, Kyla, Kylia, Kaily, Kaile

Kelly: Irish Gaelic for "warrior." Once as Irish as a shamrock, Kelly has become an all-American name for either lads or lassies.
Relatives: Kelley, Keller, Kelli, Kellen, Kellia
Namesakes: Kelly McGillis, Ellsworth Kelly, kelly green

Kelsey: From the Old Norse for "shipping harbor." A delightful variation on Casey or Chelsea.
Relatives: Kelsi, Kelsy, Kelcie, Kelson, Kelton
Namesake: Linda Kelsey

Kelvin: Irish Gaelic for "narrow river." Kelvin offers a neat little spin on the standard Kevin.

Relatives: Kelvan, Kelven, Kelvyn, Kel
Namesakes: Kelvin Bryant, Baron Kelvin of Largs

Kemp: From the Middle English for "champion." Make sure this baby starts training for the Olympics immediately.
Relatives: Kempy, Kem, Kemper, Kemplen, Kempson
Namesakes: Jack Kemp, Victor Kemper

Kendall: Celtic for "ruler of the valley." A solid, forthright name for a boy or girl. The variations offer room to maneuver.
Relatives: Kendal, Kendell, Kendel, Kendalia, Kendaline, Kenna, Kendra, Ken, Kenny
Namesake: Kay Kendall

Kennedy: Irish Gaelic for "helmeted warrior" and a clan name. Naming children for presidents has fallen off during the last few administrations, but little Kennedys are beginning to enter the job market.
Relatives: Kennady, Kenny, Ken
Namesakes: John F. Kennedy, George Kennedy, William Kennedy

Kenneth: Irish Gaelic for "handsome" and Old English for "royal oath." A cousin of Kevin and Keith, this is a noble old Irish name.
Relatives: Kennet, Kenny, Kenney, Ken, Kenn
Namesakes: Kenneth Grahame, Kenneth Cole, Kenny Rogers, Ken Rosewall, Ken Russell, Ken Kesey

Kenrick: Old English for "bold ruler."
Relatives: Kendrick, Kendric, Kenway, Kenley, Kennard

Kent: Old Welsh for "bright white." Kent has a clean-as-a-whistle sound. Although a bit hard-edged for a baby, remember they do grow up.
Relatives: Kenton, Kenyon
Namesakes: Princess Michael of Kent, "Clark Kent," Kenyon College

Kermit: Irish Gaelic for "freeman." Does Miss Piggy know this?
Namesakes: Kermit Roosevelt, Kermit Washington

Kerr: Norse for "marshland" and a Scottish surname. May be pronounced "Cur" or "Car."
Relatives: Keir, Kirby

Namesakes: Keir Dullea, Kirby Puckett, Graham Kerr, Deborah Kerr, George Kirby

Kerry: Irish Gaelic for "dark eyes." A great androgynous name that can be used as a variation on Carrie or Cary.
Relatives: Kerrie, Keri, Kerwin

Kevin: Irish Gaelic for "gentle." Saint Kevin was a sixth-century Irish saint who sought refuge from the outside world (and women specifically) on an uninhabited island.
Relatives: Kevan, Keven, Kev
Namesakes: Kevin Kline, Kevin Costner, Kevin Bacon

Kezia: From the Hebrew for "cinnamon."
Relatives: Keesha, Keziah, Ketzia, Kezzy, Keisha, Keishia, Keshia, Lakeisha
Namesake: Keshia Knight Pulliam

Kieran: Irish Gaelic for "dark one." A deeply Irish name, Kieran melds nicely with an "O" surname.
Relatives: Kieron, Key, Kerwin, Kirwin, Kerry, Kern, Kerr, Ceirnin, Carra, Ciaran
Namesakes: Kieron Moore, John Kieran

Killian: Irish Gaelic for "fighter," "cell," or "strife." A kill, in Dutch, is a small channel of water. It is often used in place names such as Catskill.
Relatives: Kilian, Kelian

Kim: Old English for "chief." Rudyard Kipling's novel *Kim* tells the story of orphan Kimball O'Hara who joins a holy man in his treks through India. Kim is also a nationally popular name in Korea.
Relatives: Kym, Kimmi, Kimmey, Kimmy, Kimball, Kimble, Kimbell, Kemble
Namesakes: Kim Novak, Kim Hunter, Kim Bassinger

Kimberly: Old English for "from the castle meadow." An engaging name with an enchanting meaning. Kimberly's popularity is attributable to the diamond-mining center in South Africa. There is another Kimberley in Western Australia where gold was discovered in 1882, setting off the country's first major gold rush.

Relatives: Kimberley, Kymberly, Kimby, Kim, Kimmi, Kimmie, Kimmy
Namesake: Kimberly-Clark

King: Old English for "ruler." Perhaps not the most democratic choice, but it certainly commands attention.
Relatives: Kingsley, Kingston, Kingswell
Namesakes: King Vidor, Kingsley Amis, Charles Kingsley

Kipp: Old English for "sharply pointed hill."
Relatives: Kinnard, Kinnell, Kippy, Kipper, Kipling
Namesakes: Galway Kinnell, Kipp's Bay

Kirk: Old Norse for "church." In Scotland, a kirk refers to a church associated with the national church of Scotland. A kirkman is a member of this church.
Relatives: Kirkley, Kirkwood, Kirby, Kurk, Kirkus
Namesakes: Kirk Douglas, Kirk Cameron, "Captain James T. Kirk"

Kirsten: Old English for "stone church." Offers a series of winsome variations on Christine, from which it is derived.
Relatives: Kristen, Kirstin, Kirstie, Kirsty, Kirsti
Namesake: Kirstie Alley

Knox: Old English for "from the hills." As in "knife," the "K" is silent.
Relative: Knoll
Namesakes: John Knox, Knox Burger, Fort Knox

Knut: From the Danish for "kindness." This monicker guarantees him a scholarship to Notre Dame.
Relatives: Knute, Knud, Cnut, Cnutte, Canute
Namesakes: Knute Rockne, King Knut

Koren: From the Greek for "maiden."
Relatives: Kori, Korry, Korrie
Namesake: Edward Koren

Kurt: An abbreviated form of Conrad.
Relatives: Kert, Kirt
Namesakes: Kurt Russell, Kurt Vonnegut

Kyle: Scottish Gaelic for "strait." LaCoste shirts, chinos, and Topsiders will look spiffy on this kid.

Relatives: Kylene, Kylie
Namesakes: Kyle Rote, Kylene Baker

Kyna: Irish Gaelic for "intelligence" and a feminine version of Conan. You'll never find preprinted balloons or key chains with this one. Dare to be different.
Relatives: Kyne, Cyna, Cyne

Myth Nomers

Greek and Roman deities and mythological heroes provide a rich collection of names, many of which endure as common proper names in Greece. The Roman names are often Latinized versions of their Greek counterparts, which, in turn, were borrowed from more ancient cultures. Venus, for example, is the Roman version of Aphrodite, the Greek goddess of love and marriage. It is believed Aphrodite is based on the Asiatic goddess Ishtar.

Keep in mind that virtually every culture has nurtured a library of myths. Consult the vivid folklore of the Australian Aborigines and American Indians as well as the legends of India, Asia, Africa, and Europe.

Arcas—a son of Zeus and Callisto
Ariadne—a princess of Crete
Arion—a musician saved from drowning by dolphins
Artemis—the Greek equivalent of Diana—Apollo's twin and goddess of the moon and the hunt. Her other names are Selene and Cynthia.
Athena—the Greek goddess of wisdom
Aurora—the Roman goddess of dawn
Berenice—a queen whose hair became a comet
Calliope—the Greek muse of epic poetry
Camilla—a warrior maiden
Cassandra—a prophetess who was never believed because of Apollo's curse
Cassiopeia—the mother of Andromeda, she was changed into a constellation

Clio—the Greek muse of history

Daphne—a beautiful nymph who was changed into a laurel tree

Demeter—the Greek goddess of agriculture and civilization

Diana—the Roman goddess of the hunt and the moon

Doris—mother of the sea nymphs known as the Nereids

Eurydice—a nymph who became the wife of Orpheus

Evander—the king of the Arcadians

Hector—a leader of the Trojan army

Helen—a daughter of Zeus and Leda; her elopement with Paris brought about the destruction of Troy

Hera—the Greek equivalent of Juno, goddess of the heavens and patroness of marriages

Hermione—a daughter of Aphrodite

Hestia—a daughter of Rhea and goddess of the hearth and home

Hippolyta—the queen of the Amazons

Hope—the one good spirit released by Pandora when she opened the forbidden box

Ida—a mountain in Crete

Ilia—one of the Titanides

Iphigenia—a daughter of Agamemnon and Clytemnestra

Iris—goddess of rainbows and an attendant of Hera

Jason—a prince of Thebes who sought the Golden Fleece

Lavinia—a daughter of Latinus

Leander—Hero's beloved who swam the Hellespont every night to visit her

Leda—the mother of Helen

Linus—a music teacher who instructed Hercules

Lyra—the name of Orpheus's lyre (and a constellation)

Maia—a daughter of Atlas and the mother of Hermes

Minerva—the Roman goddess of wisdom and the patroness of the arts and trades

Nestor—a Greek commander during the Trojan War

Nike—the Greek winged goddess of victory

Olympia—a valley in ancient Greece where the games were held in honor of Zeus

Orion—the young hunter adored by Diana

Pandora—the Greek equivalent of Eve

Penelope—the faithful wife of Odysseus

Persephone—a daughter of Demeter associated with spring

Phoebe—one of the Titanides

Phoenix—a magnificent bird that periodically makes its own funeral pyre and then rises anew from the ashes

Rhea—also known as Cybele, she was the mother of Zeus

Sibyl—a prophetess from an ancient world and an attendant of Apollo

Sylvia—a daughter of Tyrrheus

Thalia—the Greek muse of comedy

Troy—a city in Asia Minor

L

Lacy: Origin unknown; possibly derived from French place name. The delicate needlework inspired the use of this name, which seems very feminine.
Relatives: Lacey, Laycee
Namesakes: Lacy Dalton, "Cagney and Lacey"

Ladd: Middle English for "young man."
Namesake: Alan Ladd

Laird: Scottish for "lord" or "landed gentry."
Namesake: Melvin Laird

Lakeisha: A blending of "La" and "Keisha." Swahili for "favorite one." Many Swahili names have a delightful melody to them.
Relatives: Lawanna, Latasha, Latoya

Lamar: Old German for "land." A good androgynous choice.
Relatives: Lambert, Lamont
Namesakes: Lamar Alexander, Hedy Lamarr

Lance: From the Old French for "knight's attendant" and an abbreviated form of Lancelot. Sir Lancelot was the most famous of King Arthur's knights, and it was he who stole the heart of Queen Guinevere.
Relatives: Lancelot, Launcelot, Ancel
Namesakes: Lance Allworth, Lancelot Hogben

Lander: Middle English for "property owner." Lander and the variations have a proper "Main Line" spirit to them.

Relatives: Landor, Landon, Landry, Landan, **Landis, Landers,** Landman
Namesakes: Ann Landers, Michael Landon

Lane: Middle English for "narrow street."
Relatives: Laine, Layne
Namesakes: Lane Kirkland, Lainie Kazan, Cleo Laine, "Lois Lane"

Lang: From the Old English and Old Norse for "long" or "tall."
Relatives: Langdon, Langford, Langley, Langston, Langhorne, Langtry
Namesakes: Langston Hughes, Samuel Langhorne Clemens, Fritz Lang, Hope Lange, Lillie Langtry, "Auld Lang Syne," Langley Air Force Base

Lani: Hawaiian for "sky." An enchanting name from the islands. Check your Hawaiian dictionary for other possibilities.
Namesake: Kay Lani Rae

Lara: From the Latin for "shining brightly." An appealing alternative to Laura.
Relatives: Larissa, Laris, Lari
Namesakes: daughter of the river god in Roman mythology, "Lara's Theme"

Lark: From the songbird of that name. A colloquialism, "to lark" means to frolic about enthusiastically.
Relatives: Larkin, Larikin
Namesakes: Philip Larkin, Barry Larkin, Meadowlark Lemon

Latimer: From the Middle English for "interpreter."
Relative: Lattimore
Namesake: Hugh Latimer

Laura: Latin for "laurel leaves." Laurel leaves have long been a symbol of honor, victory, and academic excellence.
Relatives: Laure, Lora, Lori, Lorna, Laurie, Lorry, Laurel, Lauren, Lauryn, Lorin, Laurin, Loryn, Laureen, Laurena, Lauretta, Laurette, Lorina, Lorene, Lauriette, Loretta, Lorette, Lorita, Lorenza, Lor, Lola
Namesakes: Laura Ingalls Wilder, Lauren Bacall, Lauren Hutton, Loretta Lynn, Lori Singer

Laverne: From the Old French for "from the alder grove" and Latin for "springlike."
Relatives: Laverna, La Verne, Verna, Verne, Lally
Namesake: "Laverne and Shirley"

Lavinia: From the Latin for "purity."
Relatives: Lavine, Lavin
Namesakes: a character in Virgil's *Aeneid,* Lavinia Dickinson

Lawrence: Latin for "laurel crown." Although Lawrence was always one of the fifty most popular names in the United States in the early 1900s, it peaked at number fifteen in 1940, and slipped off in the 1980s. The interesting variations are well worth browsing through.
Relatives: Laurence, Lawrance, Lorenz, Loren, Laurens, Lorin, Lorcan, Lon, Lonnie, Loring, Lawford, Lawley, Lawton, Lawler, Laughton, Lawry, Larry, Laurent, Lorenzo, Lauritz, Lorne, Lawson, Lars, Larson, Larkin, Labhras
Namesakes: Saint Lawrence, Lorenzo de Medici, Lawrence Welk, Sir Laurence Olivier, Lawrence of Arabia, Lorenz Hart, Lorenzo Lamas

Lazarus: Hebrew for "God's help." It was Lazarus Christ raised from the dead, according to the New Testament.
Relatives: Lazare, Lazar, Lazaro, Laszlo, El'azar
Namesakes: Swifty Lazar, Emma Lazarus, "Victor Laszlo"

Leah: From the Hebrew for "weary one" and Greek for "glad tidings."
Relatives: Lea, Lia, Liah, Lee, Leatrice
Namesake: a wife of Jacob

Leander: From the Greek for "lion." The Leander of yore swam the unreliable Hellespont to court his beloved Hero, but drowned in his attempt.
Relatives: Liander, Leandre, Leandro, Leandra

Lee: Old English for "glade" or Irish Gaelic for "poet." Lee tucks in well between a first and last name and is appreciated equally by boys and girls.
Relatives: Leigh, Lea
Namesakes: Lee Remick, Lee Majors, Lee Grant, Lee Iacocca, Lee Strasberg, Robert E. Lee

Leif: Old Norse for "beloved." May be pronounced "leaf" or "life."
Namesakes: Leif Ericsson, Leif Garrett

Leila: Arabic for "dark as the night." Pronounced *"Lay*-la," this is one of those names with an unmistakable sultry quality.
Relatives: Lila, Lillah, Lyla, Leilia, Lela

Leilani: Hawaiian for "heavenly flower." We include this exquisite name to encourage parents to consult Hawaiian phone books.

Leith: Scottish Gaelic for "wide river."
Relative: Leathan

Leland: Old English for "from the meadow land." Perfect for the letterhead of a future Fortune 500 executive.
Relatives: Leighton, Layton
Namesakes: Leland Stanford, Charles Leland

Lena: From the Latin for "alluring." Does anyone know where the expression "leaping Lena" comes from?
Relatives: Lina, Lenore, Leonore
Namesakes: Lena Horne, Leonore Fleischer, Lina Wertmuller

Lennon: Irish Gaelic for "cloak."
Relative: Lenin
Namesakes: John Lennon, Vladimir Ilyich Lenin

Lennox: Scottish Gaelic for "amid the elms." You can't lose with this name. People will assume you are associated with the fine china company or are a descendant of the founders of the lovely old Massachusetts town.
Relatives: Lenox, Lenix, Lennie, Lenny, Len
Namesakes: Annie Lennox, Lenox (Mass.), Lenox china

Leola: From the Latin for "lion" and a feminine version of "Leo."
Relatives: Leonarda, Leontine, Leontyne
Namesake: Leontyne Price

Leonard: From the Old German for "lion-hearted." The hands-down perfect choice for a little Leo.
Relatives: Lennard, Lenard, Lennart, Leonardo, Leonhard, Leonid, Leon, Leo, Lennie, Lenny, Len
Namesakes: Leonard Bernstein, Leonard Nimoy, Leonardo da Vinci, Leon Spinks, Leo Tolstoy, Lenny Bruce, Leonid Brezhnev, Leon Trotsky

Leopold: From the Old German for "bold leader." This name was popular with kings of Belgium.

Relatives: Luitpold, Leupold, Leopoldo, Leopolda, Leopoldine
Namesake: Leopold Stokowski

Leroy: From the Old French for "the king."
Relatives: Leroi, Lee, Roy
Namesake: "Leroy Brown"

Leslie: Scottish Gaelic for "dweller in the gray castle" or Old English for "meadow." Once used interchangeably for girls and boys, the girls have it in the late twentieth century.
Relatives: Lesley, Lesly, Les, Lee
Namesakes: Leslie Gore, Leslie Howard, Leslie Ann Warren, Leslie Banks

Lester: From the Latin for "legion camp."
Relative: Les
Namesake: Lester Maddox

Letha: From the Greek for "forgetful."
Relatives: Lethia, Leitha, Leithia, Leda, Leta
Namesake: "Leda and the Swan"

Letitia: From the Latin for "joy." For the well-mannered baby.
Relatives: Leticia, Letice, Letizia, Letycia, Leetice, Leta, Letty, Ticia, Tish
Namesakes: Letitia Baldridge, Letty Cottin Pogrebin

Levi: From the Hebrew for "united." The international synonym for "blue jeans." You'll never have to sew labels into his denims for camp. The biblical Levi founded the tribe known as the Levites.
Relative: Lev
Namesakes: son of Jacob and Leah, Levi Strauss, Primo Levi

Liana: From the French for "vine." A particularly melodic name.
Relatives: Lianna, Lianne, Liane, Leana

Lilith: Origin unknown; possibly Sumerian for "ghost." Ancient legends depict Lilith as a hag associated with storms and demons. The Hebrew legend suggests Lilith was created at the same time as Adam but refused to be anything less than his equal. Unwilling to be his wife, she was expelled from Eden to become one with the air.
Relatives: Lilyth, Lily

Lily: From the Latin, *lilium,* for the flower. The lily, a flower of infinite varieties, is associated with purity, chastity, and innocence. The name has been making a strong comeback in the last few years.

Relatives: Lillian, Lily Ann, Lilian, Lilianne, Liliana, Lilias, Lilly, Lili, Lila, Lilia, Lil, Lis

Namesakes: Lillian Hellman, Lillian Vernon, "Lili Marlene," Lily Tomlin

Lincoln: Old English for "home by the pond." A fine old family name made famous by the sixteenth president of the United States.

Relatives: Linc, Link

Namesakes: Lincoln Steffens, Lincoln logs

Lind: Old English for "linden tree." All the variations are interesting.

Relatives: Lin, Linden, Lyndon, Lindell, Lindberg, Lindley, Lindon, Lindt, Linford, Linley, Linton

Namesakes: Lyndon Baines Johnson, Charles Lindbergh, Lindt chocolates

Linda: Spanish for "pretty." Linda, although the most popular girl's name in 1950, slipped to fifth place in 1960 and then into fiftieth place in 1970. Lindsay seems to be the choice of the new era.

Relatives: Lynda, Lindy, Lindi, Lin, Linden, Belinda

Namesakes: Linda Hunt, Lynda Carter, Belinda Carlisle

Lindsay: Old English for "pool island." This lovely name offers parents a wide choice of spelling possibilities. Be careful, though—it's a chart buster.

Relatives: Lindsey, Lyndsay, Lyndsey, Lyndsy, Lynsey, Linsey, Lindy

Namesakes: Lindsay Wagner, Vachel Lindsay

Linette: From the Middle French for "linnet bird" or "flaxen." The linnet is a small variety of finch that feeds on flax seeds.

Relatives: Linnette, Lynette, Linnet, Linetta, Linn

Linus: From the Old French for "flaxen-haired." There is something endearing about the name Linus—perhaps because of the "Peanuts" character's delightful philosophies.

Namesake: Linus Pauling

Lionel: Old French for "young lion." If Leonard is too obvious for your little Leo, try this one.

Relatives: Lyonel, Lionello, Lion, Lyon
Namesakes: Lionel Barrymore, Lionel Ritchie, Lionel Hampton

Litton: Old English for "hillside town."
Relative: Lytton
Namesake: Lytton Strachey

Llewellyn: Old Welsh for "ruling." Just look at a map of Wales to see some truly astonishing arrangements of letters into names.
Namesake: Richard Llewellyn

Lloyd: Old Welsh for "gray-haired."
Relative: Floyd
Namesakes: David Lloyd George, Lloyd Bentsen, Andrew Lloyd Webber, Floyd Patterson

Locke: Old English for "stronghold." According to some sources, Robin Hood's real name was Locksley, probably in homage to the town where he was born.
Relatives: Lockhart, Locksley, Loch (Scottish for "lake")
Namesake: John Locke

Logan: Scottish Gaelic for "little hollow" and a clan name. A sturdy name for a boy or girl.
Namesakes: Josh Logan, Logan Airport

Lon: Irish Gaelic for "fierce."
Relatives: Lonn, Lonnie, Lonny, Loni
Namesakes: Lon Chaney, Loni Anderson

Lorelei: German for "from the Rhine River" or a mythological siren. Lorelei was originally a name given to a formation of treacherous rocks that jutted into the Rhine, making navigation particularly hazardous at that point. A nineteenth-century poet wrote of a woman named Lorelei who was atop the cliff and, with her siren songs, led ships to their doom.
Namesake: "Lorelei Lee"

Lorraine: From the Old German for "where Lothar dwells."
Relatives: Loraine, Lorayne, Lorry, Lorrie, Loretta, Lorette, Lorne, Lorna, Lori
Namesakes: Loraine Newman, Loretta Lynn, "Lorna Doone," "Sweet Lorraine," quiche Lorraine

Louis: Old German for "famed warrior." Louis, the name of French kings, may be pronounced "Lewis" or "Loo-ee." But chances are he will always be Lou.

Relatives: Lewis, Lewes, Luis, Louie, Lewie, Lou, Lew, Lu, Ludwig, Ludvig, Luigi, Lodovico, Luthias, Llewellyn, Clovis

Namesakes: Saint Louis, Louis Pasteur, Louis Armstrong, Louis Brandeis, Louis Jourdan, Luis Bunuel, Lu Blue, Louisville (Ky.), Saint Louis (Mo.)

Louise: From the Old German for "warrior maiden" and a feminine version of Louis.

Relatives: Luise, Louisa, Louisiana, Luisa, Loise, Lois, Loyce, Lisette, Luana, Luane, Luwana, Lou, Lu, Lulu, Lulie, Ouise, Ouisa, Eloise, Eloisa, Aloysia, Liusadh

Namesakes: Louise Nevelson, Louisa May Alcott, Tina Louise, "Eloise," Lake Louise (Canada)

Lowell: A Boston Brahmin surname. The Lowell family has produced several generations of revered American poets, including Amy, James, and Robert.

Namesakes: Lowell Thomas, Lowell (Mass.)

Lucretia: From the Latin for "riches." A name that commands attention.

Relatives: Lucrezia, Lucrece, Lucy
Namesake: Lucrezia Borgia

Lucy: Latin for "light." Lucy does have a bright, shiny quality to it. Lucina, in Roman mythology, is a goddess of childbirth. We love Lucy.

Relatives: Lucie, Lucia, Luce, Lou, Lu, Luza, Luz, Luciana, Lucianna, Lucianne, Lucienne, Lucida, Lucinda, Lucinde, Lucile, Lucille, Lucette, Liusadh

Namesakes: Saint Lucy, Lucille Ball, Lucia Chase, Clare Boothe Luce, Charlie Brown's playmate

Luella: Old English for "elfin."
Relatives: Louella, Loella, Luelle
Namesake: Louella Parsons

Luke: From the Latin for "light bringer." Saint Luke is the patron saint of physicians and painters because he was thought to have been both.

Relatives: Luc, Lucas, Luckas, Luchas, Luca, Luka, Lukas, Lucais, Lucan, Lucian, Lucien, Lucius, Luciano

Namesakes: Jean-Luc Godard, Luciano Pavarotti, Lukas Haas, "Luke Skywalker"

Luna: Latin for "moon." An interesting choice for a baby born the night of a full moon.

Relatives: Lune, Lunetta

Luther: Old German for "warrior."

Relatives: Lutera, Lothaire, Lotario

Namesakes: Luther Adler, Luther Burbank, Luther Vandross

Lydia: From the Greek for "a woman from Persia." A pretty change from the more familiar Linda.

Relatives: Lydie, Lidia

Namesake: Lydia Pinkham

Lyle: From the Old French for "island."

Relatives: Lisle, Lyell

Namesakes: Lyle Lovett, Lyle Alzado, Sparky Lyle, "Lyle Crocodile"

Lyman: Middle English for "from the meadow."

Relative: Leyman

Namesakes: L(yman) Frank Baum, Lyman Bostock, Lyman Beecher

Lyndon: Old English for "linden tree." Appropriate name for a baby Democrat.

Relatives: Lindon, Linden

Namesakes: Lyndon Baines Johnson, *Barry Lyndon*

Lynn: Old English for "waterfall." A charming euphonic sound, this works well as a middle name or as a suffix.

Relatives: Lynne, Lyn, Lin, Linn, Linell, Linette, Lyndel, Lynna, Lina, Lynnette, Lynette, Lynley

Namesakes: Lynn Swann, Loretta Lynn

Lysander: Greek for "liberator." A little precious, but it might work for a girl.

Relative: Lysandra

The Sun, the Moon, and the Stars

There are a galaxy of intriguing name possibilities just overhead. The names of constellations, moons, and satellites adapt beautifully as choices for your baby. Many are borrowed from Greek and Roman mythology.

You may also want to consider more general names such as Sky, Star, Etoile, Aurora, or Sunny or fiddle with your child's astrological charts to find something original.

Altair—the brightest star in the constellation Aquila
Andromeda—a constellation named for a princess in Greek myth
Antares—a red-tinted star in the Scorpius constellation
Aquila (the eagle)—a part of the Milky Way
Ara (the altar)—a part of the Milky Way in the southern hemisphere
Ariel—a satellite of Uranus
Caelum (the chisel)—a small constellation
Callisto—a large satellite of Jupiter, discovered by Galileo
Capella—the seventh brightest star in the sky
Carina (the keel)—a constellation in the southern hemisphere
Cassiopeia—a large constellation named for a queen of Greek myth
Delphinus (the dolphin)—a constellation in the northern hemisphere
Dione—one of the ten moons of Saturn
Janus—one of the ten moons of Saturn
Lacerta (the lizard)—a constellation that lies near Andromeda
Lyra (the lyre)—a small constellation of the northern hemisphere
Miranda—one of the five moons of Uranus
Oberon—one of the five moons of Uranus
Orion—a major constellation named for the Greek hunter
Phoebe—one of the ten moons of Saturn
Rhea—one of the ten moons of Saturn
Titania—one of the five moons of Uranus
Triton—one of Neptune's two moons
Umbriel—one of the five moons of Uranus
Vela (the sails)—a part of the Milky Way

M

Mab: Irish Gaelic for "joy." Queen Mab was the queen of the fairies, according to ancient Irish legends. Pretty thought, but remember it rhymes with "blab," "gab," and "flab"—all unfortunate possibilities for nicknames.

Relatives: Mave, Mavis, Mabley
Namesake: Moms Mabley

Mabel: From the Latin for "lovable" and French ("ma belle") for "my beautiful one." For a generation of baby boomers, Mabel will always be associated with a "yo" whistle and Black Label beer. But take heart, fans, Tracey Ullman named her baby girl Mabel.

Relatives: Maybelle, Mable, Maibelle, Mabella, Maybelline, Mabry, Amabel
Namesakes: Mabel Mercer, Maybelle Carter, Maybelline cosmetics

Mac: Scottish, Irish, and English prefix meaning "son of." Here you have a phone book of Scottish, Irish, and English family names to peruse. Some popular examples are MacAdam, MacArthur, MacDonald, MacDougal, MacIntyre, MacKenzie, MacKinley, MacLean.

Relatives: Mc, Mack, Mackey
Namesakes: Mac Davis, Mack Sennett, Mackenzie Phillips, MacLean Stevenson, "Mack the Knife," "Old MacDonald," Mount McKinley

In 1964, former English Prime Minister Harold Macmillan refused the royal Order of the Garter, a most prestigious honor. It would have meant a name change and Macmillan didn't want that.

Macon: From the Middle English "to make." Macon is a county name in nine states and is traditionally associated with the South as a surname.

Relatives: Makon, Macomb

Namesakes: Uncle Dave Macon, Randolph Macon College

Macy: From the Old French for "from Matthew's land" and Old English for "club."

Relatives: Macey, Mace, Maceo

Namesakes: Bill Macy, Macy's department store

Maddock: Old Welsh for "champion" or "good fortune." Maddock is the sort of name you'd expect to find stenciled on a glass door in a slightly rundown office building. Maddock Jones, private eye.

Relatives: Madock, Madoc, Madog, Maddox, Madox, Maidoc, Maddy

Namesake: Ford Madox Ford

Madeira: From the sweet wine of the Madeira Islands. Why not? After all, Brandy, Margaux, and Ginny are used.

Madeline: From the Hebrew for "tower of strength." A name popular in many cultures and in a wide variety of forms. And it was a little pastry called a "madeleine" that sent writer Marcel Proust into raptures.

Relatives: Magdalene, Magdalen, Magdalena, Madeleine, Madalynn, Madelynne, Madelaine, Madalena, Madelon, Madelyn, Madlin, Madigan, Marleen, Marlene, Marlena, Marline, Maighdlin, Maudlin (check the dictionary before using this one), Malina, Madga, Mady, Maddy, Maddie, Matty, Mala, Mae, May, Lena, Lene

Namesakes: Madeline Kahn, Marlene Dietrich, the *Madeline* books by Bemelmans, *Elvira Madigan*

Madison: From the German for "'son of a mighty warrior" or "related to Maude." This has a future-presidential ring to it.

Relatives: Maddison, Maddy

Namesakes: James Madison, Dolly Madison, "Oscar Madison," Madison (Wis.)

Madra: Spanish for "mother." If the baby looks like her mother—why not? Madre mia!

Relatives: Madre, Madrona

Magdalene: From the Hebrew for "woman of Magdala," an area of Palestine associated with Mary Magdalene.
Relatives: Madeline, Magdaline, Magdalena, Magda, Lena
Namesakes: Saint Mary Magdalene, Magda Gabor

Maggie: A shortened form of Margaret. It has been used as an independent name since the nineteenth century.
Relatives: Maggy, Magee, Mag
Namesakes: Maggie Smith, "Maggie"

Magnolia: The magnolia flower and tree are named for French botanist Pierre Magnol. This fragrant blossom is associated with the deep South.
Relatives: Maggie, Nola, Nolia, Nolie, Enola
Namesake: Enola Gay

Magnus: Latin for "great."
Relatives: Manus, Magnuson, Magnum, Magna, Magnilda
Namesake: King Magnus of Norway

Mahala: From the Hebrew for "tenderness" and Arabic for "marrow." The name appears in the Old Testament (Numbers 26:33). It is also translated as "woman" in a North American Indian language.
Relatives: Mahalah, Mahalar, Mahela, Mahalia, Mahelia, Mehala
Namesake: Mahalia Jackson

Maida: Old English for "maiden." Thomas Hardy used "Maidy" in his novels as a form of address to a young woman.
Relatives: Maidie, Maidy, Mady, Maidel, Mayda

Maire: A Scottish or Welsh version of Mary.
Relatives: Mair, Mare, Mairwen (Welsh for "lovely Mary"), Mairead
Namesake: Mare Winningham

Maisie: Derived from Margery or Margaret and has always been popular in Scotland as an independent name.
Relatives: Maisy, Maysie, Mysie, Mazey, Maizie

Maitland: Old English for "dweller in the meadow" and a Norman place name. Although the derivation is rather bland, the name itself is strong and forthright.
Namesake: Maitland Jones

Major: Latin for "greater." Giving a child a "rank" name such as Major poses a problem if he or she chooses a military career. Joseph Heller had fun with the possibility in his novel *Catch-22*, naming his character Major Major.
 Relatives: Majeur, Majors, Majorie
 Namesakes: Lee Majors, *Major Barbara,* majordomo, constellation Ursa Major

Makepeace: A "virtue" name. A favorite of the original Puritan settlers, perhaps inspired by the realization that if they didn't, they wouldn't get much help from the locals.
 Namesake: William Makepeace Thackeray

Mala: From the Old French for "bad one" and Old English for "meeting hall." Ignore the French root. This is a lovely name.
 Namesake: Mala Powers

Malachi: From the Hebrew for "messenger of God." Malachi was the last of the twelve minor prophets. He foretold Christ's coming.
 Relatives: Malachy, Malachai
 Namesakes: Saint Malachy, Malachi Martin, name of the last book of the Old Testament

Malca: Hebrew for "queen."
 Relative: Malka

Malcolm: Scottish Gaelic for "disciple of Saint Columba." An extremely popular name in Scotland and Australia.
 Relatives: Mal, Colm
 Namesakes: Malcolm Cowley, Malcolm X, Malcolm Muggeridge, Malcolm McDowell, Malcolm Forbes, son of "King Duncan" in Shakespeare's *Macbeth*

Mallory: From the Old German for "army counselor" and German for "without good fortune." This name is equally favored for girls and boys.
 Relatives: Mallorie, Mallorey, Malori, Malory, Mal, Mally, Malin
 Namesakes: Sir Thomas Malory, "Mallory Keaton," Mallomars

Malvina: A Gaelic version of Malvin or Melvin. Malvina probably preceded Melvin. The name was apparently invented and popularized

by writer James Macpherson, based on a translation of the Irish "maol-mhin" meaning "smooth snow."
Relatives: Malva, Malvie, Melvina, Melvine, Mevin, Mally, Melly, Mal, Mel
Namesake: Malvinas (Falkland Islands)

Manfred: From the Old German for "man of peace."
Relatives: Manny, Fred
Namesakes: Manfred Mann, poem by Lord Byron, "Mighty Manfred"

Manley: Old English for "man of the meadow." If you are interested in establishing a sense of machismo early on, this is a bold choice.
Relatives: Manly, Manning, Mansfield, Manton, Manville, Mannix, Manchester, Manheim
Namesakes: Dexter Manley, Mike Mansfield, Manchester (England), Man Ray

Manon: A French version of Mary or Marian. The French pronunciation is essential: *"Man-on."*
Namesakes: Manon Lescaut, Manon of the Spring

Manuel: Spanish variation of Emanuel.
Relatives: Manuela, Mano, Manolo, Manny, Mani
Namesake: Manuel Ortega

Mara: From the Hebrew for "bitter," a version of Mary, and an abbreviated form of Tamara ("palm tree"). Mara has an elegant simplicity, so it works well with a long surname. In the Old Testament (Ruth 1:20), Naomi says, "Do not call me Naomi, call me Mara."
Relatives: Marah, Maraline, Marlina

Marcel: A French form of Marcellus or "little hammer."
Relatives: Marcello, Marcellus
Namesakes: Marcel Proust, Marcel Marceau, Marcello Mastroianni

Marcella: A Latin name derived from Mars, the god of war. Marcella is also the feminine version of Marcus, Marcel, and Marcello.
Relatives: Marcy, Marcie, Marcelle, Marclyn, Marcelin

Marcia: A Latin name derived from the Roman god of war—Mars. It is a feminine version of Mark, Marcius, and Marcus. It may be pronounced *"Mar-cy-a"* or *"Marsh-a."*

Relatives: Marsha, Marshe, Marcille, Marchita, Marchette, Marquita, Martia, Marcelia, Marcy, Marci, Marcie

Namesakes: Marcia Wallace, Marsha Mason

Marcus: A Latin form of Mark. Marcus has become increasingly popular, perhaps in an effort to select a traditional name with a slightly different twist.

Relatives: Marilo, Marc, Mark

Namesakes: Marcus Aurelius, Marcus Allen, Marcus Garvey, "Dr. Marcus Welby"

Marcy: A name originally derived as a nickname for any name that began with "Mar."

Relatives: Marcey, Marci, Marsi, Marsy, Marsie

Margaret: From the Latin for "pearl." This name and all its variations have been consistently popular throughout the world for generations. The wide variety of nicknames makes this a good choice for insecure parents.

Relatives: Margareta, Margarita, Margita, Margery, Margory, Marjorie, Marjory, Marget, Margret, Margette, Margalo, Marguerite, Margarida, Margiad, Margherita, Margarethe, Maergrethe, Margaretha, Margalith, Mairghread, Margo, Marjoe, Marga, Margot, Margaux, Marge, Margie, Marta, Madge, Mag, Magee, Maggie, Mamie, Maymie, Maisie, Meg, Meggie, Midge, Gretchen, Gretel, Gretle, Greta, Grete, Garet, Peg, Peggy, Reta, Rita

Namesakes: Margaret, a patron saint of Scotland and one of the virgin martyrs of the third century, Margaret Rose Charlton, Margaret Mitchell, Princess Margaret, Margaret Thatcher, Margaux (the wine and the Hemingway), Marguerite Duras, Margot Fonteyn, frozen margarita

Maria: A Latin version of Mary. There are several show-stopping numbers in various musicals dedicated to Maria. The usual pronunciation is "Ma-re-a," but you might consider using "Ma-reye-a," a pretty variation.

Relatives: Mary, Marya, Mariah, Marie

Namesakes: Maria Shriver, Maria von Trapp, Maria Callas

Mariabella: A blending of Maria and "bella" (my beautiful Mary).
Relatives: Mariabelle, Maribel, Maribelle

Mariam: A Greek form of Mary or Miriam.
Relative: Mariamne
Namesake: Mariamne, wife of Herod and subject of a play by Voltaire entitled *Mariamne*

Marian: A blending of Mary and Ann and Old French for "little Mary."
Relatives: Marion, Mariana, Mariann, Marianne, Mary-Ann, Marianna
Namesakes: Marian Anderson, Marianne Moore, "Maid Marian"

Maridel: A version of Mary.
Relative: Meridel

Mariel: A French version of Marie or Mary. The simple addition of the "l" gives the name a musical quality.
Relatives: Marielle, Mariella, Marietta, Mariette, Marette, Maretta
Namesakes: Mariel Hemingway, Marietta College (Ohio)

Marigold: A flower name. Less familiar now than Rose or Lily, perhaps, but once a popular flower name.
Relatives: Mari, Golda, Goldie

Marilee: A blending of Mary and Lee. The Mari- prefix blends well with many other names; a good combination is Marilise. Experiment.
Relatives: Marlee, Merry-Lee
Namesake: Marlee Matson

Marilyn: A blending of Mary and Lynn. A relatively modern "invention," becoming common only in this century.
Relatives: Mary-Lynn, Maralin, Marilin, Marylin, Marlyn, Marlin, Marly, Mari, Lynn
Namesakes: Marilyn Monroe, Marilyn Quayle, Marilyn Horne

Mario: A variation of Mark or Marion.
Relative: Marius
Namesakes: Mario Puzo, Mario Cuomo, Mario van Peebles

Marion: Related to Mary. This name is used for both sexes and as a surname. As a girl's name, it peaked in the twenties when it made the top-twenty list.

Relative: Mariano

Namesakes: General Francis Marion, Marion Michael Morrison (John Wayne)

Marissa: From the Latin for "of the sea." If derivations are important to you, you might enjoy giving this name to a future surfer. A pretty choice with fine nicknames.

Relatives: Marisa, Maris, Mari, Marina, Maressa, Maritza, Merisa, Merrisa, Marissah

Namesakes: Saint Marina, Princess Marina of Greece, Marisa Berenson, Marina Del Rey (Calif.)

Marjorie: From the Old French for "pearl" and a variation of Margaret.

Relatives: Marjory, Marjorey, Marjary, Margery, Margey, Margie, Marge, Margo, Marje, Marjy, Marcail

Namesakes: Marjorie Merriweather Post, "My Little Margie," *Marjorie Morningstar*

Mark: From the Latin relating to Mars, the god of war, it also translates as "hammer." Mark is a solid choice, and the relatives offer room for unique variations.

Relatives: Marc, Marcus, Marcel, Marcellus, Marcello, Marcellino, Marceau, Marque, Marco, Marek, Marko, Markus, Markos, Marks, Marx, March, Marius, Marquette, Marquis, Marky, Markie

Namesakes: Saint Mark, Mark Twain, Marco Polo, Marc Chagall, Mark Harmon, Markie Post

Marlene: A German form of Madeline or a blending of Mary or Margaret with Lena or Helen. This may be pronounced with either two or three syllables.

Relatives: Marlena, Marleen, Marline, Marly, Marlie, Marla, Lene, Lena

Namesakes: Marlene Dietrich, Marla Hansen, "Lili Marlene"

Marlon: A French name related to Merlin and Merle. This could translate into a name for either sex.

Relatives: Marlin, Marlyn, Marly, Marlo, Marlis, Marlys

Namesakes: Marlon Brando, Marlo Thomas

Marlow: Old English for "from the hillside lake."

Relatives: Marlowe, Marlo

Namesakes: Christopher Marlowe, "Philip Marlowe"

Marmaduke: Celtic for "leader on the seas." Granted it's difficult blocking the image of a Great Dane, but this is an impressive monicker.
Relative: Duke
Namesake: Duke Ellington

Marna: From the Hebrew for "rejoice."
Relatives: Marni, Marnie, Marny, Marnette, Marne
Namesake: Marne River (France)

Marsden: From the Old English for "field near water."
Relatives: Marsdon, Marston, Marland, Marley, Marden, Marwood, Mardyth
Namesake: Bob Marley

Marshall: From the English for "steward" and French for "cavalry commander." A surname that is well-suited as a first name.
Relatives: Marshal, Marschall, Marsh, Marshe
Namesakes: Marshall McLuhan, Thurgood Marshall, "Marshal Dillon"

Martha: Aramaic for "lady" or "woman." The biblical Martha (Luke 10; John 11, 12) was a bit of a drudge who complained to God about her household duties and was admonished by Him. She has since become the patron saint of housewives.
Relatives: Marth, Marta, Martina, Martella, Martita, Marti, Marty, Mattie, Matty, Marthe, Masia
Namesakes: Martha Washington, Martha Graham, Martha Stewart, Martha and the Vandellas, Marthe Keller

Martin: From the Latin for "of Mars." This is not to say a Martian but, rather, related to the Greek god of war—Mars. The planet Mars rules Scorpios.
Relatives: Marten, Martyn, Marton, Maarten, Martino, Martins, Marty, Martie, Mart, Mertin, Mertil, Martinson, Martel, Martinet, Martinique
Namesakes: Saint Martin, Martin Luther King, Jr., Martin Van Buren

Martina: A feminine version of Martin, Latin for "warrior." Perfect for the baby girl with a wicked backhand.
Relatives: Martine, Marta, Marty, Tina
Namesake: Martina Navratilova

Marvelle: From the Latin and Old French for "miracle."
Relatives: Marvel, Marvell, Marva, Marvella
Namesake: Andrew Marvell

Marvin: Celtic for "beautiful sea," Anglo-Saxon for "good friend," and a version of Mervyn. This name hasn't seen much activity in the past decade in spite of its winning derivations.
Relatives: Mervin, Mervyn, Merwin, Merwyn, Myrwyn, Murvyn, Myrvyn, Marv
Namesakes: Marvin Hamlisch, Marvin Gaye, Lee Marvin

Mary: The New Testament form of Miriam (Hebrew for "bitter"). For generations, including the first half of the twentieth century, Mary has been the most popular name in many cultures. Although it has fallen out of favor in the past few decades, it will probably become the "Jessica" of the twenty-first century. Mary is also the star of dozens of nursery rhymes, which makes story-time conveniently personal. It pairs well with a second name such as Ellen, Alice, or Jane.
Relatives: Mari, Merry, Marie, Maria, Miriam, Marian, Mame, Mamie, Maymie, Mayme, May, Mally, Molly, Polly, Mara, Maretta, Marel, Marella, Maren, Marlo, Mariette, Marieta, Meriel, Mimi, Minette, Minnie, Minny, Mitzi, Madonna, Marilla, Marla, Marya, Muriel, Manon, Manette, Marija, Marika, Maire, Mare, Marquita, Maure, Mairin, Maura, Maureen, Moira, Moire, Moya, Muire, Masha, Mairi
Namesakes: Mary Queen of Scots, William and Mary, Mary Martin, Mamie Eisenhower, "Mary Poppins," "Minnie Mouse"

Maslin: Old French for "little twin." A name to keep in mind if multiple births run in your family.
Relative: Maslen
Namesake: Janet Maslin

Mason: From the French, occupational name for a stoneworker. A solid, preppie name.
Relatives: Masen, Mase
Namesakes: Mason Williams, James Mason, Jackie Mason, Mason jar

Mather: Old English for "powerful army."
Namesake: Cotton Mather

Mathilda: From the Old German for "battle maiden" or "strength." The popular Aussie song can be her personal lullaby.

Relatives: Matilda, Matelda, Maitilde, Mathylda, Mathilde, Matty, Mattye, Mattie, Maddy, Maddie, Mala, Tila, Tilly, Tillie, Tilda, Maude, Maud

Namesakes: Queen Matilda, Matilda Cuomo, Tillie Olsen, "Waltzing Matilda"

Mattea: A feminine version of Matthew (Hebrew for "gift of God"). With the emphasis on the second syllable, Mattea has a romantic quality to it. The name suggests a heroine created by Byron.

Relatives: Matthea, Mathia, Mathea, Mathia

Matthew: From the Hebrew for "gift of God." To add a distinctive twist to this ever-popular name, consider the handsome variations.

Relatives: Mathew, Mathias, Matthias, Mattieu, Matheu, Matyus, Matthaus, Mathern, Mayhew, Mattheson, Matthieson, Matthews, Mattheus, Mathe, Mateo, Matteo, Mattison, Massey, Matt, Matty, Mats

Namesakes: Saint Matthew, Matthew Arnold, Matthew Broderick, Walter Matthau, Mats Wilander

Maud: From the Old German for "strength in battle" and a variation of Mathilda. Shake that image of Bea Arthur's character in the TV show "Maude." This is a special name.

Relatives: Maude, Maudie

Namesakes: Maud Adams, *Maud* (by Alfred Lord Tennyson)

Maureen: Irish Gaelic for "little Mary," Old French (Maurin) meaning "dark-haired," and a feminine version of Maurice. Evokes Irish beauty and Celtic strength.

Relatives: Maura, Mora, Moira, Moreen, Moria, Maurin, Maurine, Morena, Maurizia, Mo

Namesakes: Maureen O'Hara, Maureen O'Sullivan, Maureen Stapleton, Maureen McGovern

Maurice: French-Latin for "moorish" or "dark" and Old English for "moor land." This name can be pronounced with the accent on the second syllable, as the French do ("Mowr-*ees*"), or on the first, as in Morris the cat.

Relatives: Morris, Morse, Maury, Morry, Morey, Morrie, Moritz, Moriz, Morets, Meuriz, Moss, Morrell, Mauricio, Maurizio, Murray, Maryse, Morrison

Namesakes: Maurice Chevalier, Maurice Ravel, Maurice Lucas, Moss Hart

Mavis: A type of small bird related to the thrush and a variation of Mab. Many names are borrowed from nature, and birds have been popular in almost every culture. Mavis was especially popular in England at the turn of the century.

Relatives: Maves, Maeves, Maeve, Mauve, Meave

Maximilian: From the Latin for "greatest one." This name is credited to and first used by Frederick III of Germany in 1459. He wanted a special name for his son and heir, and reviewed the names of his heroes—Roman emperors. Just-plain "Max" echoed across the playgrounds of America as it climbed the popularity charts in the eighties.

Relatives: Maximilien, Maximiliano, Maximus, Maxim, Maximo, Maxwell, Maxfield, Maximino, Max, Maxey, Maxie, Mac, Maxa, Mack, Maks, Maksim

Namesakes: Maximilian Schell, Maksim Gorky, Sir Max Beerbohm, Max Factor, Maxfield Parrish

Maxine: A Latin version of Maxima meaning "the greatest."

Relatives: Maxina, Maxime, Maxima, Maxita, Maxa, Maxy, Maxie, Max

Maxwell: An Anglo-Saxon place name and Old English for "Marcus's well."

Relatives: Max, Maxey, Maxie, Maxy

Namesakes: Maxwell Anderson, Maxwell Perkins, "Maxwell Smart," Maxwell House coffee

May: An abbreviated version of Mary and Margaret. Name her two little sisters April and June.

Relatives: Mae, Mai, Maia, Maya, Maye, Mayes, Mays, Maize

Namesakes: May Britt, Willie Mays, Mayo Smith, Mayo Clinic

Mayer: German for "farmer," Latin for "greater," and Hebrew for "bringer of light."

Relatives: Meyer, Meir, Meier, Mayr, Myer, Mayor, Myerson
Namesakes: Meyer Lansky, Louis B. Mayer, Oscar Mayer, Bess Myerson

Maynard: Anglo-Saxon for "remarkable strength" and Dobie Gillis's buddy, of course.
Relative: Menard
Namesakes: Maynard Ferguson, Don Maynard, Joyce Maynard

Mead: Old English for "meadow." Aside from translating literally as a level grassland, mead is a fermented drink made from honey, malt, yeast, and water.
Relatives: Meade, Meed, Meid
Namesake: Margaret Mead

Meara: Irish Gaelic for "mirth."
Relatives: Mira, Meera
Namesake: Anne Meara

Medea: In Greek "Medeon" means "ruling," and in Latin "Media" means "middle child." The mythical enchantress Medea, it should be remembered, helped Jason win the Golden Fleece. The ungrateful Jason, however, deserted her. Medea, in turn, killed her children and vanished. An ancient soap opera, and perhaps a difficult name for a modern child.
Relatives: Medora, Media, Madora

Megan: An Irish Gaelic and Welsh version of Margaret and Greek for "mighty." Megan has become a contemporary American favorite, although it has been on the top of the list in Ireland for centuries.
Relatives: Meghan, Meagan, Megann, Meggy, Meggie, Meg

Mehetabel: Hebrew for "favored by God" or "God is doing good."
Relatives: Mehitabel, Mehitabelle, Metabel, Hetty, Hitty

Melanctha: Greek for "black flower" and the family name of Protestant leader Philipp Melanchthon.
Relatives: Melanchthon, Melancton, Melantha
Namesake: Melancton Smith

Melanie: Greek for "dressed in black" or "dark." The enduring popularity of this name is probably due to its lyrical sound.

Relatives: Melany, Melane, Melani, Melania, Melloney, Melonie, Melony, Milena, Melanya, Mellie, Melly, Mel, Mela
Namesakes: Saint Melanie, Melanie Griffith, "Melanie Wilkes"

Melba: Greek for "slender" or "soft" and Latin for "mallow flower." The mallow flower is associated with the month of September. Melba is also a variation of Melvina and Melbourne.
Relatives: Melva, Malva
Namesakes: Melba Moore, Nellie Melba

Melina: From the Latin for "yellow songbird."
Relative: Melianthe
Namesake: Melina Mercouri

Melinda: From the Greek for "gentle one." A change from the more well-known Melissa and Melanie.
Relatives: Malinda, Malina, Malinde, Malena, Melina, Minda, Mindy, Mallie, Mally, Linda, Lindy
Namesake: Melinda Dillon

Melissa: Greek for "bee" or "honey." This beautiful name deserves its continuing popularity.
Relatives: Melicent, Millicent, Melisent, Melita, Melisse, Meli, Mellie, Melly, Mel, Millie, Milly, Missy, Lisa, Lissa, Lis
Namesakes: Melissa Gilbert, Melissa Manchester

Melody: From the Greek for "song." Of all the musical names, this is the most tuneful.
Relatives: Melodie, Melly, Mellie

Melville: Anglo-Saxon for "hillside," Old English for "town by the mill." Doesn't this sound classier than Melvin?
Relative: Mel
Namesakes: Melville Fuller, Herman Melville

Melvin: Celtic for "chief."
Relatives: Malvin, Melvyn, Mel, Mal
Namesakes: Mel Gibson, Mel Brooks, Mel Blanc, Melvyn Douglas

Mendel: Hebrew for "wisdom" and Middle English for "repairer."
Relatives: Mel, Mendelssohn, Menachem, Menahem
Namesakes: L. Mendel Rivers, Menachem Begin, Felix Mendelssohn

Mercedes: Spanish for the liturgical Maria de la Mercedes (Mary of Mercies) and Latin for "ransom." Mr. Daimler named his line of luxury automobiles for his daughter.

Relatives: Mercia, Mercy

Namesake: Mercedes McCambridge

Mercer: Middle English for "storekeeper." This name works equally well for boys and girls. And remember there are at least eight counties in the United States named Mercer.

Relative: Merce

Namesakes: Merce Cunningham, Johnny Mercer, Mabel Mercer, General Hugh Mercer

Mercy: From the Middle English for "compassion" or "pity." A very popular name in Plymouth colony. Roy Orbison said it best.

Relatives: Merci, Mercia, Mercedes

Meredith: From Old Welsh for "protector of the sea." Both a family name and a first name used for either sex.

Relatives: Meridith, Merry, Meri

Namesakes: Meredith McCrea, Meredith Baxter-Birney, Meredith Wilson, Don Meredith

Merit: From the Latin for "deserving." And it is a name that deserves consideration.

Relatives: Merritt, Merriwell

Namesakes: Merritt Ranew, Frank Merriwell

Merle: From the Latin for "blackbird." Appropriate for both sexes, this may be spelled in a variety of ways.

Relatives: Merl, Myrle, Meryl, Merlina, Myrlene, Merola, Merrill, Merla

Namesakes: Merle Oberon, Merle Haggard, Meryl Streep

Merlin: Celtic for "sea" and Anglo-Saxon for "falcon." It was Merlin who guided King Arthur and foretold the story of the "once and future king."

Relatives: Merlyn, Marlin, Marlen, Marwin, Mervin, Merv, Merle

Namesakes: Merlin Olsen, Merv Griffin, Marlin Perkins, Mervyn LeRoy

Merrill: From the German for "famous" and Old English for "of the sea."

Relatives: Merral, Meril, Merrel, Meryl, Myrl, Myril, Merle, Merrick, Merton

Namesakes: Robert Merrill, James Merrill, David Merrick

Merry: Middle English for "joyful." This name never attained the same following as Joy but is pretty on its own and may be used as a substitute for Mary.

Relatives: Merri, Merrie, Merrilee, Merrily, Merrita, Merrielle

Namesake: Merry Christmas

Messina: From the Latin for "middle child."

Relative: Messena

Namesake: Jim Messina

Mia: Derived from Maria and Michaela; also "mine" in Italian. This sweet name blends nicely with a long surname.

Namesake: Mia Farrow

Michael: From the Hebrew for "who is like god?" The name Michael jumped into the top ten in the forties, having been a dark horse before then. If you are nervous about using so popular a name, peruse the list of variations.

Relatives: Michail, Mikhail, Mikas, Mikel, Michel, Miguel, Michelangelo, Micah, Michiel, Micha, Mischa, Mitchell, Mitch, Michau, Michon, Mikhos, Mihal, Mick, Mickey, Mike, Mikey

Namesakes: The Archangel Michael, Michael Caine, Michael J. Fox, Michael Jackson, Mickey Mantle, Mike Tyson, Mick Jagger, Miguel de Cervantes, Mikhail Baryshnikov, "Mickey Mouse"

Michaela: From the Hebrew for "who is like God?" and a feminine version of Michael.

Relatives: Michaelina, Michaeline, Michelina, Micaela, Mikaela, Miguela, Michael, Mike, Mickey, Micki, Mikey

Namesake: Michael Learned

Michelle: A French feminine version of Michael. A child named Michelle will consider the Beatles' classic a lullaby written just for her. This name was number one in the United States in 1970 but has dropped off recently.

Relatives: Michele, Michal, Michel, Micheline, Michelyn, Midge, Mickie

Namesakes: Michelle Pfeiffer, Michelle Phillips, Midge Dichter, "Michelle, Ma Belle"

Mildred: Anglo-Saxon blending of "mild" and "thryth" (meaning "power"). This old-fashioned monicker was in the top ten in 1900.
Relatives: Mildrid, Mildraed, Mildryd, Milly, Milli, Milley, Millie
Namesakes: Saint Mildred, *Mildred Pierce*

Miles: From the Latin for "soldier," Old German for "merciful," and Greek for "millstone."
Relatives: Myles, Milo, Milos, Milan
Namesakes: Myles Standish, Miles Davis, Venus de Milo, Milos Forman

Millard: Occupational name for "caretaker of the mill."
Namesake: Millard Fillmore

Miller: Occupational name for "one who mills."
Relatives: Mills, Millson
Namesakes: Miller Barber, Arthur Miller, Glenn Miller, Ann Miller

Millicent: Old German for "industrious" or "strength." Although this has never been wildly popular, it offers a delightful change from the standard Melissa.
Relatives: Millisent, Melicent, Milly, Millie, Mili, Melly, Melisande, Melisenda
Namesakes: Millicent Martin, Millie Marmur

Milton: English place name for a mill town.
Relatives: Milten, Milty, Milt, Melton
Namesakes: Milton Berle, Milton Eisenhower, Milton Caniff, Milton Keynes

Minerva: Greek for "power" and Latin for "thinker." The goddess Minerva was born in a full set of armor from the head of Jupiter. Your child's entry into the world will be equally astonishing.
Relatives: Minette, Minnie, Minny

Minna: From the Old German for "love" and Scottish for "mother."
Relatives: Mina, Minette, Minetta, Minny, Minnie (a Scottish form of Mary), Minda, Myna, Mindy
Namesakes: Minnie Pearl, "Minnie Mouse," "Mork and Mindy"

Minta: Greek for "mint." One of several herbal names. Take a minute to review a Spice Islands display. Don't many of these labels sound like proper names?

Relatives: Mintha, Araminta

Mira: From the Latin for "wonder" and Spanish for "aim." An ideal name for a future sharpshooter.

Relatives: Myra, Mirilla, Mirella, Mirelle, Mirielle, Myrilla

Mirabelle: Latin for "wonderful" and Spanish for "beautiful to look upon."

Relatives: Mirabel, Mirabella, Mirable, Marabel

Miranda: Latin for "extraordinary" or "to be admired." Miranda offers a twist on the more popular Amanda, and the nickname Mandy may still be invoked. In England Randy is the preferred nickname.

Relatives: Myranda, Meranda, Mira, Randy, Mandy

Namesakes: Carmen Miranda, Francisco de Miranda

Miriam: Hebrew for "bitter"—the same root as Mary. It also has the sense of "rebellious." A popular name in Jewish cultures.

Relatives: Miryam, Myriam, Mimi, Minnie, Mitzi, Miri, Mims, Mimsie, Meryem, Mirjam

Namesakes: The sister of Moses, Miriam Makeba, Mitzi Gaynor, Merriam-Webster, Mimi Hines

Missy: A form of "miss." Like Sissy for "sister," this has acquired independent identity as a proper name.

Relatives: Missie, Missye, Sissy

Namesake: Sissy Spacek

Misty: Old English for "covered by mist." Misty plays well for us.

Relative: Mistee

Namesake: Misty of Chincoteague

Modesty: Latin for "modest one" and a feminine form of Modestus. Sonny and Cher named their daughter Chastity, after all.

Relatives: Modesta, Modestia, Modestine, Modeste, Desty

Namesakes: Saint Modestus, "Modesty Blaise"

Moira: An Irish variation of Mary. This name is rarely used except by parents in Ireland or of Irish descent. Put her in a kelly-green stretchie and see how it suits her.
Relatives: Maura, Moyra
Namesakes: Moira Shearer, Moira Hodgson

Molly: A variation of Mary or Margaret. Molly has experienced a resurgence in the eighties and nineties. It evokes an image of gingham frocks and braided hair in bows.
Relatives: Molli, Molley, Mollie
Namesakes: Molly Pitcher, Molly Ringwald

Mona: Latin for "peaceful," Greek for "individual," Irish Gaelic for "noble one," and an Italian contraction of "my lady." This name is at home in many cultures.
Namesake: Mona Freeman

Monica: From the Latin for "advice."
Relatives: Monca, Mona, Monique
Namesakes: Saint Monica, Monique Van Vooren

Monroe: Celtic place name for "mouth of the Roe River" and a clan name in Scotland meaning "wheelwright." This fine old Celtic name would look terrific on the door to the Oval Office.
Relatives: Munroe, Munro, Monro
Namesakes: James Monroe, Marilyn Monroe, H. H. Munro (Saki)

Montague: French place name for "steep mountain." A sturdy family name with a rich lineage.
Relatives: Montagu, Montag, Monty, Monte
Namesakes: Ashley Montagu, Lord Montagu, "Romeo Montague"

Montgomery: French place name and French for "mountain hunter." This one is loaded with snob appeal, but the nickname Monty softens it.
Relatives: Monty, Monte
Namesakes: Montgomery Clift, Monty Hall, Monty Woolley, Elizabeth Montgomery, Robert Montgomery

Mordecai: Hebrew for "warrior." Purim is a Jewish holiday honoring Queen Esther, who saved the Persian Jews from slaughter. Boys born during this time were routinely named in honor of her cousin, Mordecai.

Relatives: Mordechai, Mort, Mordy, Morty
Namesake: Mordecai Richler

Morgan: Gaelic for "white sea" and Welsh for "bright" or "dweller by the sea." Morgan is used interchangeably for girls and boys. Nevertheless, Morgana has long been popular as a feminine variant.
Relatives: Morgen (German for "morning"), Morgana, Morganne
Namesakes: Morgan Freeman, Morgan Fairchild, Morgan le Fay, Morgana, Justin Morgan

Moria: Hebrew for "my teacher is God."
Relatives: Moriah, Moriel, Morit, Moryah
Namesake: Mount Moriah

Moriarty: Irish for "sea warrior." This was the name of Sherlock Holmes's foe.
Namesake: Michael Moriarty

Morley: English place name for "moor" or "meadow."
Relatives: Morlee, Morleigh, Morry, Morrie, Lee
Namesakes: Morley Safer, Robert Morley, Christopher Morley

Morris: Related to Maurice.
Relatives: Maurice, Morrie, Morry, Morse, Moss, Morrison
Namesakes: Morris West, Toni Morrison, Samuel Morse, "Morris the cat"

Mortimer: French place name for "still water."
Relatives: Morty, Mort
Namesakes: Mort Zuckerman, Mort Adler, John Mortimer, "Mortimer Snerd"

Morton: Anglo-Saxon place name for "city on the moor."
Relatives: Morten, Mortyn, Morty, Mort
Namesakes: Morton Downey, Jr., Mort Sahl, Jelly Roll Morton

Moselle: From the Hebrew for "taken from water" and a feminine version of Moses. Moselle is also a wine made in the Moselle valley, which extends from eastern France into western Germany.
Relatives: Mozelle, Mosheh

Moses: From the Hebrew for "saved," Egyptian for "child," and Greek for "taken from water." All the derivations for Moses have to do with the story of the baby found nestled in the rushes who became a prophet and led the Israelites out of Egypt.
Relatives: Mose, Moe, Mosya, Moey, Moss, Moshe, Moishe, Mosheh, Moyes, Moyse
Namesakes: Moses Malone, Edwin Moses, Moses Gunn

Muhammad: Arabic for "praised one." This is the name most often used by Moslems, making it one of the most popular in the world.
Relatives: Muhammed, Mohamad, Mohammed, Mohammad, Mohamet, Mahmoud, Mehemet, Mehmet, Ahmad, Ahmet, Amad, Amed, Hamid, Hamad, Hammed
Namesakes: the prophet Muhammad (founder of the Moslem religion), Muhammad Ali, Elijah Muhammad

Mull: Middle English for "grinder." Mull this one over.
Relative: Muller
Namesake: Martin Mull

Murdock: Scotch Gaelic for "victorious at sea."
Relatives: Murdoch, Murtagh
Namesakes: Rupert Murdoch, Iris Murdoch

Muriel: From the Greek "myrrh" and Irish for "sea-bright."
Relatives: Murial, Meriel, Muireall
Namesakes: Muriel Spark, Muriel Rukeyser, Muriel cigars

Murphy: Irish Gaelic for "sea warrior." The most common Irish surname in the United States and once commonly used as a slang term for the potato.
Relatives: Murphee, Murphree
Namesakes: Audie Murphy, Eddie Murphy, Dale Murphy, "Murphy Brown," Murphy's Law

Murray: Celtic for "sailor." This name made the rounds in ancient Britain.
Relatives: Murry, Moray
Namesakes: Murray Kempton, Arthur Murray, Ann Murray, Jim Murray

Musetta: From the Old French for "a ballad" and probably related to "Muse."
   Relatives: Musette, Musa
   Namesake: "Musetta" (character in *La Bohème*)

Myra: From the Latin for "wonderful." This name was coined by English poet Lord Brooke (also known as Fulke Greville). It is an anagram of "Mary."
   Namesakes: Dame Myra Hess, *Myra Breckenridge*

Myrna: Irish Gaelic for "polite one" or "gentle."
   Relatives: Muirne, Merna, Mirna, Moina, Morna, Moyna
   Namesakes: Myrna Loy, Myrna Blyth

Myron: From the Greek for "sweet oil."
   Namesake: Myron Cohen

Myrtle: From the myrtle flower, an ancient Greek symbol of victory. This neglected horticultural name deserves consideration.
   Relatives: Myrta, Myrtia, Myrtis, Mirtle, Mertle, Mertice, Mert, Myrtice, Myrtilla
   Namesake: Myrtle Beach (N.C.)

The Family's Jewel

Your baby is precious to you—so why not consider a gemstone? You may toy with the idea of the baby's birthstone or try something more exotic. There are also the metals and their offshoots, such as Gold (Goldie, Golda, Ora) and Silver (Sterling, Silva, Hi Ho).

Amber—A yellow-brown resin of pine trees that has hardened, amber is most commonly seen in the form of beads. The name is Latin for "juice."

Amethyst—A type of quartz that is usually a shade of violet or purple. Amethyst is the birthstone for February babies. It is Greek for "not drunk" because it was thought that drinking alcohol from a cup made of amethyst would keep the imbiber sober.

Anatase—A gemstone that ranges in color from blue-black to lavender.

Aquamarine—Latin for "sea water," this stone is usually blue-green. It is the birthstone for March babies.

Beryl—A general name for emeralds and amethysts.

Carnelian—A type of chalcedony, it is typically reddish orange.

Cinnabar—A stone that varies in color from scarlet to brown or gray.

Coral—From the ocean depths, coral may be white, pink, or dark red but is more commonly a salmon color. Black coral is very rare.

Crystal—A type of quartz, crystals are becoming extremely popular among New Age devotees. The name is Greek for "ice."

Diamond—From the Greek meaning "hardest steel," diamonds are not just colorless. They are found in a variety of colors, including pink, yellow, green, orange, lavender, blue, and even black. April babies will find diamonds their best friends.

Emerald—Emeralds, a type of beryl, are classically green and cut in a stylized rectangle. This is the birthstone for those born in May.

Flint—A type of very hard quartz used to strike a fire.

Garnet—Garnets run the full spectrum of color but are most commonly seen in shades of reddish brown. The name is Latin for "pomegranate seed" and is the birthstone for Januaryites.

Ivory—The creamy-white dentine that makes up an elephant's tusks.

Jade—Although most commonly seen in shades of green, jade is also found in other colors. The name is derived from a Spanish expression meaning "stone of the loins" because it was once prized for its perceived healing properties.

Jasper—A type of patterned quartz in a variety of earth tones, the so-called picture jaspers look like miniature landscapes.

Jet—Black or dark brown, jet is fossilized wood.

Mica—A type of mineral silicate. The clear variety is also known as isinglass.

Onyx—A form of chalcedony usually banded black and white, the name means "claw" in Greek.

Opal—A lovely stone that ranges from milky white to deep blue or, more rarely, black. It's the birthstone for October babies to whom it is thought to bring good luck. In Greek, *opallios* means "to see a change in color."

Pearl—The surprise inside oysters, pearls come in a variety of shapes, sizes, and colors. June babies will have an affinity for them.

Ruby—A type of corundum, rubies are most often red or dark rose-colored and will best suit July babies.

Sapphire—Also a type of corundum, usually a shade of blue, this is the birthstone for September kids.

Topaz—This stone ranges from colorless to blue but is usually seen in a form of brown or yellow. November babies will prize it.

Turquoise—Typically an opaque stone of blues, greens, or greys and associated with December babies.

N

In 1979, a candidate for the Louisiana gubernatorial primary had his name legally changed from Luther Devine Knox to None of the Above.

Nadine: Slavic for "hope." Although the Slavic interpretation works, "nada" in Spanish means "nothing."
Relatives: Nada, Nadina, Nadeen, Nadia, Nata, Nadya, Nadie, Nadezhda
Namesakes: Nadine Gordimer, Nadia Comaneci

Naida: Greek for "water nymph." Perfect for the baby who loves bath time.
Relatives: Naiad, Naia, Naiia, Nayad, Nyad
Namesake: Diana Nyad

Nairne: Scottish for "from the narrow river glade." May be used interchangeably for boys and girls.
Namesake: Nairn County (Scotland)

Nancy: A variation of Ann. Although some might say "no no" to Nanette, we fancy Nancy. It was on the top-twenty lists during the first half of the twentieth century but has inexplicably fallen out of favor.
Relatives: Nancey, Nancee, Nansey, Nansee, Nana, Nanny, Nan, Nanette, Nanine, Nanice, Nance
Namesakes: Nancy Kissinger, Nanette Fabray, Nancy Lopez, "Nancy Drew"

Naomi: Hebrew for "pleasant one." A charming name with a strong biblical link.
  Relatives: Naoma, Noami, Mimi, Mimsy, Mims
  Namesake: the biblical mother-in-law of Ruth

Napoleon: Greek for "lion of the woods" and Italian for "from the city of Naples."
  Relatives: Nappie, Nappy, Nap, Leon, Leo
  Namesakes: Saint Napoleon, Napoleon Bonaparte, Nap Lajoie

Nara: Old English for "near one" or Gaelic for "joyous." If Lara, Mara, Sara, or Tara leave you flat . . .

Narcissus: From the Greek for "self-love." The Greek myth of the beautiful Narcissus tells the story of the young man falling in love with his own reflection. He is turned into a narcissus plant for his vanity.
  Relatives: Narcisus, Narcissa, Narcisse

Nash: Old English for "cliff." This nifty choice sounds "preppily" short for something much longer.
  Relative: Nashe
  Namesakes: Ogden Nash, Graham Nash, Thomas Nash, Nash Rambler automobiles

Natalie: Latin for "birthday" or "child born at Christmas." The international collection of variations make this a rich choice.
  Relatives: Nataly, Natalee, Nataleigh, Natalia, Natalya, Natala, Nataline, Nathalia, Nathalie, Noel, Noelle, Novella, Natasha, Natasa, Natalja, Natassia, Nastassia, Natividad, Netty, Nettie, Tally, Tallie, Tasha, Talia
  Namesakes: Natalie Wood, Natalia Makarova, Nastassia Kinski, Talia Shire

Nathaniel: From the Hebrew for "gift of God." This super name could become the Matthew of the next decade.
  Relatives: Nathanielle, Nathanael, Nathan, Nathania, Nataniel, Natanielle, Nataniella, Natan, Natania, Nate, Nat, Natty
  Namesakes: Nathaniel Hawthorne, Nathan Hale, Nathanael West, Nat King Cole, "Natty Bumppo"

Neal: Irish Gaelic for "champion." Neal (or Neil) is much more common in the United Kingdom but has always been a solid choice in the United States.

Relatives: Neil, Neill, Nial, Niall, Neale, Neel, Niels, Niel, Niles, Nels, Nils, O'Neill

Namesakes: Neil Armstrong, Neil Diamond, Neal Kinnock, Nils Lundgren, Nels Van Patten

Neala: Irish Gaelic for "champion" and the feminine version of Neal.

Relatives: Niela, Nela, Neela, Neila, Nealah, Neilla, Nila

Neda: Slavic for "born on Sunday" and English for "sanctuary."

Relatives: Nedda, Neddy, Ned, Nerida

Namesake: heroine in *Pagliacci*

Nehemiah: From the Hebrew for "God's compassion."

Relative: Nemiah

Namesake: Nehemiah Wilson

Nellie: An abbreviated form of Eleanor, Helen, or Cornelia.

Relatives: Nelly, Nellis, Nelle, Nell, Nela, Nelda, Nelia, Nella, Nelita, Nelina, Nellwyn

Namesakes: Nelly Bly, Nell Gwyn, "Nervous Nelly"

Nelson: Old English for "son of a champion."

Relatives: Nealson, Neilson, Nilson, Nelly, Nellie

Namesakes: Nelson Rockefeller, Nelson Eddy, Nelson Mandela, Lord Nelson, Nellie Fox

Neroli: Italian for "orange blossom." Since the time of the Crusades when soldiers brought them back from the Middle East, orange blossoms have represented enduring love.

Relatives: Nerolia, Nerolie, Neroly, Nerole

Nessa: Old Norse for "headland."

Relatives: Nesa, Nissa, Nessie

Namesake: Nessie, the Loch Ness monster

Nestor: From the Greek for "traveler" or "wisdom."

Relatives: Nesta, Nest

Namesakes: King Nestor, Nestor Chylak

Neva: Spanish for "covered in snow." The state of Nevada is so named for its snow-capped Sierra peaks.
Relatives: Nevia, Nevea, Nevita, Nevada
Namesake: Nevada Smith

Neville: Old French for "from the new farmland." Like Nigel, Neville is more popular in the British Commonwealth.
Relatives: Nevil, Nevile, Newland, Nev, Nevelson
Namesakes: Neville Chamberlain, Neville Brand, Nevil Shute

Nevin: Irish Gaelic for "worshiper," Old English for "middle,"and Old German for "nephew." Considering Kevin and Devin have such a following, it's surprising Nevin hasn't fared better.
Relatives: Nevins, Neven
Namesake: Allan Nevins

Newell: Old English for "from the manor" and Old French for "kernel."
Relatives: Newall, Newlin, Newlyn (Old Welsh for "pool"), Newland, Newbold, Newgate, Newton
Namesakes: Andrew Newell Wyeth, Isaac Newton

Newman: Old English for "newcomer." What is a baby boy if not a new man?
Relatives: Neuman, Neumann, Numen, Newmie
Namesakes: Cardinal Newman, Paul Newman, "Alfred E. Neuman"

Nicholas: Greek for "victorious people" and Saint Nicholas, patron saint of children. Long a favorite in Greece and Russia, Nicholas has soared up the popularity charts in the 1970s and 1980s. It's one of those names that sounds good in any language.
Relatives: Nicolas, Nikolaus, Nicklaus, Nicola, Nick, Nicky, Nikki, Nikita, Nikos, Nike, Nikolai, Nikola, Nicholai, Nicanor, Nikos, Nicos, Nichol, Nichols, Nicolson, Nicol, Nicolo, Nicko, Nicodemus, Nils, Niles, Nixon, Cole, Colin, Colet, Claus
Namesakes: Nick Carter, Nick Danger, Mike Nichols, Jack Nicholson, Jack Nicklaus, Nikos Kazantzakis, Cole Porter, "Nick Adams," *Nicholas Nickleby*

Nicole: A variation of Nicholas. Like the Gaelic cousins Danielle and Michelle, Nicole has maintained a steady position in the top-ten lists for the past two decades.

Relatives: Nichole, Nicola, Nikki, Nika, Nickie, Nicky, Nichola, Nicci, Nichelle, Nikolia, Nicoline, Nicolette, Nike (Greek for "victory"), Colette, Collette, Cosette

Namesakes: Nicole Gregory, Nikki Giovanni, Nicolette Larsen, "Colette"

Nigel: From the Latin for "dark one." This is pronounced *"Nie-jil"*—not *"Knee-*gul." Ask any Englishman.

Namesakes: Nigel Bruce, Nigel Dempster

Nina: Spanish for "girl" and a Russian form of Anne. In spite of its charming brevity, Nina has an exotic cadence to it. And remember, history buffs, it served Columbus's ship well.

Relatives: Ninya, Ninette, Ninon

Namesakes: Nina Simone, Nina Ricci

Nirel: From the Hebrew for "God's field." Nirel is well off the beaten path and has a delightful sound.

Relatives: Niriel, Niria, Nira, Nir, Nyree

Nissa: Scandinavian for "elf" or "fairy." For the child who believes in the fantastic.

Relatives: Nisse, Nissi, Nisi (Hebrew for "emblem"), Nissan, Nissim

Noah: Hebrew for "comfort" or "wanderer." Like many of the Old Testament names, Noah, the original zookeeper, is making a comeback.

Relatives: Noa, Noe, Noach, Noel, Noadiah (Hebrew for "God assembles"), Noam

Namesakes: Noah Webster, Noah Berry, Noam Chomsky

Noble: From the Latin for "honorable one" or "well born."

Relatives: Nobel, Nobile

Namesakes: Nobel Peace Prize, Barnes and Noble bookstores

Noel: French for "Christmas." This name and the variations work for either a girl or a boy. It may be pronounced *"Know-*el" or *"No-well"* and is often seen with an umlaut, Noël.

Relatives: Noelle, Nowell, Natale, Natal
Namesakes: Noel Coward, Noel Harrison

Nolan: Irish Gaelic for "noble."
Relatives: Nolen, Nolin, Nolyn, Nowlan
Namesakes: Nolan Miller, Nolan Ryan, Lloyd Nolan

Nona: Latin for "nine." This would work well for a girl born in September.

Nora: Abbreviated form of Eleanora, Lenore, or Honora. An elegant, simple name.
Relatives: Norah, Norine, Noreen, Norina
Namesakes: Norah Lofts, "Nick and Nora Charles"

Norbert: From the Old German for "blond hero."
Relative: Norberta
Namesakes: Saint Norbert, Norbert Wiener

Nordica: German for "from the north." This is the name of a company that manufactures ski equipment, making Nordica an ideal choice for future schussboomers.
Relatives: Norna, Norberta

Norma: Latin for "model" and a feminine version of Norman. A favorite in the 1920s, this has yet to find a following in later generations.
Namesakes: Norma Shearer, *Norma* (opera by Bellini), *Norma Rae*

Norman: From the Old French or English for "man from the North" (especially Norsemen) as well as the people known as Normans. This name is guaranteed to give your son a sense of direction.
Relatives: Normie, Normal, Norm, Norris, Norville, Normand
Namesakes: Norman Mailer, Norman Rockwell, Norman Lear, Norris Church, Frank Norris, "Norman Bates"

North: From the Old English. If Norman doesn't thrill you, consider North and its square-jawed inference.
Relatives: Northcliff, Northrup, Norton, Norvin, Norwin, Norwyn, Norward, Norwell, Norwood, Nowles
Namesakes: Northrop Frye, Norton Simon, Henry Norwell, *North by Northwest*

Nye: Middle English for "island dweller."

Namesakes: Louis Nye, Gerald Prentice Nye, Carrie Nye

> Monday's child is fair of face,
> Tuesday's child is full of grace,
> Wednesday's child is full of woe,
> Thursday's child has far to go,
> Friday's child is loving and giving,
> Saturday's child works hard for its living,
> But the child that's born on the Sabbath day
> Is fair and wise and good and gay.

O

Oakley: Old English for "from the oak meadow." Sounds more like a private academy than a child's name, but try it out before dismissing it.
Relatives: Oakly, Oakleigh, Oakes, Oak
Namesake: Annie Oakley

Obadiah: Hebrew for "servant of God."
Relatives: Obed, Obie, Obe
Namesake: "Obi-Wan Kenobi"

Octavius: Latin for "eighth child." This name and some of the variations carry a sense of authority. Octavian was, after all, a Roman emperor.
Relatives: Octavus, Octavio, Octavia, Octavian, Octavie, Tavie, Tavy
Namesake: Octavio Paz

Odelia: From the Old German for "little wealthy one" and Hebrew for "praise God."
Relatives: Odell, Odella, Odelinda, Odilia, Odette (French for "happy home"), Odetta, Odelette
Namesakes: Odetta, Odette Brailly

Odell: Old German for "little wealthy one," Greek for "ode," and Danish for "otter." Odin is the mythological equivalent of Zeus in the Norse hierarchy.
Relatives: Odin, Ode, Odie, Odis

Odessa: Greek for "odyssey." For the born traveler.
Namesake: Odessa (Tex.)

Ogden: Old English for "from the oak valley."

Relatives: Oggie, Denny, Den
Namesake: Ogden Nash

Ogilvy: Old Scottish for "from the high peak." A proud old Scottish surname, Ogilvy lends itself to a nice selection of nicknames.
Relatives: Ogilvie, Gil, Gillie, Gilly
Namesake: David Ogilvy

Olaf: Old Norse for "talisman" or "ancestor."
Relatives: Olav, Olof, Olin, Olen, Olie
Namesakes: Saint Olaf, King Olaf

Olga: Old Norse for "holy one" and the Russian form of Helga.
Relatives: Olva, Olia, Olja, Olive, Elga, Olena, Olina, Olesia
Namesakes: Saint Olga, Olga Korbut

Olin: Old English for "holly."
Relatives: Olney, Olinda
Namesake: Olney (Md.)

Olive: A botanical name from the Latin. Olive branches are traditionally used as a symbol of peace.
Relatives: Olivia, Olivette, Ollie, Olly, Olva, Livia, Livy, Nollie, Nola
Namesakes: Olivia De Havilland, Olivia Hussey, "Olive Oyl"

Oliver: Old Norse for "kind one" and Old French for "olive tree." Perhaps because of the Dickens classic, Oliver has been an enduring favorite in the United Kingdom and has enjoyed modest popularity in America.
Relatives: Olivier, Oliviero, Olley, Olly, Ollie, Noll, Nolly
Namesakes: Oliver Cromwell, Oliver Goldsmith, Oliver Hardy, Ollie North, *Oliver Twist*

Olympia: Greek for "of Mount Olympus." For a child with her head in the clouds.
Relatives: Olympe, Olimpie
Namesake: Olympia Dukakis

Omar: Arabic for "first son" and "disciple," Hebrew for "gifted speaker," and German for "famous." Rooted in the Middle East, this name is rarely used in the West.

Relative: Omer
Namesakes: Saint Omer, Omar Khayyam, General Omar Bradley, Omar Sharif, grandson of Esau

Oona: Irish Gaelic and Latin for "unity."
Relatives: Ona, Oonaugh, Oonagh
Namesake: Oona Chaplin

Opal: Sanskrit for "jewel." The opal is the birthstone for October babies.
Relatives: Opaline, Opalina

Ophelia: Greek for "useful" or "wise."
Relatives: Ofelia, Ofilia, Ophelie, Phelia
Namesake: "Ophelia" in Shakespeare's *Hamlet*

Oralia: Latin for "golden" and Hebrew for "light."
Relatives: Oriel, Orel, Orelda, Oriole, Orielle, Orlene, Orlena, Orpah, Oralee, Oralie, Oral, Ora, Orah, Oria, Orlie, Orly, Orabel
Namesakes: Oral Roberts, Baltimore Orioles, Orel Herschiser

Oran: Irish Gaelic for "pale one" and Hebrew for "pine."
Relatives: Orin, Orren, Oren, Orran, Orrin, Oram, Orrie
Namesake: Orrin Hatch

Oriana: Latin for "dawn" and Greek for "east."
Relatives: Oralia, Orelle, Orlanna, Oria
Namesake: Oriana Fallaci

Orion: From the Latin for "dawn" and Greek for "east."
Relatives: Orien, Orienne, Orestes, Orest, Oris
Namesakes: the constellation, the mythical hunter, Orion Pictures

Orlando: An Italian form of Roland and Latin for "bright sun."
Relatives: Orlanda, Orlie, Orly, Lando
Namesakes: Orlando Cepeda, Tony Orlando, *Orlando*

Orson: Old English for "spearman's son" and Latin for "bear."
Relatives: Orsen, Orsin, Orsini, Sonny
Namesakes: Orson Welles, Orson Bean

Orville: Old French for "from the golden village" and thought to be the invention of novelist Fanny Burney in 1779. For the baby with the right stuff.
Relatives: Orvalle, Orval
Namesakes: Orville Wright, Orville Redenbacher

Osbert: Old English for "inspired" or "divine."
Relatives: Osborn, Osborne, Osmar, Osmond, Osmund, Osred, Osric, Osmen, Osman, Ossie
Namesakes: Osbert Sitwell, Donnie and Marie Osmond, John Osborne

Oscar: Old Norse for "divine spear." The Academy Award, a knight holding a sword and standing on a reel of film, is called an Oscar because an actress once remarked the statuette looked like her uncle Oscar.
Relatives: Osgood, Oskar
Namesakes: Oscar Wilde, Oscar Hammerstein, Oscar de la Renta, "Oscar the Grouch"

Oswald: Old English for "divinely powerful."
Relatives: Oswell, Ossie, Ozzie, Osvald, Oswall, Oswell, Oswaldo
Namesakes: Ozzie Nelson, Ossie Davis

Otis: Greek for "acute" and Old German for "wealthy."
Relatives: Otto, Odo, Otho, Othello, Otello, Otilio
Namesakes: Otis Redding, Otis Pike, Otto von Bismarck, Otto Rank, Otto Preminger

Owen: Old Welsh for "warrior" and Greek for "well born." This handsome name should be used more often.
Relatives: Owyn, Evan, Ewen, Owens
Namesakes: Owen Wister, Owen Davis, Jesse Owens

Oxford: Old English for "from where the oxen ford." You can't get much more academic than this.
Relatives: Oxton, Oxon
Namesake: Oxford University

Oz: Hebrew for "strength." This child will certainly be a wiz at whatever he does.
Namesakes: Amos Oz, Frank Oz

WISCONSIN TOP TWENTY

1987

Girls	*Boys*
Ashley	Michael
Amanda	Andrew
Jessica	Matthew
Jennifer	Joshua
Sarah	Ryan
Nicole	Nicholas
Samantha	Christopher
Megan	Daniel
Melissa	Kyle
Stephanie	Justin
Emily	Adam
Elizabeth	David
Danielle	Benjamin
Amber	Jacob
Heather	Joseph
Rachel	Brandon
Amy	Eric
Katie	James
Brittany	Tyler
Kayla	John

Information supplied by the State of Wisconsin Department of Health.

P

Page: French for "young attendant." Page is finding a place for itself, especially as a distinctive middle name.

Relatives: Paige, Payge, Padgett

Namesakes: Page Smith, Patti Page, Geraldine Page

Palmer: Old English for "palm-bearing pilgrim." This surname is making a stab at becoming a first name.

Relatives: Palma, Palmyra, Palmira

Namesakes: Palmer Pyle, Betsy Palmer, Arnold Palmer

Paloma: Spanish for "dove." A child named Paloma is destined to keep the peace.

Relatives: Palometa, Palomita, Palita

Namesake: Paloma Picasso

Pamela: Greek for "honeyed." This name was "invented" by Sir Philip Sidney in 1590 for a character in his novel *Arcadia* and was picked up again some two hundred years later by Samuel Richardson in his novel *Pamela.*

Relatives: Pamyla, Pamilla, Pamella, Pamelia, Pamelyn, Pamelina, Pammy, Pammie, Pam

Namesakes: Pamela Mason, Pam Dawber

Pandora: From the Greek for "talented one." Ideal for a little girl who is always getting into things.

Relatives: Pan, Dora, Dory

Namesake: the mythological Pandora's box

Pansy: A flower and French for "thought." Although a charming name, this could be a tough one to carry off.
Relatives: Pansee, Pansie, Pense

Parker: Old English for "cultivated land." Parker scored high on the preppy scale. You decide.
Relatives: Parke, Park, Parkley, Parks
Namesakes: Parker Stevenson, Dorothy Parker, Gordon Parks, Parker pens

Parr: Old English for "from the stable." For the baby born with a silver tee in his mouth.
Namesake: Jack Parr

Pascal: Italian for "born at Easter." You would always remember his birthday.
Relatives: Paschal, Pasqual, Pascali, Pascha, Pace
Namesake: Blaise Pascal

Patience: Latin for "suffering." A virtue name.
Relatives: Patty, Patsy, Pat
Namesakes: Patience and Prudence, *Patience*

Patricia: From the Latin for "noble one" and a feminine variation of Patrick. Patricia has fallen off the charts recently but will no doubt make a comeback when your children are using this book.
Relatives: Patrice, Patrizia, Patsy, Patty, Pattie, Patia, Pat, Tricia, Trish, Tish, Rickie, Ricky
Namesakes: Patricia Neal, Patsy Kline, Pat Nixon, Tricia Nixon Cox, Tish Alsop

Patrick: From the Latin for "noble one." Saint Patrick is the patron saint of Ireland honored every March 17. The name also shares the Latin root "patres," which refers to the nobility or patricians.
Relatives: Patrice, Padraic, Padraig, Padruig, Pat, Paddy, Patterson, Paterson, Pattison, Rick, Ricky
Namesakes: Patrick Henry, Patrick Swayze, Patrick McGoohan, Pat Boone

Paul: Latin for "little one." A biblical standard, Paul hasn't seen much action in recent years. Start a trend.

Relatives: Pol, Pawl, Pablo, Paolo, Pauly, Pauley, Pawley, Pavel, Paulin, Pavlo, Paulo, Paulus, Powell

Namesakes: Saint Paul, Paul McCartney, Paul Revere, Paul Newman, Pablo Picasso, Pablo Casals, Paolo Soleri

Paula: Latin for "petite" and a feminine variation of Paul.

Relatives: Pauline, Paulette, Paulina, Paulita, Poalina, Paola, Pauly, Polly, Pavla, Pavlina

Namesakes: Paula Prentiss, Paulina Porizkova, Paulette Goddard

Payne: Latin for "villager" or "country person."

Relative: Paine

Namesake: Thomas Paine

Payton: Old English for "warrior's estate." Payton has an "old money" ring to it and should be considered for girls as well as boys.

Relatives: Peyton, Paxton, Patton, Patten, Paton, Pattin, Pat

Namesakes: Walter Payton, General George Patton, *Peyton Place*

Peace: From the Latin. Give it a chance.

Relatives: Paix, Pachem, Paxton, Pax

Pearl: From the Middle English for "gemstone."

Relatives: Pearla, Perle, Pearle, Purlie, Pegeen

Namesakes: Pearl Bailey, Pearl Buck, Perle Mesta, *Purlie Victorious*

In 1942, Ms. Pearl Harbour enlisted in the WACs.

Pelagia: Greek for "from the sea."

Relatives: Pelga, Pelgia, Pelagie

Namesake: Saint Pelagie

Pell: Old English for "scarf" and a distinguished surname.

Relatives: Pelton, Pelham

Namesake: Claiborne Pell

Pembroke: Welsh for "from the headland" or "rocky hill."

Namesakes: Earl of Pembroke, Pembroke College, Pembroke Welsh corgi

Penelope: From the Greek for "weaver." Although popular in the 1950s, this lovely old name has dropped off the charts. Reevaluate it.

Relatives: Penny, Penney, Pen

Namesakes: Ulysses's faithful wife, J. C. Penney's department stores

Penina: Hebrew for "jewel" or "coral."
Relatives: Peninah, Peninit, Penny, Peni, Nina

Penrod: From the Old German for "esteemed commander." What about Penn for a future writer?
Relatives: Penn, Penley (Old English for "enclosed meadow")
Namesakes: William Penn, Sean Penn, *Penrod*

Pepin: Old German for "perseverance."
Relatives: Peppy, Pepi, Pippin, Pip, Pippi
Namesakes: King Pepin (Charlemagne's father), Jacques Pepin, *Pippi Longstocking, Pippin*

Percival: Old French for "pierce the veil." Although this now has a prissy image, Percival was a brave knight of the Round Table.
Relatives: Perceval, Percheval, Parsifal, Parsefal, Perce, Percy, Perci
Namesakes: Percy Bysshe Shelley, Percy Faith, Percy Grainger

Perdita: Latin for "lost."
Relatives: Perdea, Perda
Namesake: character in Shakespeare's *The Winter's Tale*

Perry: Middle English for "pear tree" and Welsh for "son of Harry." Perry, though traditionally used for boys, should also be considered for a girl.
Relatives: Pierrey, Parry, Perianne, Perian, Perrin, Perin, Peregrine (Latin for "wanderer")
Namesakes: Perry Ellis, Perry King, "Perry Mason"

Persephone: Greek goddess of the underworld.
Relatives: Persa, Perse, Percy, Fanny

Perth: Old Celtic for "thorny bush."
Namesakes: Perth County (Scotland), Perth (Australia)

Peter: From the Latin for "rock." This standard is solid as a rock. Experiment with the variations.
Relatives: Pete, Petey, Pietor, Pytor, Petr, Pieter, Piotr, Pietro, Pedro, Pierre, Piers, Pierce, Peer, Pero, Piero, Peder, Per, Peadair, Petrus, Peterson, Perrin, Perkin, Perkins, Parnell, Parle, Parkin, Parkinson, Petrie, Petri, Pierson

Namesakes: Saint Peter, Peter the Great, Peter Stuyvesant, Peter Yarrow, Peter Jennings, Pierre Trudeau, Pierre Boulez, Oscar Peterson, *Peer Gynt*

Petra: From the Latin for "rock."
Relatives: Petronia, Petronella, Petronilla, Pierette, Perrine, Petronille, Petrina, Petrine, Pete, Petie, Petula
Namesake: Petula Clark

Phedra: From the Greek for "shining one." A thoughtful choice for a future rock star.
Relative: Phaidra
Namesake: wife of Theseus

Phelan: Irish Gaelic for "little wolf." O. Henry wrote a short story about a couple who argued over whether their son would be named Pat or Phelan. Try Phelan.

Philana: Greek for "adoring."
Relatives: Philene, Philina, Philida, Philantha, Philander, Philadelphia (Greek for "brotherly love"), Falana
Namesakes: Philander Knox, Lola Falana

Philip: From the Greek for "horse lover." It's hard to go wrong with this fine old name. It has served the royal houses of ancient Rome and Macedonia, France, Spain, Germany, and England.
Relatives: Phillip, Philipe, Philippos, Philo, Phillips, Phelps, Phipps, Philipson, Phillips, Philby, Phil, Philly, Felipe, Filippo, Filip, Filbert
Namesakes: Saint Philip, Prince Philip, Phil Donahue, John Philip Sousa

Philippa: From the Greek for "horse lover" and a feminine variation of Philip. Philippa is most popular in the United Kingdom and is almost always abbreviated as Pippa.
Relatives: Philippine, Felipe, Felipa, Philly, Philia, Pippa
Namesakes: Philippa Carr, "Pippa Passes"

Philomena: Greek for "song lover" or "friend."
Relatives: Philomen, Filomena

Phineas: From the Hebrew for "oracle" and Egyptian for "dark-skinned." Until he is elected to the bench or establishes himself as the senior partner, Phinny will suffice.

Relatives: Phinny, Phin, Finn, Pincus, Pinchas, Pinchos

Namesakes: Phineas T. Barnum, Pinchas Zuckerman, "Phineas T. Firefly"

Phoebe: Greek for "bright one." This is an off-the-beaten-track name with an ancient lineage.

Relatives: Phebe, Phoebus

Namesakes: Saint Phoebe, Phoebe Snow, Phoebe Cates

Phoenix: The mythical bird that rises from the ashes.

Relative: Phoena

Namesakes: River Phoenix, Phoenix (Ariz.)

Phyllis: Greek for "leafy branch."

Relatives: Phillis, Phylys, Philicia, Philida, Filida, Philly, Phil, Phyl

Namesakes: Phyllis Newman, Phylicia Rashad

Pia: Italian for "devout." A sweet name that solves the problem of working with a long surname.

Namesakes: Pia Lindstrom, Pia Zadora

Pierce: From the Old Anglo-French for "rock."

Relatives: Pearce, Piercy, Pears, Piers, Pearson

Namesakes: Pierce Brosnan, Franklin Pierce, Drew Pearson, Piers Paul Read, "Hawkeye Pierce"

Pilar: Spanish for "pillar." The derivation refers to the Virgin Mary as the "pillar" of Christianity.

Piper: Old English for "bagpipe player."

Relative: Pyper

Namesakes: Piper Laurie, William Piper, Piper Cub

Placida: From the Latin for "tranquillity."

Relative: Placido

Namesake: Placido Domingo

Polly: A nickname for Mary and Paula. Whoever first called a parrot Polly tainted this fine name.

Relatives: Pollie, Pollyanna

Namesakes: Polly Bergen, "Pollyanna"

Porter: From the French for "gatekeeper" or "carrier." Like similar occupational surnames (Carter and Tyler), Porter is finding a place as a first name.
Relative: Porteur
Namesakes: Porter Waggoner, Cole Porter

Portia: From the Latin for "a gift." This is a lovely name and a fast car.
Relatives: Porsha, Porsche
Namesakes: wife of "Brutus" in Shakespeare's *Julius Caesar,* major character in Shakespeare's *The Merchant of Venice*

Powell: Old Welsh for "son of Howell."
Relatives: Powers, Power
Namesakes: Powers Boothe, Dick Powell

Prentice: Middle English for "apprentice." An attractive choice that tends to defy nicknames.
Relative: Prentiss
Namesake: Paula Prentiss

Preston: Old English for "dweller at the church" or "priest's settlement." It's surprising that this one has not inspired a wider following.
Relatives: Prescott, Presley, Priestley, Priestly, Priest
Namesakes: Preston Sturges, Preston Tucker, Prescott Bush, Robert Preston

Prewitt: Old French for "valiant one."
Relatives: Pruitt, Pruit, Prue
Namesake: Greg Pruitt

Price: Old Welsh for "urgent one." A staunchly WASP-y name.
Relative: Pryce
Namesakes: Reynolds Price, Vincent Price, Leontyne Price, Price Waterhouse

Primo: Italian for "first one." An appropriate choice for a firstborn, but a hard act to follow.
Relative: Prime
Namesake: Primo Levi

Priscilla: Latin for "from ancient times." And this name suggests a gentler time of lemonade and porch swings.

Relatives: Priss, Prissy, Prisca, Silla, Cilla, Cyla
Namesakes: Saint Priscilla, Priscilla Presley, Priscilla Mullins

Prudence: From the Latin for "foresight." Prudence is one of the enduring virtue names.
Relatives: Prudy, Prue, Pru

Pryor: From the Old French for "head of the priory."
Relative: Prior
Namesake: Richard Pryor

Purvis: French for "provide."
Namesake: Purvis Ellison

Putnam: Old English for "from the sire's estate." In tribute to the Revolutionary War general, Israel Putnam, there are ten counties named for him in New England.
Relative: Putney

A Flower by Any Other Name

The plant world offers a garden of opportunities for unique names. There are the generic possibilities, such as Fleur, Petal, Flora, and Blossom, and the classics (Rose, Lily, and Daisy, for example). Some of the more provocative names are based on the surname of successful naturalists. But take care to tiptoe through the choices; only creations of Lewis Carroll or William Shakespeare could carry names like Mugwort, Toadflax, and Scuppernong.

Andromeda—This name pops up in astronomy and mythology lists as well. It is a flowering plant found in wooded areas and heaths.

Anemone—A spring flower, the name means "breath" in Greek. The flower is associated with Venus, whose tears for the slain Adonis first caused anemones to grow.

Artemisia—A type of sagebrush named for Artemis, the Greek goddess of the moon.

Aster—This flower comes in a vast array of varieties and colors. The name means "star" in Greek and refers to the rays of the blossom. Asters are associated with September.

Azalea—The flowering azalea bushes come in a wide variety of colors and hybrids. They bloom in the spring.

Betony—A fernlike plant considered by herbalists to be a cure-all.

Calla—A water arum, calla lilies are made up of a single white petal around a small clublike center. Calla is Greek for "beautiful."

Celandine—A type of buttercup. The flower is named for swallows because they were thought to bloom when the birds arrived and fade when they left.

Columbine—Greek for "dove," columbine blossoms resemble a circlet of doves. In religious art, the flower signifies the Holy Ghost. It is also the state flower of Colorado.

Daisy—The sunny daisy gets its name for "day's eye" because it opens at sunrise and closes at sunset.

Fern—Found all over the world in thousands of varieties. Fern is Anglo-Saxon for "feathered wing."

Ginger—The fragrant root has long been prized by many cultures for its medicinal powers.

Heather—Refers to the purple or white flowering shrub that grows across wastelands. The Scots use it for cattle feed as well as thatching for rooftops. It symbolizes good luck and prosperity.

Hyacinth—The sweet-smelling plant is named for a Greek youth who was adored by Apollo. There are about thirty species of hyacinth.

Iris—This flower comes in a variety of colors. Iris was a member of Juno's court and is associated with rainbows. Since the reign of Clovis I, it has also been associated with the royal houses of France in the form of the fleur-de-lis.

Ivy—The botanical name for these evergreen vines—Hedera—is rather alluring.

Laurel—The botanical name for the laurel tree is Kalmia, for Swedish naturalist Peter Kalm. According to Greek myth, when the lovely nymph Daphne was being pursued by Apollo, she called upon her father, the river god, to help her. To frustrate Apollo, the god changed his daughter into a laurel tree—to remain forever chaste.

Lily—These flowers come in a bouquet of varieties and colors. They are associated with Easter.

Mariposa—A variety of sego lily whose roots are edible. The name means "butterfly" in Spanish. The markings on the flower are similar to those on a butterfly's wing.

Narcissus—This lovely flower was once thought to induce comas if you inhaled the fragrance too deeply. The term "narcissistic" comes from the myth of Narcissus—a young man who fell in love with his own reflection. Daffodils and jonquils are varieties.

Rose—This universally admired flower has inspired poets for centuries. It was the flower sacred to Venus and eventually became a Christian symbol of holiness, associated with Mary.

Tansy—The yellow flower is framed by feathered leaves. The name is from the Greek for "immortality."

Tulip—These dazzling spring blooms get their name from a Latinized version of the Turkish word for "turban."

Valerian—This plant is used in perfumes and was once thought to promote sleep.

Violet—Shares its name with the color, although the flowers come in a variety of colors.

Other plant and tree names include:

Abelia (for Dr. Clarke Abel)	Bay
Aira	Birch
Alder	Branch
Allamanda	Brya (for J. T. de Bry)
Althaea	Calanthe
Alyssum	Calliandra
Angelica	Camellia (for Georg Kamel)
Ania	Carissa
Arnica	Carya
Ash	Cassandra
Aspen	Cassia
Azara (for J. N. Azara)	Cherry
Basella	Chloris (Greek goddess of flowers)

Clover
Conifer
Cosmos
Dahlia (for Dr. Anders Dahl)
Daphne
Davidia (for Abbe Armand David)
Ebony
Emilia
Eria
Erica
Eugenia (for Prince Eugene)
Fabiana (for Archbishop Francisco Fabian)
Freesia
Gardener
Gilia (for Filippo Gilii)
Hazel
Heath
Hepatica
Holly
Inga
Itea
Ivy
Jasmine
Kerria (for William Kerr)
Larch
Latania
Laurel
Leaf
Linden
Magnolia (for Pierre Magnol)
Mahogany
Marguerite
Marica (a nymph in Roman mythology)
Marigold (Mary's gold)
Melica

Melissa
Michelia (for Pietro A. Micheli)
Mimosa (from the Greek for "to mimic")
Moss
Myrtle (associated with Aphrodite and fidelity)
Neillia (for Patrick Neill)
Nicandra (for Nikander of Colophon)
Nyssa (a water nymph)
Oak
Olea
Oleandra
Olinia (for Johan H. Olin)
Olive
Ottelia
Petrea
Petunia
Phylicia
Piper
Poppy
Portea (for Marius Porte)
Prunella
Quassia (for Gruman Quassi)
Quince
Randia (for Isaac Rand)
Robinia (for Jean Robin)
Rose
Rue
Sagina
Sequoiah
Serissa
Sorrel
Tamarind
Thalia (for Johannes Thal)
Thea

Tiarella

Tristania (for Jules Tristan)

Twiggy

Ursinia (for Johannes H. Ursinus)

Valeriana

Veronica (for Saint Veronica)

Viola

Willow

Wyethia (for Nathaniel J. Wyeth)

Zea

Quennel: Old French for "dweller by the oak tree." This is not to be confused with the poached dumpling, "quenelle."
Namesake: Peter Quennel

Quentin: Latin for "fifth child" and from the Old English for "from the queen's land." William Faulkner immortalized this name in his novel *The Sound and the Fury.* And Loni Anderson and Burt Reynolds selected Quintin for the name of their baby.
Relatives: Quenten, Quenton, Quintin, Quinton, Quent, Quint, Quintilian, Quintus
Namesakes: Saint Quentin, Quentin Crisp, Quentin Compson, *Quentin Durward*

Quincy: From the Old French for "dweller on the fifth son's estate."
Relatives: Quince, Quincey, Quin
Namesakes: Quincy Jones, John Quincy Adams

Quinlan: Irish Gaelic for "muscular." Ideal for a future bodybuilder.
Relatives: Quinlan, Quinlyn, Quin

Quinn: Irish Gaelic for "wise" or "queen." A unique choice for a boy or girl.
Relatives: Quin, Quinton, Cuin, Quillan
Namesakes: Quinn Cummings, Quinn Buckner, Anthony Quinn

Quinta: Latin for "fifth-born daughter."
Relatives: Quin, Quintilla, Quintelle

Birth Rites

Every month is associated with a birthstone and a flower. And, thanks to the nursery rhyme, every day is associated with a personality trait. Months, days of the week, birthstones, and flowers all make for interesting name choices. And don't feel limited by the Gregorian calendar. Consult the Chinese, Hebrew, and Mohammedan calendars as well.

January	garnet (constancy)	carnation
February	amethyst (sincerity)	violet
March	aquamarine (courage)	jonquil
April	diamond (eternal love)	sweetpea
May	emerald (success)	lily of the valley
June	pearl (health)	rose
July	ruby (security)	larkspur
August	peridot (joy)	gladiolus
September	sapphire (stability)	aster
October	opal (hope)	calendula
November	topaz (fidelity)	chrysanthemum
December	turquoise (prosperity)	narcissus

R

Rachel: Hebrew for "little lamb." This beautiful name has always been a favorite but has mercifully never become too trendy.

Relatives: Rachael, Rachele, Rochelle, Rahel, Raquel, Rae, Ray, Shelley, Shelly, Shellie, Chelle, Chellie

Namesakes: wife of Jacob, Rachel Carson, Rachel Ward, Rachel Roberts, Raquel Welch, Shelley Long

Radclif: Old English for "red cliff." A bit hefty unless the child looks particularly studious.

Relatives: Radcliff, Radcliffe, Radclyffe, Radclyf, Radford, Radley, Radnor, Rad

Namesakes: Radcliffe College, Radnor (Penn.)

Rae: Old English for "doe."

Relatives: Ray, Rai

Namesakes: Rae Dawn Chong, *Norma Rae*

Rain: From the Latin for "ruler." This could also refer to the meteorological phenomenon.

Relatives: Raine, Rein, Reign, Raine, Rayne, Rana, Rane

Rainier: From the Latin for "ruler."

Relatives: Rainer, Raner

Namesakes: Rainer Fassbinder, Prince Rainier of Monaco, Rainer Maria Rilke

Raissa: From the Old French for "thinker" and Greek for "rose." In the spirit of *glasnost,* consider Raisa.

Relatives: Raisa, Raizel, Rayzel, Razel
Namesake: Raisa Gorbachev

Raleigh: Old English for "dweller by the deer meadow."
Relatives: Rawley, Rawly, Rawls, Leigh, Lee
Namesakes: Sir Walter Raleigh, Lou Rawls, Raleigh (N.C.)

Ralph: Old English for "wolf" or "wise counsel." After a dry spell, Ralph and the variations are once again gaining favor.
Relatives: Ralf, Raff, Raffi, Rolf, Rolph, Raoul, Raul, Ralston
Namesakes: Ralph Waldo Emerson, Sir Ralph Richardson, Ralph Lauren, Ralph Nader, Raul Julia

Ramona: Spanish for "wise protector."
Relatives: Ramonda, Ray, Rae, Mona
Namesake: "Ramona Quimby"

Ramsey: Old English for "ram's land." If astrology amuses you, take a close look at this for an Aries baby.
Relatives: Ramsay, Ramsden
Namesakes: Ramsey Clark, Ramsey Lewis, Ramsay MacDonald

Randolph: Anglo-Saxon for "shield-wolf." A handsome choice with solid nickname choices.
Relatives: Randolf, Randall, Randal, Randell, Randl, Randle, Randy, Rankin, Rand, Ran
Namesakes: Randolph Scott, Randolph Macon, Randall Jarrell, Ayn Rand

Ranger: From the Old French for "dweller in the field" and an occupational name for "forest guardian."
Relative: Rainger
Namesakes: "The Lone Ranger," "Ranger Rick"

Ransom: Old English for "son of the shield" and Latin for "redeemer." A third baseman for the Chicago Cubs, Ransom Jackson, was nicknamed "Handsome Ransom."
Relatives: Ransome, Ranson, Rankin, Ransford ("raven's ford"), Ransley ("raven's meadow"), Rance
Namesakes: John Crowe Ransom, Arthur Ransome

Raphael: From the Hebrew for "healed by God." An appealing name with a poetic quality.

Relatives: Rafael, Rafaelle, Rafaello, Rafe, Rafer, Rafi, Raff, Raph, Rafferty, Raphaella

Namesakes: Rafer Johnson, Rafael Palmeiro

Rashid: Swahili for "wise adviser."

Relative: Rasheed

Ravinder: From "ravine." A variation for a little girl might be Ravinia, like the summer home of the Chicago Symphony.

Relatives: Ravi, Ravinia

Namesake: Ravi Shankar

Rawlins: Old English for "son of a little wise wolf."

Relatives: Rawlings, Rawson

Namesakes: Marjorie Rawlings, Rawlings sporting goods

Rayburn: Old English for "from the deer stream."

Relatives: Ray, Rayfield, Rayford

Namesakes: Sam Rayburn, Sir Henry Raeburn

Raymond: Old German for "worthy protector." This name faded in the 1960s and 1970s but is beginning to find a foothold again.

Relatives: Raymund, Ramon, Raimundo, Raimund, Reamonn, Raynor, Rainer, Ray, Rae, Wray

Namesakes: Raymond Massey, Raymond Chandler, Ray Charles

Read: Old English for "red-haired" or "reed." We are particularly fond of this choice, no matter how you spell it.

Relatives: Reed, Reid, Reading, Reade

Namesakes: John Reed, Ishmael Reed, Reading Railroad

Rebecca: From the Hebrew for "bound." Rebecca is keeping apace with Rachel in the biblical-names category.

Relatives: Rebekah, Rebeccah, Rebeca, Rebeka, Rebeque, Rebequa, Becky, Bekki, Becca, Becha, Becka, Riba, Reba, Riva, Reeba, Rivka, Rifka, Rivca

Namesakes: wife of Isaac, Dame Rebecca West, Reba McEntire, "Becky Sharp," *Rebecca of Sunnybrook Farm*

Redford: Old English for "from the red ford." Both the name and the variations are handsome. Farrah Fawcett and Ryan O'Neal chose Redmond for their son.

Relatives: Redfield, Redgrave, Redman, Redmond (Old German for "adviser"), Redwald, Redd, Redding, Red

Namesakes: Red Smith, Robert Redford, Vanessa Redgrave

Reece: Old Welsh for "enthusiastic." A pleasant name, it offers a variety of spelling choices.

Relatives: Riece, Reace, Reese, Rase, Rice, Rhys, Rhett

Namesakes: Pee Wee Reese, Jean Rhys, "Rhett Butler," Reese's pieces

Reeve: Middle English for "bailiff."

Relatives: Reave, Reeves

Namesakes: Christopher Reeve, George Reeves

Regan: Irish Gaelic for "little king." King Lear's second daughter was named Regan.

Relatives: Reagan, Rayghun, Reagen, Regen, Regino, Regent

Namesake: Ronald Reagan

Regina: Latin for "queenly." Appropriate for little girls destined for greatness.

Relatives: Reggie, Gina, Rina, Regan, Reyna, Reine, Rein, Reina, Rain, Rane, Reyna, Rani, Raina

Namesake: Regina College

Reginald: Old English for "powerful one."

Relatives: Reggie, Reggy, Reg, Regis, Reynolds, Reynold, Reinwald, Regnauld, Reinald, Renault, Rene, Rinaldo, Renato, Reinhold, Raghnall

Namesakes: Regis Philbin, Reggie Jackson, Mary Renault, Judge Reinhold, Reynolds Wrap

Remington: Old English for "from the raven's home." It's possible the fleeting but popular television show "Remington Steele" in the early 1980s spawned a group of little Remingtons.

Relatives: Remmy, Remy, Remmie, Remme

Namesakes: Remy Martin, Frederic Remington, Remington automatic

Remus: Latin for "swift oarsman."
Namesakes: Uncle Remus, Romulus and Remus

Renee: From the Latin for "reborn." Renee is most often used for girls and Rene for boys.
Relatives: Rene, Renata, Rennie, Renate, Renette, Renita, Renny
Namesakes: Renee Richards, Renata Adler

Renfrew: Old Welsh for "from the still waters." And we all know still waters run deep.
Relatives: Renfred, Renshaw, Renton

Reuben: From the Hebrew for "behold a son." One of those biblical names that should be more popular.
Relatives: Rube, Ruben, Reubin, Rubin, Reuven, Reuby, Ben, Benny
Namesakes: Rube Goldberg, "Hey, Rube," Reuben sandwich

Rex: Latin for "king." He may not grow up to be king, but he can shoot for the Senate.
Relatives: Rei, Roi, Rexford, Rexer
Namesakes: Rex Harrison, Rex Stout, Rex Chapman

Reynard: From the Old German for "brave one."
Relatives: Raynard, Renard, Reinhard, Reinhart, Rinehart, Renaud, Reynaud, Reynart, Reyner, Rey, Ray
Namesakes: Mary Reinhart, Fernando Rey, Satyajit Ray, "Reynard the fox"

Rhea: From the Greek for "stream" or "mother" and Latin for "poppy."
Relatives: Ria, Rea
Namesakes: the mother of the Greek gods, Rhea Perlman

Rhoda: From the Greek for "rose." The River Rhonda flows through Wales, and in Celtic Rhonda means "mighty river."
Relatives: Rhonda, Rhodanthe, Rhodia, Rhodie, Rodie, Roe
Namesakes: Rhonda Fleming, Roe vs. Wade, "Rhoda Morgenstern," "Help Me, Rhonda"

Rhodes: Middle English for "dweller by the crosses" and Greek for "roses."

Namesakes: Cecil Rhodes, Dusty Rhodes, Colossus of Rhodes, Rhodes scholar

Richard: From the Old German for "powerful ruler" and Old English for "brave one." Once a leader in the name game, there have been fewer and fewer little Richards in recent years. But this is a can't-miss name with scads of variations.
Relatives: Ricard, Ricardo, Richerd, Richman, Ricker, Richmond, Richardson, Rickward, Rickert, Rickard, Richart, Riocard, Ritchie, Rich, Rick, Rickie, Ricky, Rico, Rocco, Dick, Dickie, Dicky
Namesakes: Richard the Lion-Hearted, Richard Strauss, Richard Burton, Ricardo Montalban, Ricky Nelson, "Richie Rich," Ritchie Valens, Dick Cavett, "Ricky Ricardo," "Dick and Jane," *Poor Richard's Almanack*

Rider: Old English for "horseman." Nice for a future equestrian.
Relative: Ryder
Namesakes: Rider Haggard, Charles Ryder, Rider College

Rigby: Old English for "valley of the ruler." This is very "old school" and yet has a charming youthful ring to it.
Namesakes: Cathy Rigby, "Eleanor Rigby," Rigby (Idaho)

Riley: Irish Gaelic for "valiant."
Relatives: Ryley, Reilly
Namesakes: James Whitcomb Riley, General Bennett Riley, *The Life of Riley*

Ring: From the Old German.
Relatives: Ringling, Ringo
Namesakes: Ring Lardner, Ringling Brothers, Ringo Starr

Riordan: Irish Gaelic for "poet."
Relative: Reardon

Ripley: Old English for "dweller in the noisy meadow."
Relatives: Rypley, Rip
Namesakes: Rip Torn, "Rip Van Winkle," *Ripley's "Believe It or Not"*

Risa: From the Latin for "laughing one." For the baby girl who comes out smiling.

Relative: Risë
Namesake: Risë Stevens

Rishon: Hebrew for "first." A feminine version is Rishona.

Risley: Old English for "from the wild meadow."
Relative: Riston

Rita: An abbreviated form of Margaret. Although an abbreviated form, Rita has come to stand well on its own.
Namesakes: Rita Hayworth, Rita Moreno

Ritter: From the Old German for "knight."
Relative: Ritt
Namesakes: John Ritter, Thelma Ritter, Tex Ritter

Riva: From the French for "river" and a shortened version of Rebecca.
Relatives: Rivy, Reeva, Rive, Rivi, Ria, Reva
Namesake: Rive Gauche

Rivers: From the Latin and French for "stream of water." Like Sky, Sunshine, and Freedom, this has a 1960-ish air to it. Nevertheless, it still clicks.
Relatives: River, Rio
Namesakes: River Phoenix, Joan Rivers, Mickey Rivers

Roarke: Irish Gaelic for "famous ruler" and Old English for "rock." Sounds as solid as Gibraltar.
Relatives: Ruark, Rourke, Rorke
Namesake: Robert Ruark

Robert: From the Old English for "bright" or "famous." A perennial favorite, Robert lends itself well to nicknames.
Relatives: Roberto, Rupert, Rubert, Robertson, Robin, Robinson, Robbins, Robben, Riobard, Robby, Robbie, Robey, Rober, Rab, Rob, Bobby, Bob, Bert, Berty, Tito, Dob, Dobbs
Namesakes: Robert the Bruce, Robert E. Lee, Robert Redford, Robert De Niro, Bobby Knight, "Christopher Robin," Robin Hood, Robinson Jeffers

Roberta: From the Old English for "bright" or "famous" and a feminine variation of Robert. Although never as popular as the masculine version, Roberta is a proper proper name.

Relatives: Ruperta, Robin, Robyn, Robbin, Robinette, Robina, Bobbi, Bobbie, Bobby, Bert, Berta, Bertie, Berthe
Namesakes: Roberta Peters, Roberta Flack, Roberta Muldoon

Rochelle: French for "from the little rock."
Relatives: Rochella, Rochette
Namesake: New Rochelle (N.Y.)

Rochester: Old English for "rock fortress." Jack Benny's butler, who else?
Relatives: Rocky, Rock, Rocho, Roche, Rockley, Rockwell, Rockne, Rocker
Namesakes: Rock Hudson, Rocky Graciano, Knute Rockne, Norman Rockwell, Rochester (N.Y.)

Roderick: From the Old German for "famous one."
Relatives: Rodrick, Broderick, Rodrigo, Roderich, Rodrigue, Rodney, Rod, Rodd, Roddy, Rodman, Rodmond, Rory, Rick, Ricky, Roderica
Namesakes: King Roderick, Roderick Thorp, Rod Steiger, Rod Stewart, Roddy McDowall, Broderick Crawford

Rodney: Old English for "famous one's island."
Relatives: Roddy, Rod, Rodman
Namesakes: Rodney Dangerfield, Rod Laver

Rogan: Irish Gaelic for "red-haired." This delightful Irish name would work beautifully for a girl or a boy.
Relative: Roan

Roger: From the Old German for "famous spearman." A fun choice for the son of a C.B. aficionado. That's a Roger.
Relatives: Rodger, Rodgers, Rogers, Rogerio, Rog, Ruggiero, Rudiger, Rodiger, Rutger
Namesakes: Roger Moore, Roger Maris, Rutger Hauer, Kenny Rogers, Will Rogers, Roy Rogers, Richard Rodgers, *Jolly Roger*

Roland: From the Old German for "from the famous island."
Relatives: Rolland, Rowland, Rollan, Rollin, Rollins, Rolando, Rodhlann, Rowe, Rollo, Rolly, Orlando, Rolt, Rolanda
Namesakes: Roland Barthes, Charlemagne's heroic nephew, Rollo May, Howard Rollins

Romeo: Italian for "pilgrim to Rome." Although Juliet has found a home in the twentieth century, Romeo remains more firmly planted in the fifteenth.

Relatives: Rome, Roman, Romain, Roma, Romy, Romana

Namesakes: Roman Gabriel, Roman Polanski, Romain Gary, Romy Schneider, *Romeo and Juliet*

Ronald: Old Norse for "mighty." Former President Reagan may have breathed life back into Ronald.

Relatives: Ronnie, Ronny, Ron, Rona, Renaldo, Ronan, Naldo, Ronalda

Namesakes: Ronald Coleman, Ron Greschner, Ron Howard, "Ronald MacDonald"

Rooney: Irish Gaelic for "red-haired." A delightful name that, sadly, rhymes with "looney," "gooney," and "puny." Such unfortunate rhyming possibilities should be kept in mind because classmates are likely to select one of them as a nickname for your child.

Relatives: Roon, Roone, Rune

Namesakes: Roone Arledge, Mickey Rooney, Andy Rooney

Roosevelt: From the Dutch for "field of roses." Many New Deal babies were given this name in honor of then-president Franklin Delano Roosevelt.

Relatives: Rosey, Rosie

Namesakes: Roosevelt Brown, Rosie Grier, Theodore Roosevelt

Rory: Irish Gaelic for "red king." This adorable name can be carried with equal grace by boys or girls.

Relatives: Rurik, Roric, Ruaidhri

Namesakes: Rory Calhoun, Rory Kennedy

Roscoe: Old Norse for "from the deer forest." This is a wonderful but seldom-used name.

Namesakes: Roscoe Tanner, Roscoe Lee Brown

Rose: From the Latin or Greek for the flower. This charming name has hundreds of variations when linked with other names. It also stands alone beautifully as a first or second name.

Relatives: Rosa, Rosie, Rosey, Roz, Rozsi, Rosalie, Rosalee, Rosalia, Rosetta, Rosette, Rosina, Rosena, Rasia, Rois, Rosita, Rosebud, Rosabell, Rosalinda, Rosalind, Rosalyn, Roslyn, Roslin, Roseline, Rosamund, Rosmund, Rosemonde, Rozamund, Rosanne, Rosanna, Roanne, Roanna, Rosaleen, Rosellen, Roselle, Rosemary, Rosemarie, Chara, Charo

Namesakes: Rose Kennedy, Princess Margaret Rose, Roseanne Barr, Rosa Parks, Tokyo Rose, Rosemary Clooney, Pete Rose, Rosetta Stone

Roslin: From the Old French for "little red-haired one" and a blending of Rose and Lynn. This offspring of Rose has quaint variations.
Relatives: Rosselin, Roslyn, Rose-Lynn, Rosalyn, Rosalind, Rosalinde, Rosalinda, Rosalynda
Namesake: Rosalynn Carter

Ross: Scottish Gaelic for "from the peninsula," Anglo-Saxon for "horse," and a clan name. This handsome name commands respect. It has recently found a following as a strong second name and as an alternative to the overworked Scott.
Relatives: Rossano, Roswald
Namesakes: Ross Martin, H. Ross Perot, Betsy Ross, Rossano Brazzi, Diana Ross

Rowan: Irish Gaelic for "red-haired" and Old English for "rugged."
Relatives: Rowen, Rowe, Rowell, Rowley, Rowson, Rowena
Namesakes: Carl Rowan, Dan Rowan

Roxanne: From the Persian for "brilliant one." This might strike an old-fashioned chord in some, but the name is a noble one well worth considering.
Relatives: Roxane, Roxann, Roxanna, Roxie, Roxy, Rox
Namesakes: Cyrano de Bergerac's love, Roxanne Pulitzer

Roy: From the Old French for "regal one." This works for the boy who would be king.
Relatives: Royal, Royale, Royall, Roi, Royce
Namesakes: Roy Rogers, Roy Acuff, Roy Lichtenstein

Ruby: From the Old French for "red gem." The ruby is the birthstone for July babies.

Relatives: Rubie, Rubee, Rubia, Rubina
Namesakes: Ruby Keeler, Ruby Dee, "Ruby Begonia," ruby slippers

Rudolph: From the Old German for "wolf." Rudolph has faded into the Name Hall of Fame perhaps because of the red-nosed reindeer song, but Rudy and Dolph are interesting.
Relatives: Rudolf, Rodolf, Rodolphe, Rodolfo, Raoul, Rudy, Rudie, Rolf, Rolph, Rollo, Rollin, Dolph
Namesakes: Rudolph Valentino, King Rudolf, Rudolf Nureyev, Rudy Vallee, Rollo May, Dolph Lundgren, Wilma Rudolph, "Rudolph the Red-Nosed Reindeer"

Rudyard: Old English for "from the red gate."
Relatives: Ruddy, Rudy
Namesake: Rudyard Kipling

Rue: An herb name from the Greek and Latin. Rue, a delightful choice, also means "regret." But don't let that stop you. The herb signifies "remembrance."
Namesake: Rue McClanahan

Rufus: From the Latin for "red-haired one." There are several names similar to Rufus for redheads; peruse all the choices before settling on one for your carrot top.
Relatives: Ruphus, Rufe, Ruff, Rufford
Namesake: Rufus Thomas

Rush: From the French for "red-haired." A great name for a tackle. He wouldn't have to wait around for a nickname.
Relatives: Rousse, Rusk, Ruskin, Rust
Namesakes: Bob Rush, Dean Rusk, Mount Rushmore

Russell: From the Old French for "red-haired" or Old English for "foxlike."
Relatives: Russel, Russ, Rusty
Namesakes: Russell Baker, Russell Long, Rusty Staub, Bertrand Russell

Ruth: From the Hebrew for "compassionate friend." Not as popular as Rachel and Rebecca, but usage is on the rise.
Relatives: Ruthie, Ruthanne

Namesakes: daughter-in-law of Naomi, Ruth Gordon, Ruth Benedict, Ruth St. Denis, Babe Ruth

Rutherford: Old English for "from the cattle ford" or "from the ford of red stones." Perfect for the baby with the gray flannel layette.
Relative: Ruthren
Namesakes: Rutherford B. Hayes, Dame Margaret Rutherford

Ryan: Irish Gaelic for "little king." This trendy choice has caught on with girls as well as boys.
Relatives: Ryen, Rian
Namesakes: Ryan O'Neal, Nolan Ryan, "Ryan's Hope"

Rylan: Old English for "dweller in the rye field." The added letter gives Ryan an entirely different spin.
Relatives: Ryland, Ryle, Rycroft, Ryman, Ryton
Namesakes: Gilbert Ryle, Ryman Auditorium

Some Names That Are Good Enough to Eat

A long list of endearments are based on a favorite major food group—sweet stuff. No one can coo to a new baby without calling him or her "honey"—even if the baby's proper name is Spike. Typical endearments from the food category include:

Babycake	Muffin
Cookie	Pudding
Cupcake	Pumpkin
Dumpling	Sugar
Honeybun	Sweetie Pie
Lambie Pie	

Southerners in particular seem gifted at inventing these syrupy nicknames. You need to have a facility for tossing the ingredients together and then throwing in a suffix such as "-kins." For example, Honeypiesugarlumpkins.

Other food group choices may be found by meandering down the aisles of gourmet shops and grocery stores. But tread carefully here. Yes, Brie is rather pretty, but consider the other cheeses. Roquefort? Gouda? Well, maybe Stilton. And though Stew is nice, we wouldn't name a baby Pot-a-feu on a bet. Keep in mind the advertising slogan, "With a name like Smuckers—it *has* to be good."

Berry	Mirabelle
Brie	Morel
Candy	Olive
Charlotte	Peaches
Cherry	Quince
Chili	Rennet
Chutney	Rye
Ginger	Savarin
Ham	Shallot
Madeleine	Stew
Melba	Stilton
Melon	Taffy
Mignon	Vacherin
Millet	

S

Sabina: Latin for "Sabine woman."
Relatives: Sabine, Savina, Saidhbhin, Saba

Sabra: From the Hebrew "to rest." A Sabra is also a native-born Israeli.

Sabrina: From the Latin for "from the border land." It was in the movie *Sabrina* that a brilliant casting agent brought Audrey Hepburn together with Humphrey Bogart. Hepburn, as everyone knows, played the title role.

Sacha: From the Russian, a pet form of Alexander or Alexandra. Like Mischa, Sacha has become an independent name with a Cyrillic spirit.
Relatives: Sasha, Sascha

Salina: From the Latin for "by the salt water."
Relative: Saleena

Salome: From the Hebrew for "peace." Salome was the biblical temptress who demanded (and got) John the Baptist's head on a platter.
Relatives: Saloma, Salomi

Salvador: Spanish for "savior." Salvador and Salvatore are enduring favorites in Spain and Italy, respectively.
Relatives: Salvatore, Sauveur, Sal, Sally
Namesakes: Salvador Dali, Sal Bando, San Salvador

Samantha: From the Aramaic for "listens well." Bewitching.

Relatives: Sammy, Sammi, Sam, Samara
Namesakes: Samantha Eggar, Samantha Fox

Samara: From the Hebrew for "guarded by God" and Latin for "seedling." A pretty choice.

Samson: From the Hebrew for "shining man." Buy this child a set of weights early and let him wear his hair long.
Relatives: Sampson, Sanson, Sansone, Sam, Sammy
Namesakes: Samson and Delilah, Ralph Sampson

Samuel: From the Hebrew for "His name is God." Samuel has fallen in and out of favor in this century but lately is back—with a bullet. The little-used Samuela is quite lovely for a girl.
Relatives: Samuela, Samuella, Samuele, Samuelson, Samella, Samelle, Sam, Sammy, Sammie, Shemuel, Schmuel, Shem
Namesakes: Samuel Goldwyn, Samuel Adams, Samuel Beckett, Samuel Taylor Coleridge, Samuel McKenzie Newman, "Uncle Sam"

Sanders: Middle English for "Alexander's son."
Relatives: Sander, Sandor, Sandy, Sands, Sanderson, Saunders, Saunderson
Namesakes: Sander Vanocur, Sandy Richardson, Tommy Sands, George Sanders, George Sand

Sandra: A form of Alexandra. Sandra was in the top twenty in the fifties—perhaps because of the matinee heroine Sandra Dee.
Relatives: Sondra, Sandie, Sandy, Sandee
Namesakes: Sandra Day O'Connor, Sandy Duncan

Sanford: Old English for "dweller at the sandy ford."
Relatives: Sanborn, Sandy, Sandford
Namesakes: Georg Sanford Brown, Mount Sanford, Chase and Sanborn coffee

Sapphira: From the Greek for the jewel and the color. Sapphire, the blue gem, is the birthstone for September babies.
Relatives: Saphira, Sapphire
Namesake: Sapphira and the Slave Girl

Sarah: From the Hebrew for "princess." This biblical name has always been popular and deservedly so. It blends beautifully with other names.

Relatives: Sara, Sari, Sarene, Sarai, Sarina, Sarine, Sarita, Sairne, Sarette, Salaidh, Sally, Sallye, Salli, Sallie, Sal, Sadie, Sadey, Zarah, Zara, Zaria

Namesakes: wife of Abraham, Sarah Bernhardt, Sara Teasdale, Sally Jessie Raphael, Zara Phillips (daughter of Princess Anne)

Sargent: From the Old French for "officer." For the hierarchy-conscious child, first take a look at Major.

Relatives: Sargeant, Sergent, Sarge
Namesake: Sargent Shriver

Saul: From the Hebrew for "asked for." Saul hasn't been able to compete with the more popular Samuel but has held its own since biblical times.

Relatives: Sol, Sauly, Solly
Namesakes: King Saul, Saul Steinberg, Saul Bellow

Savanna: Old Spanish for "from the open plain." If Sarah seems too popular, consider Savanna as a change of pace.

Relative: Savannah
Namesake: Savannah (Ga.)

Sawyer: Middle English for "woodsman." This occupational name is rarely used but is pleasant sounding.

Namesakes: Sawyer Brown, Diane Sawyer, "Tom Sawyer"

Sayer: Welsh for "carpenter."

Relatives: Sayers, Sayre, Sayres
Namesakes: Dorothy Sayers, Gale Sayers

Scarlet: Middle English for "deep red." For *Gone with the Wind* fans, is there any other choice?

Relative: Scarlett
Namesakes: "Scarlett O'Hara," *The Scarlet Pimpernel,* "The Scarlet Empress"

Schuyler: From the Dutch for "shield" or "scholar." The actress Sissy Spacek chose this name for her baby girl. Sky is a captivating nickname.

Relatives: Skyler, Skylar, Sky, Skye, Ciel
Namesakes: Schuyler Huntoon, James Schuyler, Isle of Skye

Scott: Old English "from Scotland." Scott peaked in the seventies but has held steadily in the top-fifty list—especially as a second name.
Relatives: Scot, Scotty, Scottie, Escott
Namesakes: Scott Joplin, Scott Carpenter, F. Scott Fitzgerald, Sir Walter Scott

Scully: Irish Gaelic for "town crier." A "scull" is a small, lightweight rowboat and sculling is an Olympic event. This name would work well for the child of an oarsperson.
Namesake: Vincent Scully

Seabert: Old English for "sea-glorious."
Relatives: Seabright, Sebert, Seberg, Seabrook, Seabury, Sea
Namesakes: Samuel Seabury, Jean Seberg

Sean: Irish form of John. This name has become so popular (for girls as well as boys) that it no longer seems distinctly Irish.
Relatives: Shawn, Shaun, Shawna, Shaune, Sian
Namesakes: Sean O'Casey, Sean Connery, Sean Penn, Sean Young

Season: From the Latin for "planting time." Spring, Summer, and Winter work well, so why not consider Season?
Namesake: Season Hubley

Seaton: Old Anglo-French for "from Baron Sai's estate" and English for "sea town."
Relatives: Seeton, Seton, Seetin
Namesakes: Elizabeth Seton, Ernest Thompson Seton, Seton Hall

Sebastian: From the Latin for "revered one." Sebastian is the patron saint of archers and pin makers. This is a superb name and worthy of a comeback.
Relatives: Sebastiane, Sebastianne, Sebastiana, Sebastien, Sebastiona, Bastien, Bastian
Namesakes: Saint Sebastian, Sebastian Cabot, John Sebastian, "Sebastian Flyte"

Selby: Old English for "of the manor house farm." Think about this for a girl.
Relatives: Selden, Seldon, Selwin, Selwyn

Selena: From Greek for "moon." Selena is an ancient, mythological name for the goddess of the moon.
Relatives: Selina, Selene, Selinda, Selly, Sellie, Sela, Selia, Sena, Celena, Celina, Celene, Celie, Celia
Namesake: Selina, Countess of Huntingdon

Sennett: From the French for "wise one." This could be interpreted as akin to naming your child Congress or President. Then again, why not?
Relatives: Senet, Senta
Namesakes: Mack Sennett, Senta Berger

Septima: From the Latin for "seventh born." If you have six already, celebrate with this enchanting name.
Relatives: Septimus, Seven
Namesake: Lilibet Septima

Seraphina: From the Hebrew for "afire" or "angel." This exotic name can be shortened to Sara until she is old enough to "carry" Seraphina.
Relatives: Serafina, Sarafina, Serafine, Seraphine, Seraphim, Sera, Sara

Serena: From the Latin for "peaceful one." For the contented child.
Relatives: Serene, Serenity

Serge: From the Latin for "attendant." Sergius is a widely revered saint in Russia.
Relatives: Sergei, Sergius
Namesakes: Sergei Prokofiev, Sergei Eisenstein

Seth: From the Hebrew for "appointed." Seth was popular with the Puritans and so is about due for a revival. Try it on a girl.
Namesakes: third son of Adam and Eve, Seth Thomas

Seward: Old English for "from the sea."
Relatives: Sewell, Severn
Namesakes: Anna Sewell, Seward's Folly, Severn River (Britain)

Seymour: Old French contraction for Saint Maur and Old English for "tailor." A distinguished name with Olde English flair.

Relatives: Seymor, Seemour, Sy, Skip
Namesakes: Seymour Chwast, Jane Seymour

Shaina: From the Yiddish for "beautiful."
Relatives: Shaine, Shanie, Shayne, Shayna, Shanna, Shana
Namesake: Shana Alexander

Shannon: Irish Gaelic for "wise one." A distinctive choice for a girl or boy.
Relatives: Shanley, Shandy, Shanahan, Shanon, Shanna, Shane, Shana, Sean, Shan
Namesakes: Del Shannon, *Shane,* River Shannon (Ireland)

Sharon: From the Hebrew for "princess" or "of the plain." The popularity of Sharon dropped sharply after World War II.
Relatives: Sharen, Sharyn, Sharron, Charon, Sharry, Shari, Sherry
Namesakes: Shari Lewis, Ariel Sharon, "The Rose of Sharon"

Shaw: Old English for "a grove."
Namesakes: George Bernard Shaw, Artie Shaw

Shea: Irish Gaelic for "ingenious" or "majestic."
Relative: Shay
Namesakes: Milo O'Shea, John Shea, Shea Stadium

Sheehan: Irish Gaelic for "little peaceful one."
Relative: Sheen
Namesakes: Fulton Sheen, Martin Sheen

Sheena: Irish Gaelic for "God's grace."
Namesakes: Sheena Easton, "Sheena, Queen of the Jungle"

Sheila: Irish Gaelic for Cecilia. In Australia, "sheila" is a generic term for woman.
Relatives: Sheilah, Sheela, Sheelah, Shelah (Hebrew for "request"), Selia, Sheilagh
Namesake: Sheila MacRae

Shelley: Old English for "sloping meadow." Nifty for a girl; spiffy for a boy.
Relatives: Shelly, Shelli, Shell, Shelby, Sheldon, Shelton

Namesakes: Shelley Winters, Shelley Long, Shelley Berman, Percy Bysshe Shelley

Shepherd: From the Old English for one who herds sheep. Shep is a darling nickname.
Relatives: Shepard, Sheppard, Shepley, Shep
Namesakes: Shep Woolley, Alan Shepard, Sam Shepard

Sheridan: Irish Gaelic for "wild one."
Namesakes: General Philip Sheridan, Richard Sheridan, "Sheridan Whiteside"

Sherlock: Old English for "white-haired." Oh, if only deerstalkers came in infant sizes.
Namesake: "Sherlock Holmes"

Sherman: Old English for "wool cutter." This is a grand name, but Sherm is not an easy nickname to carry.
Relatives: Sherwin, Sherborne, Sherm
Namesakes: Sherman Billingsley, Sherman Helmsley, Sherwin Williams, Sherman Oaks (Calif.)

Sherry: From the French for "cherished." Sherry is also a type of wine named for the Spanish town of Jerez and, like Brandy and Margaux, is used as a girl's name.
Relatives: Sherrey, Sheri, Sherrie, Cherie, Sherye, Sheree, Cherry
Namesake: Sherry Lansing

Sherwood: Old English for "bright forest." Robin Hood's favorite haunt.
Namesakes: Sherwood Anderson, Robert Sherwood

Shipley: Old English for "from the deep meadow."
Relative: Shipton

Shira: From the Hebrew for "song."
Relatives: Shirah, Shiri

Shirley: Old English for "from the bright meadow."
Relatives: Shirlee, Sherlie, Shurlie, Shirleigh, Shirleen, Sheryl, Shirl, Shyrl, Shir
Namesakes: Shirley Temple, Shirley Booth, Shirley Jones, Shirley MacLaine

Shoshannah: From the Hebrew for "rose." An exquisite choice for traditionalists who like the concept of Rose.
Relatives: Shoshanna, Shoshana, Shoshanah, Shosha
Namesake: "Shosha"

Shulamith: From the Hebrew for "peaceful" and a form of Salome.
Relative: Shulamit
Namesake: Shulamith Firestone

Sibyl: From the Greek for "prophetess." In ancient times Sibyls were thought to be capable of predicting future events. Imagine a sibilant sibling named Sibyl with a multiple personality.
Relatives: Sybyl, Sybil, Sybille, Sibille, Sibylle, Sibeal, Sybilline, Sibby, Sibbi, Sib, Cybil, Cybill
Namesakes: Sybil Thorndike, Cybill Shepherd, *Sibyl*

Siddell: Old English for "from the wide valley."
Relatives: Sydell, Sidwell

Sidney: Old French contraction of Saint Denis. This name has always been used interchangeably for girls and boys as well as for place names.
Relatives: Sydney, Sydny, Sid, Sidne, Sidoney, Sidonia, Siddie, Syd, Sydell, Sidell, Sydel
Namesakes: Sidney Poitier, Sydney Biddle Barrows, Sid Caesar, Sir Philip Sidney, Sydney (Australia)

Sigmund: Old German for "victorious protector." Don't overanalyze your ultimate choice for a name. Go with one you like.
Relatives: Siegmund, Sigismond, Sigismundo, Siegfried, Sigfrid, Siffre, Sigvard, Siggy, Ziggy
Namesakes: Sigmund Freud, Siegfried Sassoon, "Ziggy Stardust"

Sigrid: Old Norse for "winning adviser."
Relatives: Sigrath, Sigwald, Sigurd

Silas: From the Latin for "wood." Put Silas on the birth certificate and call him Woody.
Namesake: Silas Marner

Simon: From the Hebrew for "listener." Simon says consider Simon.
Relatives: Simeon, Siomonn, Sim, Shimon

Namesakes: Saint Simeon, Simon Bolívar, Paul Simon, Shimon Perez, "Simon Legree"

Simone: From the Hebrew for "listener." Long popular in France, this pretty name could withstand more usage.
Relatives: Simona, Simonette
Namesakes: Simone Signoret, Simone de Beauvoir

Sinclair: A French contraction of Saint Clair. There are several contractions akin to Sinclair (such as Sinjon for St. John). Sinclair would work well for a girl, too.
Namesakes: Sinclair Lewis, Upton Sinclair

Skeet: Middle English for "speedy." Skeets are also the clay "birds" used in target shooting.
Relatives: Skeets, Skeat, Skeeter
Namesake: Skeeter Davis

Skipp: Old Norse for "ship owner." Skip is often used as a nickname in lieu of a more formal given name. It also stands well alone and proves convenient if you own a boat or a kangaroo.
Relatives: Skipper, Skippy, Skip

Sloan: Irish Gaelic for "warrior." Has a distinctive pedigreed ring to it.
Relative: Sloane
Namesakes: Sloan Wilson, John French Sloan

Smith: From the Old English for "hammer worker" or "artisan." This is such a popular surname, it's a wonder it isn't invoked more often for a first name.
Relatives: Smyth, Smythe, Smitty, Smits
Namesakes: Bessie Smith, Smith-Barney, John Smith, Smith & Wesson

Snowden: Old English for "from the snow-covered hill." Because it means so much to their way of life, Eskimoes have hundreds of words for "snow."
Relatives: Snowdun, Snow
Namesakes: Lord Snowden, Edgar Snow

Solomon: From the Hebrew for "peaceful." Solomon was a king of Israel famous for his profound wisdom.

Relatives: Soloman, Salomon, Salmon, Sholem, Shalom, Sholom, Schlomo, Shlomo, Solly, Sol (Latin for "sun")

Namesakes: Solomon Guggenheim, Salmon Chase, Sholem Aleichem, Sol Hurok, Solomon Brothers, *Song of Solomon*

Somerset: Old English for "where the summer people settle." A marvelous name with rich poetic undertones.

Relatives: Somerton, Somerville, Somer, Summer

Namesake: Somerset Maugham

Sophie: Greek for "wisdom." Once considered a bit dowdy by some, Sophie has rightfully charged up the popularity lists in recent years. Bette Midler selected it for her baby girl.

Relatives: Sofie, Sophy, Sophia, Sofia, Sonja, Sonya, Sophronia, Sadhbh

Namesakes: Sophie Tucker, Sophia Loren, Sonja Henie, *Sophie's Choice, Red Sonya*

Spalding: Old English for "from the divided meadow."

Relative: Spaulding

Namesakes: Spalding Grey, Spalding sporting goods

Spencer: Middle English for "provider." This is a name with integrity and sincerity.

Relatives: Spenser, Spence

Namesakes: Spencer Tracy, Spencer Christian, Edmund Spenser, "Spenser for Hire"

Spring: Old English for the season. Only Fall seems to stretch the use of seasonal names too far. Winter, Summer, and Autumn as well as Season have been used.

Namesake: Spring Byington

Stacey: From the Latin for "stable." An unlikely derivation for so pretty a name. Stacey is used for either sex.

Relatives: Stacy, Staci, Stasia, Stasya, Tasia

Namesakes: Stacy Keach, Stacy Ladislaw, James Stacey

Stanislaus: Slavic for "stand in glory."

Relatives: Stanislav, Stanislas, Stanislavsky, Stan, Aineislis

Namesakes: Saint Stanislaus, Stanislaus Richter, Konstantin Stanislavsky

Stanley: Old English for "from the rocky meadow." This name was cast in bronze when Tennessee Williams chose it for his brutish hero in *A Streetcar Named Desire.*
Relatives: Stanly, Stanleigh, Stanbury, Stanberry, Standish, Stanfield, Stanford, Stanhope, Stanmore, Stanton, Stanway, Stanwick, Stanwyck
Namesakes: Stanfield Turner, Stanford White, Stan "The Man" Musial, Stan Laurel, Stanley and Livingston, Miles Standish, Barbara Stanwyck, Stanley Cup

Stein: German for "stone." A stein is also an earthenware mug designed to hold a pint of beer.
Relatives: Steyn, Stine, Styne, Steiner, Steen, Steinway, Steinbeck, Steinberg, Steinmetz
Namesakes: Stein Erickson, Gertrude Stein, Jule Styne, John Steinbeck, Saul Steinberg, Steinway pianos

Stella: Latin for "star." If the child seems unfazed by the lights, camera, and action in the delivery room, this might be the right choice for your little star.
Relatives: Stela, Stellar, Star, Starr, Starla, Starling
Namesakes: Stella Stevens, Stella Adler, Star Lawrence, Bart Starr, "Stella Dallas," "Brenda Starr"

Stephanie: From the Greek for "crowned." This dark horse has emerged as a leader in recent years.
Relatives: Stefanie, Stephania, Stephana, Stephanya, Steffie, Steffi, Stef, Stepha, Stefa, Fannie, Fanny
Namesakes: Saint Stephana, Stephanie Zimbalist, Stefanie Powers, Steffi Graf

Stephen: From the Greek for "crowned." You can't go wrong with Stephen. It has endured the slings and arrows of decades of popularity polls.
Relatives: Stephan, Steven, Stefan, Stefano, Steve, Stevie, Stephens, Stevens, Stevenson, Stephenson, Etienne, Esteban, Estevan

Namesakes: Stephen Crane, Stephen King, Stevie Nicks, Steve McQueen, Stevie Wonder, Stefan Edberg

Sterling: From the Middle English for "pure" and Old Welsh for "from the yellow house." Perfect for the baby born with a silver spoon in his mouth.
Relative: Stirling
Namesakes: Sterling Moss, Sterling Hayden, sterling silver, British Sterling

Sterne: Middle English for "serious-minded." Some babies have that serious-minded look even moments after birth. This might just work.
Relatives: Stern, Stearn, Stearne
Namesakes: Laurence Sterne, Isaac Stern

Stewart: Old English for "steward" and Scottish clan name. This elegant old family name, a royal one in Scotland, is always in good taste, as long as you don't mind the inevitable Stew or (worse!) Stewie.
Relatives: Stuart, Steward, Stew, Stu
Namesakes: Stewart Granger, Jackie Stewart, James Stewart, "Stuart Little"

Stockley: Old English for "from the tree-stump meadow."
Relatives: Stockton, Stockwell, Stockman, Stokley, Stockard
Namesakes: Stokley Carmichael, Stockard Channing, David Stockman, Stockton (Calif.)

Storm: From the Old English for "tempest." An appropriate name for a child born in the middle of one.
Relatives: Storme, Stormy, Stormie
Namesakes: Storm Field, "Stormy," "Stormy Weather"

Stroud: Old English for "from the thicket."
Relatives: Stroude, Stod
Namesakes: Don Stroud, Robert Stroud (the Birdman of Alcatraz)

Sullivan: Irish Gaelic for "black eyes." Sullivan is much more popular as a surname but makes a nice first name, too.
Relatives: Sullyvan, Sully
Namesakes: John L. Sullivan, Ed Sullivan, Susan Sullivan

Sumner: Middle English for "summoner."

Relatives: Sumenor, Sumnor, Summer
Namesakes: Sumner Welles, James Sumner

Sunny: From the English for "bright disposition" or "cheerful."
Relatives: Sunnie, Sunnee, Sonny, Sunday
Namesakes: Sunny von Bulow, Sonny Bono

Susan: From the Hebrew for "lily." Susan has been a persistently favorite choice in the twentieth century. The more traditional Susannah is particularly melodic.
Relatives: Susanne, Suisan, Susanna, Susannah, Suzanne, Suzanna, Shoshannah, Sosana, Susette, Suzette, Sue Anne, Sue Ellen, Susy, Susie, Soos, Suzy, Suzie, Soozie, Sue, Suki ("beloved" in Japanese), Sukie, Sukey, Zsa Zsa
Namesakes: Saint Susanna, Susan Sontag, Susan B. Anthony, Suzanne Somers, Zsa Zsa Gabor, crepes suzette, Suzy Q, "Old Susannah"

Sutherland: Old Norse for "people from the south land" and a clan name. It would be safe to assume that, for Norwegians, everyone they encountered was from the south.
Relatives: Sutton, Sutcliff, Suffield, Sundy
Namesakes: Donald Sutherland, Joan Sutherland, Rick Sutcliff, Sutton Place (N.Y.)

Sven: From the Scandinavian for "youth." Remember that first names should jibe with surnames. And Sven jibes best with surnames having Scandinavian roots.
Relatives: Swen, Svend, Svenson, Svensen, Swensen, Swenson
Namesake: Bo Svenson

Swain: Middle English for "knight's attendant." The word "swain" is used in poetry of earlier centuries to describe a young man from the country.
Relatives: Swaine, Swayne, Swayze
Namesakes: Patrick Swayze, Swains Islands (American Samoa)

Sweeney: Irish Gaelic for "little hero." Sweeney Todd was the infamous barber of Fleet Street.
Relative: Sweeny

Sylvester: From the Latin for "from the forest." This name has jumped in popularity since Sly Stallone has become so familiar to moviegoers.
Relatives: Silvester, Sylvestro, Silvestre, Sly, Silvanus, Silas, Syl, Sil
Namesake: "Sylvester the cat"

Sylvia: From the Latin for "from the forest." Sylvanus was a mythological patron of woodcutters and farmers.
Relatives: Silvia, Silvie, Sylvie, Silva, Sylva, Silvana, Sylvana, Zilvia
Namesakes: Sylvia Plath, Sylvia Porter

Some Spirited Names

A stroll through your local wine and liquor shop might yield some names that strike your fancy. Wines and liqueurs are probably your best bets, and you can always put aside a few bottles of the chosen vintage to await that twenty-first birthday toast.

Legend has it that Margaux Hemingway was named for the bottle of wine her parents drank the night she was conceived. She's probably very glad they weren't guzzling Riunite.

Alsace	Dubonnet
Amaretto	Gamay
Amboise	Gibson
Ambrosia	Ginny
Anisette	Harvey Wallbanger
Barbera	Lancer
Bourbon	Madeira
Brandy	Margarita
Brandy Alexander	Margaux
Brittany	Marsala
Cabernet	Mead
Chablis	Mickey Finn
Champagne	Moselle
Chardonnay	Port
Claret	Porter

Remy Martin   Tattinger
Rickey   Tisane
Rob Roy   Tom Collins
Sauterne   Tom and Jerry
Sherry   Vouvray
Shirley Temple   Whiskey
Syrah

T

In 1974, the Board of Registrar of Voters in Worcester, Massachusetts, removed a woman's name from the rolls because she refused to be listed under her husband's name.

Tab: Old German for "brilliant" and Middle English for "drummer." An enchanting selection that's short, sweet, and unusual.
Relatives: Taber, Tabor, Tabbert, Taburer, Tabby
Namesake: Tab Hunter

Tabitha: From the Greek for "gazelle." Beatrix Potter named one of her little animal characters Tabitha Twitchet. For TV triviologists, Tabitha was the name of Darren and Samantha's witchlette daughter in "Bewitched."
Relatives: Tabatha, Tabbie, Tabbi, Tabby
Namesake: Tabitha King

Taggart: Irish Gaelic for "son of the prelate." Taggart is an agreeable-sounding name suggesting a strong character and a lethal slapshot.
Relatives: Taggard, Tagg, Tag, Gary
Namesake: Genevieve Taggard

Talbot: From the Old French for "reward." The baby will want suede elbow patches on his tweed stretchie.
Relatives: Tally, Tallie
Namesake: Talbot's catalog

Talia: From the Hebrew for "dew from heaven," which sounds like the final line of a delicately crafted haiku.
Relatives: Talya, Tally, Tai, Talitha
Namesakes: Talia Shire, Tai Babilonia

Tallulah: Choctaw Indian for "leaping water." This name is closely associated with its famous namesake.
Relatives: Tally, Tallie
Namesake: Tallulah Bankhead

Tamara: From the Hebrew for "palm tree."
Relatives: Tamarah, Tamar, Tammy, Tammie, Tamarind, Tamika

Tammy: From the Hebrew for "perfect one." Tammy, like Gidget, was a teen queen of the fifties and sixties. The character starred in a series of saccharine movies, including the classic *Tammy Tell Me True.*
Relatives: Tammie, Tam
Namesakes: Tammy Grimes, Tammy Wynette

Tanner: Old English for "leather worker." Appropriate for a little sun-worshiper.
Namesakes: "Henry Tanner," Roscoe Tanner

Tanya: From the Russian for "fairy princess."
Relatives: Tania, Tan, Tani, Tatiana
Namesake: Tanya Tucker

Tara: Irish Gaelic for "rocky hill." No fan of Margaret Mitchell will ever forget Scarlett O'Hara's vow to return to her beloved Tara. The name can now be heard at most playgrounds.
Relatives: Taria, Taryn
Namesake: the ancient capital of Ireland

Tate: Middle English for "cheerful." Short and endearing.
Relative: Tatum
Namesakes: Tatum O'Neal, Allen Tate, Art Tatum, Tate Gallery

Tavis: Scottish for "twin."
Relatives: Tevis, Tav, Tavish, Tamsin

Taylor: Middle English for "tailor." Taylor is an occupational surname that has often been pressed into service as a first name.
Relatives: Tailor, Tay, Tie

Namesakes: Taylor Caldwell, Elizabeth Taylor, Paul Taylor, General Matthew Taylor

Teague: Irish Gaelic for "poet." Is your baby rhyming "goo goo" with "boo hoo"? This name could prove prophetic.
Relatives: Tadhg, Tegan (Celtic for "doe")
Namesake: McTeague

Tempest: From the Old French for "storm." So far we've seen Raine, Storm, and Misty. Tempest is fine for a passionate child.
Relative: Tempestt
Namesake: Tempestt Bledsoe

Tennyson: Middle English for "son of Dennis."
Relatives: Tennison, Tennessee, Tenny
Namesakes: Alfred Lord Tennyson, Tennessee Williams

Terence: From the Latin for "polished." Terence has a faithful following in England but is seldom used in the United States. Give it a go.
Relatives: Terrence, Terance, Terencio, Terentius, Terry, Teri, Terris
Namesakes: Terence Stamp, Terry Bradshaw, "Terry and the Pirates"

Terrell: Old English for "thunderer."
Relatives: Terrill, Tirell, Terris, Tyrell, Tarrant
Namesake: Robert Terrell

Tess: From the Greek for "fourth born." Once used as an abbreviation of Teresa, Tess has come to stand on its own. It's a sweet name.
Relatives: Tessa, Tessie
Namesakes: Tess Harper, *Tess of the D'Urbervilles*

Thaddeaus: From the Latin for "courageous" or "praiser."
Relatives: Thaddaus, Thaddea, Thada, Taddeo, Tadeo, Tadeusz, Tadgh, Thad, Taddy, Tadda, Tad, Ted
Namesakes: an apostle, Tadeusz Kościuszko

Thalassa: Greek for "from the sea." Thalasso mud wraps are a sought-after form of therapy at seaside spas.
Namesake: Thalassa Cruso

Thalia: From the Greek for "blooming." Thalia blends nicely with a flower name, making such combinations as Thalia Rose and Thalia Lily.
Namesakes: one of the three Graces, the Muse of comedy

Thea: From Greek for "goddess." An exquisite name.

Thelma: From the Greek for "nursing."
Namesake: Thelma Ritter

Theobald: Old German for "the boldest."
Relatives: Teoboldo, Tibalt, Tybalt, Thebault, Thibaud, Thibaut, Theo
Namesakes: "Tybalt" (character in Shakespeare's *Romeo and Juliet*)

Theodora: From the Greek for "gift of God." This was rock star Keith Richards and wife Patti Hansen's choice for one of their baby girls.
Relatives: Theora, Theda, Teodora, Theodosia, Thedora, Thera (Greek for "wild"), Tedra, Feodora, Dora, Theone, Theophania, Theophila
Namesake: Theda Bara

Theodore: From the Greek for "gift of God." How Theodore Cleaver became "the Beaver" rather than Teddy is beyond us.
Relatives: Theodor, Teodore, Teodoro, Teddy, Ted, Feodor, Fyodor
Namesakes: Theodore Roosevelt, Theodore Dreiser, Theodore Roethke, Ted Turner, Ted Williams, Fyodor Dostoyevsky, "Theodore the Chipmunk"

Theophilus: From the Greek for "beloved of God."
Namesake: "Theophilus North"

Theresa: Greek for "reaper." No matter how you spell it, this is an exquisite name with an assortment of nickname possibilities.
Relatives: Teresa, Teressa, Therese, Toireasa, Teri, Terri, Terry, Tessa, Tess, Tessie, Tessy, Tracey, Tracie, Tracy, Tressa, Thera
Namesakes: Saint Theresa, Mother Teresa, Tracy Chapman, Tracey Ullman, Teri Garr

Thirza: From the Hebrew for "sweet-natured" or "cypress tree." The "h" is silent, giving this name a melodic sound.
Relatives: Thyrza, Tirza

Thisbe: From the Greek place name for "where the doves live." Rhymes with the flying disk.
Namesake: Pyramus and Thisbe

Thomas: From the Greek for "twin." Tom is terrific.

Relatives: Tomas, Tomaso, Tom, Thom, Thos, Tommy, Thompson, Thomson, Massey

Namesakes: Saint Thomas, Thomas Jefferson, Thomas Wolfe, Dylan Thomas, Tom Selleck, "Tom Thumb," Thom Gunn, Tom Cruise

Thomasa: From the Greek for "twin" and a feminine variation of Thomas. Tamsin might be the prettiest choice from this group.

Relatives: Thomasina, Thomasine, Tomasina, Tommie, Tommy, Tammy, Tamsen, Tamsin, Tamson

Namesake: "Thomasina"

Thor: Old Norse for "thunder." Thor was the Norse equivalent of Zeus—the god of war who was often depicted as tossing lightning bolts.

Relatives: Thora, Thorbert, Thordis, Thordia

Namesakes: Thor Heyerdahl, Thorstein Veblen

Thorne: Old English for "thorn tree." This baby may be nicknamed Spike, so think this one through.

Relatives: Thorn, Thorndyke, Thornton, Thornley

Thorpe: Old English for "from the village."

Namesake: Jim Thorpe

Thurlow: Old English for "from Thor."

Relatives: Thurston, Thorald, Thorbert, Thorburn, Thorley, Thurmon, Thurman, Thurmond, Thurber, Thormond, Torold, Terrell

Namesakes: Thurmon Munson, Strom Thurmond, James Thurber

Tiernan: Irish Gaelic for "lord."

Relative: Tierney

Namesake: Gene Tierney

Tiffany: From the Old French for "appearance of God." Tiffany glass and New York's famous jeweler, Tiffany and Company, are both known for their exquisite designs. The name leaped onto some top-ten lists in the United States in 1982 and 1983.

Relatives: Tifany, Tiphany, Tifanee, Tiffy, Tiffie, Fanny

Namesakes: Tiffany Chin, Louis Comfort Tiffany

Timothy: Greek for "honoring God." Timothy is also a type of prairie grass named for Timothy Hanson. Whereas Timothy would suit a girl as well as a boy, consider Timothea only for a daughter.

Relatives: Timotheus, Timoteo, Timothea, Timmy, Timmie, Tim, Timon, Timo, Timora, Thea

Namesakes: Timothy Hutton, Timothy Leary, Tim Matheson

Titania: From the Greek for "giant." An ideal choice for a sprite-child.

Relatives: Tatiana, Titian (red-gold)

Namesake: queen of the fairies in Shakespeare's *A Midsummer Night's Dream*

Titus: Greek for "of the giants." Have any plans to turn this child into an N.B.A. star?

Relatives: Tito, Titan

Namesake: "Titus Moody"

Tobias: From the Hebrew for "God is good." Tobias is a book of the Old Testament in the Douay Bible. A toby is a ceramic mug in the shape of a human head or body.

Relatives: Tobia, Tobiah, Toby, Tobit, Tobin, Tova

Namesakes: Toby Harrah, Tovah Feldshuh, Andrew Tobias, "Toby Tyler"

Todd: Middle English for "fox." This strong one-syllable name enjoyed a run of popularity in the sixties but has since retreated.

Namesakes: Todd Stottlemyer, Mary Todd Lincoln, Mike Todd

Tomkin: Old English for "little Tom." Has a sweet sound and offers a change from Thomas.

Relatives: Tompkin, Tomlin

Namesake: Lily Tomlin

Topaz: From the Latin for the yellow gemstone. An unusual jewel name that suits a bright-eyed child. It is the birthstone for November babies.

Torrance: Anglo-Irish for "from the low hills." This puts a different spin on Terence.

Relatives: Torey, Torrey, Torry, Tori, Torr

Namesake: Torrance (Calif.)

Townsend: Old English for "from the end of town." A solid name for a future real estate mogul.

Relatives: Towne, Townley, Townes

Namesake: Townsend Hoopes

Travis: Old French for "crossing." Although traditionally a boy's name, this would certainly work well for a girl.
Relatives: Travers, Trever
Namesakes: Travis Jackson, Randy Travis, "Travis Magee"

Tremayne: Old Cornish for "house by the stones." Has an Old World cachet.
Relative: Tremaine
Namesake: Johnny Tremain

Trent: From the Latin for "torrent." A potent name for a child who debuts during a rainstorm.
Namesakes: Terrance Trent D'Arby, Trent Tucker, Council of Trent

Trevor: Irish Gaelic for "cautious." This name has long been in fashion in England.
Namesakes: Trevor Howard, Trevor Nunn, Hugh Trevor-Roper

Trey: Middle English for "third born." Trey may be used as a nickname for a child who has the same name as a parent and a grandparent.
Relative: Tray
Namesake: "Old Dog Tray"

Tripp: Old English for "traveler" and common abbreviation for "the third." Like Trey, Tripp is used as a nickname for a child named for a parent and a grandparent. A good choice if the child is destined for an exclusive prep school.

Tristan: Old Welsh for "noisy one" and Latin for "laborer." The love story of Tristan and Isolde (or Iseult) is a classic literary folk tale. Tristan (sometimes appearing as Tristram) was also one of the knights of King Arthur's Round Table.
Relative: Tristram
Namesakes: Tristan de Cunha, Tristram Coffin, *Tristram Shandy*

Troy: From the French place name "Troyes," and the ancient city in Asia Minor. Troy weight refers to a system of measuring precious metals. According to Greek mythology, Troilus was killed by Achilles.
Relative: Troilus
Namesakes: Troy Donahue, Helen of Troy, *Troilus and Cressida*

Truman: Old English for "disciple."

Relatives: Truesdale, True
Namesakes: Truman Capote, Harry S Truman

Tucker: Middle English for "tailor." In Great Britain, "tuck" or "tucker" is a colloquialism for food. To eat is to "tuck it in." But you may feel too tuckered out to worry about details.
Relatives: Tuckman, Tuck
Namesakes: Tucker Frederickson, Sophie Tucker, "Friar Tuck," Tucker automobiles

Tuesday: From the Old English for "the day of the week." Of the days of the week, this is the most popular.
Namesakes: Tuesday Weld, "Ruby Tuesday"

Tully: Irish Gaelic for "a people" or "peaceful one." The derivations for Tully make this a special choice.
Namesake: Alice Tully

Turner: Middle English for "carpenter."
Namesakes: Nat Turner, Tina Turner, Lana Turner

Turpin: Old Norse for "thunder-Finn." Good for a boisterous Scandinavian.
Namesakes: Dick Turpin, Archbishop Turpin

Twain: Middle English for "two pieces." Samuel Langhorne Clemens took the pseudonym Mark Twain from Mississippi River slang. It means "two fathoms deep."
Namesake: Mark Twain

Tye: Old English for "enclosed." For trivia buffs, Buster Brown's dog was named Tighe.
Relatives: Tie, Tigh, Tighe, Tiegh, Tynan, Tai
Namesakes: Tai Babilonia, Kenneth Tynan

Tyler: Middle English for "tiler" or "roofer." It's hard to go wrong evoking a president's name: John Tyler was the tenth president of the United States.
Namesakes: Mary Tyler Moore, Tyler (Tex.)

Tyne: Old English for "river."
Relatives: Tain, Tine, Tyna
Namesake: Tyne Daly

Tyrone: From the Greek for "king." Tyr was the god of battle in Nordic mythology. As Thor's brother, he possessed a magic sword, and despite losing a hand to a treacherous wolf, he never lost a fight.
Relative: Tyron
Namesake: Tyrone Power

Tyrus: From the Latin for "person from Tyre."
Relative: Ty
Namesake: Ty Cobb

Tyson: From the Old French for "son of a German." Perhaps the boxing champ will inspire a bevy of little Tysons.
Namesake: Mike Tyson

FLORIDA TOP TWENTY
1986

Girls	*Boys*
Jessica	Michael
Ashley	Christopher
Amanda	Matthew
Jennifer	James
Brittany	Joshua
Sarah	David
Stephanie	Robert
Heather	Daniel
Nicole	John
Tiffany	Joseph
Melissa	William
Amber	Justin
Christina	Ryan
Danielle	Andrew
Lauren	Brandon
Elizabeth	Jonathan
Megan	Anthony
Samantha	Jason
Crystal	Brian
Kimberly	Steven

1980

Jennifer	Michael
Amanda	Christopher
Jessica	James
Melissa	Jason
Christina	David
Kimberly	Robert
Heather	John
Tiffany	Joseph
Michelle	William
Sarah	Joshua
Nicole	Matthew
Stephanie	Daniel
Angela	Brian
Elizabeth	Justin
Amy	Ryan
Crystal	Richard
Kelly	Jonathan
Rebecca	Eric
Lisa	Charles
April	Thomas

1970

Jennifer	Michael
Kimberly	James
Lisa	Robert
Michelle	John
Angela	David
Melissa	William
Tammy	Christopher
Mary	Richard
Tracy	Charles
Stephanie	Joseph
Elizabeth	Thomas
Amy	Mark
Patricia	Kevin
Pamela	Steven

Karen	Brian
Shannon	Timothy
Dawn	Anthony
Laura	Eric
Susan	Jason
Kelly	Jeffrey

Information provided by the State of Florida Department of Health and Rehabilitative Services.

U

Ula: Old German for "inherited estate." Edgar Allan Poe's poem "Ulalume" is the story of a lost love. The name alone is poetry.

Ulric: Old German for "wolf ruler."
Relatives: Ulrica, Ulrick, Ulrich, Udolf, Ulger, Ulfred, Ull, Ulu
Namesake: Ulu Grossbard

Ulysses: From the Greek for "anger." Ulysses is the Roman version of Odysseus, the ultimate traveler who wandered the earth looking for adventure in Homer's *Odyssey.*
Relatives: Ulises, Uillioc
Namesakes: Ulysses S. Grant, *Ulysses* (by James Joyce)

Una: From the Latin for "wholeness" or "unity." Una appears in Edmund Spenser's *The Faerie Queene* symbolizing truth. It is thought Spenser was paying homage to Queen Elizabeth with this character.
Relative: Oona
Namesake: Oona O'Neill

Undine: From the Latin for "wave." Friedrich von Fouque's *Undine* is the ill-fated romance between a water nymph and a knight. The story inspired a musical interpretation and a play (*Ondine*) by Jean Giraudoux.
Relatives: Unda, Onde, Ondine

Upton: Old English for "upper town." In ancient times, well-protected cities prospered. The "upper towns" were hilltop fortresses built to watch over the "lower towns" in the valleys.
Relative: Upshaw
Namesake: Upton Sinclair

Urania: From the Greek for "heavenly." A proper choice for parents who believe in star-gazing. John Milton evokes her name in *Paradise Lost*.
Namesake: Greek Muse of astronomy

Urban: From the Latin for "from the city."
Relatives: Urbano, Urbanus, Urbaine, Urbane, Urbana
Namesake: Urbana (Ill.)

Uriel: From the Hebrew for "flame of God" or "angel of light." Uriel was one of the seven archangels in Jewish religious texts.
Relatives: Urie, Uri
Namesake: Uri Geller

Ursula: From the Latin for "bear."
Relatives: Ursola, Ursule, Orsola, Ursa, Ursie, Orsa
Namesakes: Saint Ursula, Ursula Le Guin, Ursula Andress, constellations Ursa Major and Ursa Minor

Uta: Diminutive of Ottilie.
Namesake: Uta Hagen

Location, Location, Location

Place names are becoming increasingly popular as first names, but be wary. State names can be tricky. Tex, Florida, and Georgia may sound terribly romantic to you, but to someone else these sound like the names of short-order cooks. Cities and countries are generally less risky. India (pronounce "*Ind*-ya," please) is lovely and oh-so-British, and any kid called Salisbury is going to be taken seriously as well.

Just remember as you peruse your atlas that while some names transcend their location, others don't. Shelby, Savannah, and Dixie are best suited for those with the appropriate Southern heritage.

Alabama	Binghamton
Alberta	Bismarck
Augusta	Brittany
Austin	Calgary
Beaumont	Carolina
Berne	Casper

Charleston	Lansing
Charlotte	Lucerne
China	Odessa
Cleveland	Olympia
Cornwall	Paris
Dakota	Perth
Dallas	Phoenix
Dixie	Pierre
Edmonton	Raleigh
Erin	Regina
Eugene	Reno
Florence	Richmond
Florida	Sahara
Geneva	Salem
Georgia	Salisbury
Halifax	Savannah
Hartford	Shannon
Helena	Stratford
Houston	Tennessee
India	Tex
Indiana	Troy
Jackson	Victoria
Jersey	Virginia
Kerry	Washington
Lancaster	

And for the environmentally aware or just down-to-earth parent, here are a few more names to consider.

Bay	Ocean
Brook	Range
Channel	River
Delta	Rock
Desert	Sandy
Forrest	Savannah
Isle	Sierra
Lisle	Tundra
Monte	Woody

V

Vachel: From the French occupational name for "cow tender."
Namesake: Vachel Lindsay

Vail: From the Old French for "from the valley."
Relatives: Vayle, Vale, Valle, Val
Namesakes: Val Kilmer, Jerry Vale, Vail (Colo.)

Valentine: From the Latin for "good health." Sometimes you've got to have heart.
Relatives: Valentina, Valentin, Valentino, Valeda, Valina, Vally, Val
Namesakes: Saint Valentina, Rudolph Valentino, Karen Valentine, Valentine's Day

Valerie: From the Old French for "valor." Valerie has been used moderately in the past few decades. Give it a try.
Relatives: Valeria, Valery, Valerian, Vally, Vallie, Val
Namesakes: Saint Valerie, Valerie Perrine, Valerie Harper

Van: Dutch for "from" or "of."
Namesakes: Van Heflin, Van Johnson, Van Cliburn, Van Halen, Martin Van Buren, Vincent Van Gogh, Dick Van Dyke

Vance: Middle English for "dweller at the windmill."
Namesakes: Vance Bourjaily, Vance Law, Vivian Vance

Vanessa: From the Latin for "butterfly." Butterfly is an enchanting name in every language: mariposa (Spanish), papillon (French), schmetterling (German).
Relatives: Vannia, Vanna, Vannie, Van, Vanora, Nessa
Namesakes: Vanessa Bell, Vanessa Redgrave, Vanna White

Vania: From the Old Russian for "God's gift" and a feminine variation of Ivan.
Relative: Vanya
Namesake: Uncle Vanya

Varden: From the Old French for "from a green hill."
Relative: Vartan
Namesake: Vartan Gregorian

Vaughan: Old Welsh for "small one." You so rarely hear this, and it's so classy.
Relative: Vaughn
Namesakes: Vaughan Monroe, Vaughn Meader, Robert Vaughn, Ralph Vaughan Williams

Veda: Sanskrit for "eternal knowledge." The Vedas are the four sacred books of the Hindu religion consisting of prayers, hymns, poems, chants, and incantations.
Relative: Vedis
Namesake: Ved Mehta

Vega: Arabic for "falling star."
Namesakes: Susan Vega, Lope de Vega

Velvet: Middle English for the "fabric." Velvet is known for its softness and luster, as in Velveeta cheese.
Namesake: National Velvet

Vera: From the Latin for "truth." Vera may seem a bit old-fashioned, so try Verity.
Relatives: Verin, Verina, Verine, Verenia, Vere, Verity, Verita
Namesakes: Vera Miles, Vera Lynn

Vernon: From the Latin for "springlike." This name suggests the cool bright green of springtime.
Relatives: Verda, Verne, Verney, Verna, Verneta, Vernita, Vernis, Virna, Vernal, Laverne, Lavinia
Namesakes: Vern Stephens, Jules Verne, "Laverne and Shirley," vernal equinox, Mount Vernon

Veronica: From the Latin for "true likeness" as well as a plant. A veronica is a cloth with an impression of the face of Christ. Veronica followed Christ up to Calvary and wiped his face with her handkerchief. An image of his face was found on the cloth.
Relatives: Veronique, Vera, Ronnie, Ron, Nica, Nicky
Namesakes: Saint Veronica, Veronica Hamel, Veronica Lake

Vesper: From the Latin for "evening." Vesper is the evening star, and vespers are sung at late afternoon services. The name is like a whisper.
Relative: Vespera
Namesake: Vesper Presley (Elvis's uncle)

Victor: Latin for "winner." A blue-ribbon, gold-medal, first-place name.
Relatives: Viktor, Vitorio, Vittorio, Vick, Vic
Namesakes: Victor Borge, Victor Hugo, Vic Morrow

Victoria: Latin for "victory." Queen Victoria of Great Britain ruled from 1837 to 1901. Her name is used to describe the tastes and mores of a generation. And like Victorian antiques, this one is making a comeback.
Relatives: Viktoria, Vitoria, Victoire, Victory, Vicky, Vickie, Vicki, Vic, Toria, Torey, Torri, Tori
Namesake: Victoria Principal

Vida: From the Hebrew for "beloved."
Relatives: Vide, Vidal
Namesakes: Vida Blue, Vidal Sassoon, Gore Vidal

Vincent: From the Latin for "conqueror." A well-liked name around the world.
Relatives: Vincente, Vincenz, Vincenzo, Vicente, Vinson, Vince, Vinnie
Namesakes: Saint Vincent de Paul, Vincent Van Gogh, Vincent Price, Vince Lombardi

Violet: Old French for "violet flower." This name is sweet. It is a tiny blue-purple blossom as well as the color of Elizabeth Taylor's eyes.
Relatives: Violette, Violeta, Viola, Viole, Iolanthe, Yolanda, Yolande, Yolanthe
Namesake: "Viola" (character in Shakespeare's *Twelfth Night*)

Virgil: From the Latin for "staff bearer" or "flourishing."
Relatives: Vergil, Virgille, Virgilio, Virgie, Virge, Virgilia
Namesakes: the poet Vergil, Virgil Grissom, Virgil Stallcup

Virginia: From the Latin for "maiden." The state of Virginia is named in honor of Queen Elizabeth I, the Virgin Queen.
Relatives: Virginie, Virgie, Virgy, Gina, Ginia, Ginny, Ginni, Ginger, Jinny
Namesakes: Gina Lollobrigida, "The Virginian"

The first baby born on American soil to English parents was named Virginia Dare, in tribute to Queen Elizabeth, the Virgin Queen.

Vita: Latin for "life."
Relatives: Vitas, Veta, Vitia, Vito
Namesakes: Vita Sackville-West, Vitas Gerulaitis

Vivian: From the Latin for "living." A beautiful name that hasn't been popular in decades. Revive it.
Relatives: Vivien, Vivianne, Viviana, Vivienne, Vyvyan, Vivyen, Vivyan, Viviana, Vivie, Viv, Vibiana, Viveca
Namesakes: Saint Vivian, Vivian Vance, Vivien Leigh, Viveca Lindfors, Emilia Viviani

Vladimir: Old Slavic for "regal." This fine old name suggests caviar and iced vodka in lieu of cigars and champagne.
Relatives: Vlad, Vladislav
Namesakes: Saint Vladimir, Vladimir Horowitz, Vladimir Nabokov, Vladimir Ashkenazy

Well-Seasoned Names

Herb (and let's pronounce the "h") is an abbreviated form of Herbert. Herbs (and spices) also provide a terrific list of name possibilities. Although a few selections sound like proper names for pixies, many of the following are delightful choices for a baby.

Herbs are used medicinally and as seasonings. It was once thought they were also endowed with magical properties. If you are seriously pondering one of these names, consult an herbal (a book describing the traits of each herb). It might be fun to know the properties and history of the plant.

Allium	Curry
Angelica	Dhuma
Anise	Dill
Basil	Dittany
Bay	Estragon
Burnet	Fennel
Camomile	Ginger
Caraway	Juniper
Cardamom	Mace
Cassia	Marjoram
Cayenne	Mint
Chili	Paprika
Ciceley	Pepper
Cilantro	Poppy
Cinnamon	Rosemary
Clove	Rue
Comfrey	Saffron
Coriander	Sage

Wade: Old English for "advancer" or "river crossing." This may turn out to be the sort of child who walks on water.
Relatives: Wadley, Wadsworth
Namesakes: Wade Boggs, Virginia Wade, Henry Wadsworth Longfellow

Wakefield: Old English for "wet field."
Relatives: Wake, Wakeley, Wakeman
Namesakes: Dan Wakefield, *The Vicar of Wakefield*

Waldo: From the Old German for "ruler" and Old English for "mighty."
Relatives: Waldemar, Waldorf, Walfred
Namesakes: Ralph Waldo Emerson, Waldo Frank, Waldorf Astoria

Walker: Middle English for "cloth worker." This child is destined to write prize-winning books about the South.
Namesakes: Walker Percy, Walker Evans, Alice Walker

Wallace: Old English for "Welshman." A great choice for a girl. But be forewarned, Wally is a British colloquialism for a wimp.
Relatives: Wallis, Wallas, Wally, Wallie, Walsh, Welsh, Welch, Wallach
Namesakes: Wallace Stevens, Wallace Beery, Wallace Stegner, George Wallace, Wallis Simpson, "Wally Cleaver"

Walter: From the Old German for "powerful warrior." An impressive list of namesakes bodes well for a child named Walter.

Relatives: Walt, Wally, Walther, Watson, Watkins, Gautier, Gauthier, Ualtar

Namesakes: Sir Walter Raleigh, Sir Walter Scott, Walter Cronkite, Walter Reed, Walter "Red" Smith, Walter Winchell, Walt Disney, Barbara Walters

Walton: Old English for "dweller by the wall."
Relative: Waller
Namesakes: Bill Walton, Fats Waller, "John Boy Walton"

Wanda: From the Old German for "wanderer."
Relatives: Wenda, Wandis, Wendeline, Wendy
Namesake: Wanda Landowska

Ward: From the Old English for "to guard." A person is called a ward who is under guard or protection.
Relatives: Wardell, Warden, Wardley, Warfield, Warford, Warley, Warmond, Warton, Warwick
Namesakes: Ward Bond, Douglas Ward, Dionne Warwick, Marsha Warfield

Warner: From the Old German for "defending army."
Relative: Werner
Namesakes: Werner Ehrhardt, Werner von Braun, Sylvia Townsend Warner, John Warner, David Warner, Warner Communications

Warren: From the Old German for "watchman" and Middle English for "game keeper." A splendid choice that refuses to submit to lightweight nicknames.
Relatives: Wareine, Warin, Warrener
Namesakes: Warren G. Harding, Warren Beatty, Jennifer Warren, Robert Penn Warren, Earl Warren, Warren Burger

Washington: Old English for "from the estate of the wise one." Some might question whether our nation's capital was aptly named.
Namesakes: Washington Irving, George Washington

Watson: Old English for "son of Walter."
Relatives: Watkins, Watt
Namesakes: James Watson, Watkins Glen, "Dr. Watson"

Waverly: Old English for "from the tree-lined meadow." Sir Walter Scott wrote some thirty books under a pseudonym, and the first of these was the novel *Waverly*.
Namesakes: Viscount John Waverly, Waverly Place (N.Y.)

Wayland: Old English for "from the path land."
Relatives: Waylon, Way
Namesakes: Waylon Jennings, Way Bandy

Wayne: Old English for "wagon maker." Wayne too plain? Try Wainwright.
Relatives: Wagner, Waggoner, Wain, Wainwright
Namesakes: Wayne Gretzky, John Wayne, Jonathan Wainwright

Webster: Old English for "weaver." An expedient selection for a future philologist.
Relatives: Weber, Webley, Webb
Namesakes: Noah Webster, Daniel Webster, W. E. B. Du Bois

Wells: Old English for "from the springs." These rather formal-sounding names hint at a family estate in the country.
Relatives: Welles, Weller, Welborne, Welby, Weldon, Welford, Welton
Namesakes: H. G. Wells, Orson Welles, Wells Fargo, Wells College

Wendell: Old German for "wanderer." You can have Wendell on her birth certificate but call her Wendy.
Namesake: Wendell Willkie

Wendy: Old English for "fair" and a pet form of Gwendolyn. Peter Pan's girlfriend.
Relatives: Wendie, Wendee, Gwendolyn
Namesake: Wendy Wasserstein

West: From the Old English. This name demands a navy-blue blazer and an old school tie.
Relatives: Weston, Westbrook, Westby, Westcott, Weston, Wes, Wesley, Westleigh
Namesakes: Adam West, Morris West, Anthony West, Edward Weston, John Wesley, Westbrook Pegler

Wetherby: Old English for "ram's meadow." A well-grounded name for a little Aries.
Relatives: Wetherell, Wetherly

Wheaton: Old English for "wheat town." Before you fall in love with this name, keep in mind there is a breed of dog called the Wheaton terrier.
Relatives: Wheatley, Wharton
Namesakes: Edith Wharton, Phillis Wheatley, Wheaton College

Whit: Old English for "white." Whitney is the most popular of the Whit names and works equally well for a boy or girl.
Relatives: White, Whitey, Whitcomb, Whitby, Whitelaw, Whitfield, Whitford, Whitley, Whitlock, Whitman, Whitmore, Whitney, Whittaker
Namesakes: Whitey Ford, Whitney Houston, Whittaker Chambers, E. B. White, James Whitcomb Riley, Walt Whitman, James Whitmore, Eli Whitney

Whoopi: Popular exclamation for "I'm having a good time now."
Relatives: Yahoo, Yippee, Wahoo
Namesake: Whoopi Goldberg

Wilhelmina: Old German for "fierce protector." This powerful name is also a feminine variation of William. The nickname Billie takes the starch out of this one.
Relatives: Willamina, Wilhemine, Wihelma, Willette, Wilmette, Wyla, Willa, Wilma, Willie, Willy, Will, Mina, Minnie, Minny, Billie, Billy, Helma, Vilma, Guillelmine, Guillemette, Vilhelmina
Namesakes: Queen Wilhelmina of the Netherlands, Willa Cather, Wilma Rudolph, Billie Jean King, Billie Holliday, "Wilma Flintstone"

William: Old German for "valiant protector." Although a popular name for centuries, Prince Charles and Princess Diana may have rekindled interest in this classic by choosing it for their firstborn son.
Relatives: Willem, Wilhelm, Wilson, Williams, Williamson, Will, Wills, Willie, Willy, Wiley, Wyley, Wilkie, Willkie, Wilkes, Wylkes, Willis, Wilton, Wilmer, Wilmar, Winton, Willard, Wilbur, Wilford, Wilfred, Wilfrid, Guillaume, Guillermo, Vilhelm, Vilem, Viliam, Vasili, Vasily, Uilleam, Uilliam

Namesakes: William the Conqueror, William Hurt, William Carlos Williams, Willie Mays, Will Rogers, Wilfrid Sheed, Wilfred Owen, Wilbur Wright, Willard Scott, Wilt Chamberlain, Willie Nelson

Wilson: Old English for "son of William." This is Ronald Reagan's middle name.
Namesakes: Wilson Pickett, Woodrow Wilson, Lanford Wilson

Winifred: From the Old German for "peaceful friend."
Relatives: Winnie, Winny, Winni, Win, Winn, Wyn, Fred, Freddie, Freddy
Namesakes: Winnie Mandela, "Winnie the Pooh"

Winona: Sioux Indian for "firstborn daughter."
Relatives: Winonah, Wenona
Namesakes: Hiawatha's mother, Winona Ryder, Winona (Minn.)

Winslow: Old English for "from the friend's hill."
Relatives: Winchell, Windsor, Winfield, Winfred, Wingate, Winthrop, Winton, Wynton, Winward, Winfrey
Namesakes: Winslow Homer, Wynton Marsalis, Walter Winchell, Dave Winfield, John Winthrop

Winston: Old English for "from the friend's estate." England's grand old prime minister inspired many little Winstons after World War II.
Relatives: Wynston, Winnie, Win
Namesakes: Winston Churchill, Winston-Salem (N.C.)

Winter: From the Old English for the season. An off-the-beaten-track name for a girl or boy.
Relatives: Wynter, Winters, Win
Namesakes: Jonathan Winters, Dana Winters

Witt: Old English for "wise." For the baby with a sly sense of humor.
Relatives: Witter, Witton, Witley, Wit
Namesake: Katarina Witt

Wolfgang: Old German for "advancing wolf." This perennial favorite in Germany has never established itself elsewhere.
Relatives: Wolf, Wolfe, Wolfie, Wolcott, Woolsey
Namesakes: Wolfgang Amadeus Mozart, Wolfman Jack, Alexander Woolcott, Cardinal Thomas Wolsey, Tom Wolfe

Woodrow: Old English for "forester."
Relatives: Woodruff, Woodward, Woodie, Woody
Namesakes: Woodrow Wilson, Woody Guthrie, Woody Allen, Woodie Harrelson, Bob Woodward

Wren: Old Welsh for "chief." Aside from being a small songbird, this is an acronym for the Women's Royal Naval Service.
Namesake: Christopher Wren

Wright: Old English for "craftsman." Impossible to go wrong with this name.
Namesakes: Steven Wright, Frank Lloyd Wright, Richard Wright, the Wright brothers

Wyatt: From the Old French for "little warrior" and Old English for "water." Goldie Hawn and Kurt Russell chose this name for their son.
Relative: Wyeth
Namesakes: Wyatt Earp, Andrew Wyeth

Wylie: Old English for "enchanting."
Relative: Wiley
Namesakes: Wiley Post, Philip Wylie, "Wile E. Coyote"

Wyndam: Old English for "the field with the winding path."
Relatives: Windham, Wyn
Namesake: Windam Hill

Wynn: Old Welsh for "fair." A subtle lifelong message from competitive parents.
Relatives: Wynne, Wyn, Wynnie, Winnie, Winny, Win, Winn
Namesake: Keenan Wynn

Wystan: Anglo-Saxon for "battle stone" and a variation of Winston.
Namesake: W(ystan) H(ugh) Auden

POPULAR MEXICAN-AMERICAN
BAPTISMAL NAMES

Girls	*Boys*
Guadalupe	Guadalupe
Margarita	Jesus

Maria	Jose
Mary	Juan
Gloria	Luis
Juanita	Manuel
Marta (or Martha)	David
Francisca	Francisco
Juana	Martin
Linda	Miguel

Xavier: Spanish place name, Basque for "new house," and Arabic for "splendid." Xavier is responsible for all those middle initials in Catholic schools. Xaviera, the feminine form, is quite melodic.
Relatives: Xaviera, Xaver, Xever, Javier, Giaffar, Jaffar
Namesakes: Saint Francis de Xavier, Xavier Cugat, Xaviera Hollander

Xenia: Greek for "hospitality."
Namesake: Xenia (Ohio)

Xerxes: Persian for "prince." Xerxes I was the king of Persia (519–465 B.C.) who went to war with the Greeks after creating a bridge of boats across the Hellespont.

Weather Report

With a few exceptions, these meteorological phenomena make better nicknames than proper ones. A parent may be inspired by the weather conditions on the day the baby is born or by the child's disposition. But remember, a child's name must last a lifetime. Think twice before sticking your baby with a name that sounds as though it jumped off the pages of a romance novel, a racing form, or a Dairy Queen menu.

Aurora	Dewey
Blizzard	Dusty
Breeze	Frosty
Dawn	Gale

Gusty	Sparky
Hail	Storm
Ice	Stormy
Misty	Sunny
Rain	Tempest
Rainbow	Thunder
Snow	Wind

Here are some real-life examples:

Dewi Sukarno	Edgar Snow
Dustin Hoffman	Sparky Lyle
"Frosty the Snowman"	Storm Field
Gale Storm	Sunny von Bulow
Muddy Waters	Tempestt Bledsoe
Raine McCorquodale	"The Velvet Fog" (Mel Torme)

Y

Yale: Old English for "corner of land." This ivy-covered name wins the Preppie Award hands down.
Relative: Yael
Namesakes: Yale Lary, Elihu Yale, Yale locks

Yancy: American Indian interpretation of "Yankee."
Namesake: "Yancy Derringer"

Yardley: English for "of the yard." A sentimental choice for anyone who wore white frosted lipsticks and ice-blue eye shadow, compliments of Yardley cosmetics.
Namesake: George Yardley

Yates: Middle English for "gate keeper." Has a clean, crisp sound.
Relative: Yeats
Namesake: William Butler Yeats

Yedda: Old English for "singing."
Relative: Yetta

Yehudi: From the Hebrew for "praise God."
Relative: Yehuda
Namesake: Yehudi Menuhin

Yolanda: Greek for "violet."
Relatives: Yolande, Iolanthe, Iolande, Eolande

York: Old English for "yew tree" and a place name.
Relative: Yorick

Namesakes: Duke and Duchess of York, Michael York, "poor Yorick," *Sergeant York*, New York

Yul: Mongolian for "from the far horizon." The baby may be bald now, but it won't last forever.
  Namesake: Yul Brynner

Yves: A French variation of Ives. Far more popular in France than in the United States.
  Relatives: Yvette, Yvo, Yvon, Yvonne, Ives
  Namesakes: Saint Yves, Yves Montand, Yves Saint Laurent, Yvette Mimieux, Yvonne De Carlo, Yvonne Goolagong

Naming Your Baby After an Institution of Higher Learning

Colleges, universities, and prep schools offer some choice names. Some may be a bit self-consciously preppie for your taste, but in general they have a high recognition factor and a certain amount of built-in prestige. Do avoid the community colleges and any schools with too many initials. RPI, for example, while a fine school, would not be an appropriate name for your child. And remember that just because your child carries the name Yale, it is no guarantee that he or she will be admitted to that college eighteen years from now.

Amherst	Clark
Andover	Clarkson
Auburn	Clemson
Babson	Colby
Barnard	Colgate
Bates	Cornell
Baylor	Creighton
Bowdoin	Dartmouth
Bradley	Davidson
Brown	Dickinson
Carleton	Drew
Chaffee	Duke

Emory
Harvard
Hobart
Holyoke
Hotchkiss
Howard
Kenyon
Loomis
Mary Baldwin
Radcliffe
Randolph Macon
Reed
Regis
Rollins
Sarah Lawrence
Simmons

Skidmore
Smith
Spelman
Stanford
Virginia
Washington
Wayne
Wellesley
Wells
Wesleyan
Wheaton
William (and Mary)
William Smith
Xavier
Yale

Z

In 1943, an Argentine criminal court fined a couple for naming their children Jupiter and Zoroaster. The children were ordered renamed.

Zachary: From the Hebrew for "God remembers" or "renowned is God." Zachary is a newcomer to the top-fifty most popular boys' names in the United States, first becoming noticeable in the eighties.
Relatives: Zacharias, Zakary, Zacarius, Zaccheus, Zaccaria, Zachariah, Zechariah, Zackry, Zach, Zack, Zak
Namesakes: Saint Zachary, Zachary Taylor

Zane: A variation of John. Buy this baby cowboy boots and a typewriter.
Namesake: Zane Grey

Zara: Hebrew for "dawn" and Arabic for "princess." An unusual shift from the more standard Sara. Princess Anne and Mark Phillips chose this name for their daughter.
Relatives: Zarah, Zarry, Zari, Zerlinda

Zebulon: From the Hebrew for "home." This may sound like an Italian dessert, but it has a pleasant derivation.
Namesake: Zebulon Weaver

Zelda: An abbreviated version of Griselda. For baby boomers, Zelda will forever be associated with "Dobie Gillis."
Namesake: Zelda Fitzgerald

Zenobia: From the Greek for "of Zeus." Zenobia was the queen of Palmyra in the third century and was the epitome of ambitious zeal.
Relatives: Zenobie, Zena, Zenna, Zenina

Zephyr: From the Greek for "wind." According to ancient mythology, Zephyr was the god of the west wind. This is really quite pretty.
Namesake: "Zephyr" (monkey in the Babar books)

Zera: From the Hebrew for "seeds."
Relative: Zero
Namesake: Zero Mostel

Zev: From the Hebrew for "deer." Since Zachary has become so popular, why not consider the lesser-known "Z's" such as Zev?
Relatives: Zvi, Zevie, Zivia, Ziva, Zeva

Zinnia: A flower named in honor of J. G. Zinn.
Relatives: Zinia, Zin, Zina
Namesake: Zina Garrison

Zippora: From the Hebrew for "trumpet" or "sparrow."
Relatives: Zipporah, Sippora, Sipporah
Namesakes: the wife of Moses, Zippo lighters

Zoë: From the Greek for "life." A gem of a name with a meaningful derivation.
Namesakes: Zoë Wanamaker, Zoe Caldwell

Zora: Slavic for "golden dawn."
Relatives: Zorah, Zohra, Zarya, Zoranna, Zorina, Zori, Zorie, Zorry, Zorro
Namesakes: Zora Neale Hurston, "Zorro"

Zuleika: From the Arabic for "fair-haired." In Max Beerbohm's novel, *Zuleika Dobson*, the heroine destroys young men with her beauty.
Namesakes: wife of Potiphar, Byronic heroine in "The Bride of Abydos"

Zuriel: Hebrew for "God is my rock." An interesting spin on Muriel.

Middle-Age Nomenclature for New-Age Babies

As with any fashion, trends in naming babies run in cycles. The 1960s and 1970s mirrored the times that were a-changing. Barbara, Susan, and Mary were shunned in favor of Starlight, Sunshine, and Moonbeam. However, in recent years, "old-fashioned" choices have become fashionable. Rose-water and lace-hanky names such as Molly, Sophia, and Emma are once again stylish. But if you are looking for true antiquity—a name with a legacy centuries old—try one that was in vogue during the Middle Ages.

	Girls	*Boys*
Old English	Alditha	Ailsi
	Edild	Coleman
	Ediva	Edstan
	Godiva	Harding
	Golyva	Ingulf
	Livilda	Osmund
	Milda	Theodric
	Wakerilda	Wymond
Norman	Amice	Amery
	Constance	Bevis
	Emmeline	Drew
	Jocelyn	Gilbert
	Laura	Hugh
	Majorie	Joel
	Oriel	Rayner
	Rose	Warren
Christian	Anne	Augustine
	Barbara	Benedict
	Chloë	Crispin
	Dorcas	Gregory
	Ellen	Marcus
	Gillian	Philip

Juliet	Sebastian
Katharine	Simon
Lydia	Timothy
Priscilla	Vincent
Tabitha	Zebedee

Star-Gazing

Okay, we may not really *believe* in astrology, but we cannot resist reading our daily forecast in the newspaper. True believers say that astrology offers a window into your child's future, and questions of compatibility, talents, and characteristics may be addressed.

Whether or not you follow your chart, each sign offers ideas for names for your baby.

Aries (March 21–April 19) the Ram
Taurus (April 20–May 20) the Bull
Gemini (May 21–June 21) the Twins
Cancer (June 22–July 22) the Crab
Leo (July 23–August 22) the Lion
Virgo (August 23–September 22) the Virgin
Libra (September 23–October 23) the Scales
Scorpio (October 24–November 21) the Scorpion
Sagittarius (November 22–December 21) the Archer
Capricorn (December 22–January 19) the Goat
Aquarius (January 20–February 18) the Water-bearer
Pisces (February 19–March 20) the Fish

Chinese Astrology

Chinese astrology has been practiced and highly regarded in that country since ancient times. Believers say that humans are just temporary custodians of the planet and that they should follow astral advice as interpreted by the sages or chaos would reign. The Chinese zodiac, which is based on a twelve-year cycle, is approximately one thousand years old and a relatively modern concept. The ancient astrologers based this cycle on what they called "the Great Year"—the twelve years it took Jupiter to complete an orbit of the sky. In order to make the study more accessible to laymen, they assigned an animal to each year or "house."

The twelve animals are: Dragon, Snake, Horse, Sheep, Monkey, Rooster, Dog, Pig, Rat, Ox, Tiger, and Hare. Each animal represents a year in the cycle as well as a person's individual characteristics. But don't be put off if, for example, your baby is born in the year of the Rat. The Chinese interpretation of the Rat is that he is a master of ingenuity.

The astrologers fine-tune a person's chart according to the month and time of birth and are able to predict personality, compatibility with others, and, to a certain extent, fate and fortune.

> The Dragon is extroverted, imaginative, and decisive—February 17, 1988–February 5, 1989
>
> The Snake is cultured, subtle, and crafty—February 6, 1989–January 26, 1990
>
> The Horse is sporty, conversational, and eager—January 27, 1990–February 14, 1991
>
> The Sheep is selfless, affectionate, and artistic—February 15, 1991–February 3, 1992
>
> The Monkey is quick-witted, curious, and mischievous—February 4, 1992–January 22, 1993
>
> The Rooster is determined, aggressive, and bold—January 23, 1993–February 9, 1994
>
> The Dog is honest, faithful, and entertaining—February 10, 1994–January 30, 1995
>
> The Pig is industrious, home-loving, and goal-oriented—January 31, 1995–February 18, 1996
>
> The Rat is charming, creative, and adaptable—February 19, 1996–February 6, 1997
>
> The Ox is practical, reliable, and loyal—February 7, 1997–January 27, 1998
>
> The Tiger is competitive, authoritative, and sincere—January 28, 1998–February 15, 1999
>
> The Hare is sociable, truthful, and perceptive—February 16, 1999–February 4, 2000

In Closing

If, after reviewing the entries in this book, you *still* haven't found the perfect name for your baby, don't despair. There are other sources you can consult. We recommend:

works of literature
movie and television credits
the Bible
song charts
racing forms
fables and legends from different countries
color charts
social registers
Who's Who
foreign dictionaries and phone books
atlases and road maps of places with special significance
calendars (for days of the week, months, and holidays)
wedding and birth announcements in your local newspapers

INDEX

Abba; see Abbott
Abbe; see Abbott
Abram; see Abraham
Adalee; see Ada
Adalia; see Ada, Adelaide
Adara; see Ada
Adelbert; see Albert
Adele; see Adelaide, Ethel
Adeline; see Adelaide
Adolphus; see Adolph
Adrea; see Adrian
Adren; see Aldrich
Adriana; see Adrian
Adrie; see Adrian
Agace; see Agatha
Agenta; see Agnes
Agnesa; see Agnes
Ahmad; see Muhammad
Ahmet; see Muhammad
Aineilis; see Stanislaus
Ainsworth; see Ainsley
Akim; see Joachim
Alaine; see Elaine
Alana; see Elaine, Alan
Alanna; see Ilana
Alban; see Auburn
Albin; see Alban
Albion; see Alban
Albrecht; see Albert
Alby; see Albert
Aldo; see Aldous
Aldred; see Aldrich

Aldridge; see Aldrich
Aldwin; see Alden
Alejo; see Alexander
Aleksey; see Alexandra
Alethea; see Althea
Alette; see Alida
Alexine; see Alexandra
Alexis; see Alexandra,
    Alice
Aliki; see Alexandra, Alice
Aline; see Adelaide
Alise; see Elise
Alison; see Alice
Alix; see Alice
Allie; see Alice, Althea
Alonzo; see Alphonse
Aloysia; see Louise
Alwyn; see Alvin
Alya; see Alexandra
Amabel; see Mabel
Amadis; see Amadeus
Amado; see Amadeus
Ambrosia; see Ambrose
Amia; see Amy
Amity; see Amy
Anca; see Anne
Ancel; see Lance
Ancelot; see Ancel
Anika; see Anne
Anselm; see Ancel
Aria; see Ariadne
Arianne; see Ariadne

Ario; see Ariel
Arkady; see Archibald
Arlen; see Arland
Arles; see Arland
Arliss; see Arland
Arlo; see Arland
Armand; see Herman
Arnaud; see Arnold
Arnell; see Arnold
Artie; see Artemis
Aubert; see Albert
Aubin; see Auburn
Aurora; see Aurelia
Ava; see Eve, April
Aveline; see Evelyn
Avery; see Athol
Avital; see Aviva
Avraham; see Abraham
Avram; see Abraham
Avril; see April
Avrom; see Abraham
Axtel; see Axel

Babette; see Barbara
Bard; see Baird
Barney; see Barnabas,
    Bernard
Barret; see Barnett
Bart; see Hobart,
    Bartholomew
Barton; see Bartholomew

Basia; see Bathsheba
Bastien; see Sebastian
Bat; see Bartholomew
Baylor; see Bayard
Becca; see Rebecca
Becky; see Rebecca
Belinda; see Linda
Belle; see Anabelle
Ben; see Reuben
Berenice; see Bernice
Berkley; see Barclay
Bert; see Robert
Berta; see Roberta
Berthe; see Roberta
Bertolt; see Bertram
Betsy; see Elizabeth
Bijou; see Beryl
Billy; see Wilhelmina
Bjorn; see Bernard
Blancha; see Bianca
Blanchard; see Blake
Blanche; see Bianca
Blanco; see Blake
Bliss; see Blase
Bobbie; see Barbara
Bobby; see Robert
Bonita; see Bonnie
Bosworth; see Boswell
Bourne; see Burne
Bowie; see Bowen
Bradford; see Bradley
Bram; see Abraham
Brant; see Brandon
Braxton; see Brock
Brenden; see Brandon
Brie; see Bridget
Brigada; see Bridget
Brit; see Bridget
Broderick; see Roderick
Bruin; see Brown
Bruno; see Brown
Bryant; see Brian
Buckminster; see Buckley
Bunny; see Bernice
Burton; see Burt
Byram; see Byron

Caddie; see Acadia
Cadie; see Acadia
Cadmus; see Caldwell
Caine; see Kane
Cal; see Caleb
Cale; see Caleb
Calla; see Callis
Callie; see Calandra
Calvinnia; see Calvin
Camelia; see Camille
Camp; see Campbell
Candy; see Candace
Cane; see Kane
Canute; see Knut
Caren; see Karen
Carlisle; see Carl
Carlotta; see Charlotte,
   Carl
Carmel; see Carmen
Carmelita; see Carmen
Carolyn; see Caroline
Carra; see Kieran
Carrie; see Karen
Casmir; see Kasmira
Casper; see Jasper
Cathleen; see Catherine
Cecil; see Cecilia
Cecily; see Cecilia
Celene; see Selena
Celia; see Selena
Channa; see Hannah
Charmaine; see Charlotte
Charo; see Rose
Charon; see Sharon
Chauncy; see Chancellor
Chelle; see Rachel
Cher; see Cheryl
Cherie; see Sherry
Chet; see Chester
Chevalier; see Chevy
Chip; see Charles
Chriselda; see Griselda
Ciaran; see Kieran
Cicely; see Cecilia
Ciel; see Schuyler
Cilla; see Priscilla

Cindy; see Cynthia
Cinta; see Cynthia
Cissy; see Cecilia
Clarendon; see Clarence
Clarissa; see Claire
Clayton; see Claiborne,
   Clay
Cleavon; see Cleveland
Cleopatra; see Clio
Clive; see Cleveland
Cloris; see Chloë
Clovis; see Louis
Cnut; see Knut
Cobb; see Jacob
Colby; see Cole
Cole; see Nicholas
Coleman; see Cole
Colin; see Nicholas
Collette; see Nicole
Corbett; see Corbin
Coretta; see Cora
Cornelius; see Cornelia
Cort; see Conrad
Corwin; see Corbin
Cosette; see Nicole
Court; see Courtland
Crispus; see Crispin
Cuin; see Quinn
Curren; see Currier
Cybill; see Sibyl
Cyna; see Kyna

Dabney; see David
Dagmar; see Dag
Dailey; see Dag
Dallin; see Dale
Dalton; see Dale
Damon; see Damien
Dane; see Dakin
Danice; see Danielle
Dara; see Darren
Dare; see Darrell
Darian; see Darius
Darleen; see Darrell
D'Artagnan; see Arthur

Dawson; see David
Dayton; see Dag
Deena; see Dinah
Della; see Adelaide
Demi; see Demelza
Denny; see Ogden
Denzel; see Dennis
Dermot; see Jeremy
Desmond; see Esmond
Desty; see Modesty
Devorah; see Deborah
Dewi; see Dewey, David
Dick; see Richard
Dicken; see Dickinson
Dimitri; see Demetrius
Dion; see Dennis
Dionne; see Diana
Dixon; see Dixie
Dob; see Robert
Dolly; see Dorothy
Dolph; see Rudolph
Donnel; see Donnelly
Donner; see Donnelly
Dora; see Isidore, Pandora,
   Dolores, Eudora,
   Theodora
Dot; see Dorothy
Drew; see Andrew
Duke; see Marmaduke
Durante; see Durand

Eamon; see Amon
Ebenezer; see Eben
Eberhardt; see Everett
Eda; see Ada
Edda; see Edith
Edie; see Eden, Edith
Egedio; see Giles
Elaine; see Helen
Elbert; see Albert
Elder; see Alder
Eleanor; see Helen
Elfred; see Alfred
Elga; see Olga
Elgar; see Alger

Eliana; see Eleanor
Elijah; see Elias
Elisha; see Ellis
Ellie; see Eleanor
Ellison; see Elias
Elmo; see Elmer
Eloise; see Louise
Emaline; see Emily
Emelia; see Amelia
Emery; see Amory
Emilio; see Emily
Enola; see Magnolia
Enrica; see Henrietta
Enrique; see Henry
Eolande; see Yolanda
Erlene; see Earl
Erma; see Irma
Ermanno; see Herman
Errol; see Earl
Escott; see Scott
Esteban; see Stephen
Etan; see Ethan
Etta; see Harriet, Ada
Evan; see Ivan, Owen
Evander; see Eve
Evelyn; see Eileen
Everill; see Averill
Evette; see Evelyn
Evita; see Eve

Fairfield; see Fairfax
Falana; see Philana
Fannie; see Stephanie
Fanny; see Persephone,
   Tiffany
Faron; see Farrar
Felice; see Felicia
Felipe; see Philip
Feodora; see Theodora
Fernando; see Ferdinand
Ferrell; see Ferris
Fidel; see Faith
Fifi; see Josephine
Filbert; see Philip
Filida; see Phyllis

Filip; see Philip
Finley; see Finnian
Finn; see Phineas
Fitzgerald; see Fitz
Fitzpatrick; see Fitz
Florida; see Florence
Flower; see Florence
Floyd; see Lloyd
Fred; see Manfred, Alfred,
   Winifred
Fyodor; see Theodore

Gail; see Abigail
Galina; see Helen
Garret; see Gareth
Garth; see Gareth
Garvey; see Gary
Gary; see Gareth, Taggart
Gaspar; see Jasper
Gautier; see Walter
Gavrila; see Gabriel
Gemma; see Jemima
Gene; see Eugene
Genny; see Genevieve
Geoffrey; see Jeffrey
Georgette; see Georgia
Georgina; see Georgia
Geraldo; see Gerald
Gerome; see Jerome
Gerrit; see Gerald
Gervase; see Gary
Gibson; see Gilbert
Gil; see Ogilvy
Gillette; see Gilbert
Gillian; see Julia, Giles
Gilroy; see Gilford
Gina; see Georgia,
   Regina, Virginia
Giordano; see Jordan
Giorgia; see Georgia
Giorgio; see George
Giovanna; see Jane
Gipper; see Gilbert
Giulo; see Julian
Giuseppe; see Joseph

Gleda; see Gladys
Glenda; see Glen
Glory; see Gloria
Goddard; see Godfrey
Godfrey; see Jeffrey
Gorham; see Gordon
Gorton; see Gordon
Graham; see Ingram
Graydon; see Gray
Graza; see Grace
Greta; see Margaret
Gretchen; see Margaret
Griffith; see Griffin
Griswold; see Gray
Guillaume; see William
Guillelmine; see
  Wilhelmina
Guillermo; see William
Guiseppina; see Josephine
Gunter; see Gunnar
Gus; see August
Gwendoline; see Guinevere
Gypsy; see Gitana

Hadrian; see Adrian
Hal; see Harold
Hamid; see Muhammad
Hamilton; see Hamlet
Hamish; see James
Hammond; see Hamlet
Hampton; see Hamlet
Hans; see John
Hanson; see John, Anson
Happy; see Harriet
Harford; see Harlan
Harley; see Harlan
Harpo; see Harper
Harrison; see Harry
Harry; see Henry
Haslett; see Hazel
Hatty; see Harriet
Haverel; see Averill
Havis; see Haven
Hawkins; see Henry
Haywood; see Hayes

Heathcliff; see Heather
Hedda; see Hedwig
Helma; see Wilhelmina
Hersh; see Hershel
Herve; see Harvey
Hester; see Esther
Heywood; see Hayes
Hi; see Hiram
Hiraldo; see Harold
Hogan; see Haven
Holbrook; see Holden
Holm; see Hume
Hubbell; see Hubert

Iago; see Jacob
Ian; see John
Ibrahim; see Abraham
Igor; see Ingrid
Ilario; see Hilary
Ilene; see Eileen
Immanuel; see Emanuel
Ines; see Agnes
Inez; see Agnes
Iolanthe; see Violet,
  Yolanda
Irvin; see Ervin
Irving; see Ervin
Isoep; see Joseph
Ita; see Ida
Ivan; see John
Ives; see Yves
Ixsander; see Alexander

Jackson; see Jacob, John
Jaffar; see Xavier
Jamal; see Gamal
Janet; see Jane
Javier; see Xavier
Jeanne; see Jane
Jelena; see Helen
Jenner; see John
Jera; see Gertrude
Jeremiah; see Jeremy
Jermaine; see Germain

Jerry; see Gerald
Jinny; see Virginia
Joan; see Jane
Joaquin; see Joachim
Jolene; see Jolie
Jolson; see Joel
Jonah; see Jonas
Jorge; see George
Jose; see Joseph
Josiah; see Joseph, Joshua
Joyce; see Joy
Justine; see Jocelyn, Justin

Kamille; see Camille
Kara; see Karen, Cara
Karla; see Carl
Karmen; see Carmen
Kate; see Catherine
Kathryn; see Catherine
Katrina; see Catherine
Keisha; see Kezia
Kellen; see Kelly
Kelsey; see Chelsea
Kenyon; see Kent
Kerry; see Carey
Kiefer; see Keefe
Kingston; see King
Kinnard; see Kipp
Kirby; see Kerr
Kirsten; see Christina
Kirwin; see Kieran
Kitty; see Catherine
Konrad; see Conrad
Kordelia; see Cordelia
Krispen; see Crispin
Kristen; see Christina
Kristian; see Christian
Kristofer; see Christopher
Krystal; see Crystal
Kyla; see Kelilah
Kyril; see Cyril

Laine; see Elaine
Lakeisha; see Kezia

Lambert; see Lamar
Lamont; see Lamar
Lando; see Orlando
Laney; see Elaine
Laris; see Lara
Latoya; see Lakeisha
Laughton; see Lawrence
Lauren; see Laura
Laverne; see Vernon
Lavinia; see Vernon
Lawanna; see Lakeisha
Lawford; see Lawrence
Lawton; see Lawrence
Layton; see Leland
Leigh; see Raleigh
Leighton; see Leland
Lena; see Helen
Lene; see Madeline
Lenora; see Helen
Leon; see Napoleon
Leonore; see Lena, Eleanor
Leontyne; see Leola
Lida; see Alida
Lila; see Delilah
Linda; see Belinda
Lindy; see Melinda,
    Lindsay
Linford; see Lind
Link; see Lincoln
Linton; see Lind
Lisa; see Melissa
Lise; see Elise
Livia; see Olive
Lodovico; see Louis
Lois; see Louise
Lola; see Laura
Lorcan; see Lawrence
Loretta; see Laura,
    Lorraine
Lorna; see Laura, Lorraine
Lorne; see Lawrence
Lottie; see Charlotte
Luana; see Louise
Luce; see Lucy
Lucian; see Luke
Ludvig; see Louis

Lyndon; see Lind
Lynn; see Marilyn

Mabley; see Mab
MacKay, see Kay
Mackey; see Mac
Macomb; see Macon
Madge; see Margaret
Madonna; see Donna
Mae; see May
Magdalene; see Madeline
Malin; see Mallory
Mamie; see Mary
Manchester; see Manley
Mandy; see Miranda,
    Amanda
Manny; see Emanuel
Mansfield; see Manley
Manuel; see Emanuel
Marcello; see Marcel
Marclyn; see Marcella
Marcy; see Marcella,
    Marcia
Mariette; see Mariel
Marilo; see Marcus
Marleen; see Madeline
Marley; see Marsden
Marlin; see Merlin
Marnette; see Marna
Marquita; see Marcia
Marta; see Margaret
Marva; see Marvelle
Mary-Ann; see Marian
Massey; see Thomas
Matty; see Madeline,
    Martha, Mathilda
Maude; see Mathilda,
    Maud
Mavis; see Mab
Maxfield; see Maximilian
Maxwell; see Maximilian
Maya; see May
McGregor; see Gregory
Meg; see Margaret
Menachem; see Mendel

Mercy; see Mercedes
Merlina; see Merle
Merriwell; see Merit
Midge; see Michelle
Millicent; see Melissa
Mimi; see Jemima, Naomi
Mina; see Wilhelmina
Minda; see Melinda,
    Minna
Mindy; see Melinda
Minnie; see Minerva,
    Wilhelmina
Mitzi; see Mary
Mona; see Ramona
Monique; see Monica
Monte; see Montague,
    Montgomery
Morrison; see Maurice
Mort; see Mordecai
Mosheh; see Moselle
Moss; see Maurice
Murray; see Maurice
Musa; see Mussetta

Nadia; see Nadine
Naldo; see Ronald
Nana; see Nancy
Nanette; see Nancy
Nap; see Napoleon
Natal; see Noel
Natasha; see Natalie,
    Anastasia
Nate; see Jonathan
Nathan; see Jonathan
Ned; see Edward
Nelda; see Nellie
Nelina; see Nellie
Nell; see Eleanor
Nelly; see Helen
Nels; see Neal
Nerida; see Neda
Nessa; see Agnes, Vanessa
Newland; see Neville
Newton; see Newell
Neza; see Agnes

Nica; see Veronica
Nick; see Dominick
Nina; see Penina
Ninette; see Nina
Nixon; see Nicholas
Noel; see Natalie
Nola; see Magnolia, Olive
Nollie; see Olive
Nolly; see Oliver
Nora; see Honor
Norna; see Nordica
Norville; see Norman
Norvin; see North

Odelinda; see Odelia
Odin; see Odell
Olena; see Olga
Olin; see Olaf
Ondine; see Undine
Oona; see Una
Orlando; see Roland
Orrin; see Oran
Orsola; see Ursula
Osgood; see Oscar
Osmond; see Osbert
Osric; see Osbert
Othello; see Otis
Otto; see Otis
Oxton; see Oxford

Paddy; see Patrick
Palita; see Paloma
Paolo; see Paul
Parkinson; see Peter
Parkley; see Parker
Parnell; see Peter
Paterson; see Patrick
Patsy; see Patricia
Patton; see Payton
Patty; see Patricia
Pauline; see Paula
Pavel; see Paul
Pavlina; see Paula
Pearson; see Pierce

Pedro; see Peter
Pegeen; see Pearl
Peggy; see Margaret
Pelton; see Pell
Pepe; see Joseph
Pepita; see Josephine
Percy; see Persephone
Perdea; see Perdita
Perianne; see Perry
Perkin; see Peter
Perrin; see Perry, Peter
Perrine; see Petra
Perry; see Henry
Petula; see Petra
Phelia; see Ophelia
Philadelphia; see Philana
Philicia; see Felicia
Philida; see Philana
Phipps; see Philip
Phylicia; see Felicia
Pierre; see Peter
Pincus; see Phineas
Pollyanna; see Polly
Power; see Powell
Prescott; see Preston
Priest; see Preston
Prissy; see Priscilla
Pruit; see Prewitt

Rad; see Radclif
Radnor; see Radclif
Rahel; see Rachel
Ralston; see Ralph
Ramsden; see Ramsey
Rana; see Rain
Randall; see Randolph
Randy; see Miranda
Rankin; see Randolph,
  Ransom
Ransford; see Ransom
Raoul; see Ralph,
  Rudolph
Raquel; see Rachel
Ravinia; see Ravinder
Ray; see Rachel

Rayford; see Rayburn
Raynor; see Raymond
Razel; see Raissa
Redgrave; see Redford
Redman; see Redford
Redwald; see Redford
Regis; see Reginald
Reinhard; see Reynard
Reinhold; see Reginald
Renaldo; see Ronald
Renata; see Renee
Renault; see Reginald
Renton; see Renfrew
Reynolds; see Reginald
Rhett; see Reece
Rhonda; see Rhoda
Ria; see Riva
Riba; see Rebecca
Richmond; see Richard
Rick; see Broderick
Rickie; see Patricia
Ricky; see Roderick,
  Patrick
Rina; see Regina
Riston; see Risley
Rita; see Margaret
Riva; see Rebecca
Roan; see Rogan
Robin; see Robert
Rochette; see Rochelle
Rockwell; see Rochester
Roderica; see Roderick
Roderick; see Broderick
Rodman; see Roderick,
  Rodney
Rollin; see Rudolph
Rollo; see Rudolph
Rolt; see Roland
Romana; see Romeo
Ronnie; see Veronica
Rosalyn; see Rose
Rosanna; see Rose
Rosette; see Rose
Roswald; see Ross
Rowell; see Rowan
Royal; see Roy

Royce; see Roy
Rube; see Reuben
Rubia; see Ruby
Rufford; see Rufus
Rupert; see Robert
Rurik; see Rory
Rusk; see Rush
Ruskin; see Rush
Rusty; see Russell
Rutger; see Roger
Rycroft; see Rylan
Ryton; see Rylan

Sacha; see Alexander
Sadie; see Sarah
Salvatore; see Salvador
Samara; see Samantha
Samuela; see Samuel
Sanborn; see Sanford
Sandor; see Alexander
Sandra; see Cassandra
Sandro; see Alexander
Sandy; see Cassandra,
  Alexandra
Sanson; see Samson
Santiago; see James
Sarette; see Sarah
Sarina; see Sarah
Sarita; see Sarah
Saunders; see Sanders
Savina; see Sabina
Schlomo; see Solomon
Sean; see John
Selda; see Griselda
Selden; see Selby
Selinda; see Selena
Selwin; see Selby
Sena; see Selena
Senta; see Sennett
Seosaidh; see Joseph
Serenity; see Serena
Sergei; see Serge
Seven; see Septima
Severn; see Seward
Sheba; see Bathsheba

Sheldon; see Shelley
Shelley; see Rachel
Shelton; see Shelley
Shem; see Samuel
Sherborne; see Sherman
Sherryl; see Cheryl
Sherwin; see Sherman
Shimon; see Simon
Shipton; see Shipley
Shirleen; see Shirley
Sian; see Sean
Sidwell; see Siddell
Siegfried; see Sigmund
Sigwald; see Sigrid
Sile; see Julia
Simonette; see Simone
Sinead; see Jane
Siobhan; see Judith
Sippora; see Zippora
Sissy; see Cecilia
Skip; see Seymour
Sky; see Schuyler
Sly; see Sylvester
Smits; see Smith
Somerton; see Somerset
Sonja; see Sophie
Sonny; see Orson
Stacy; see Eustace,
  Anastasia
Stanbury; see Stanley
Standish; see Stanley
Stanfield; see Stanley
Stanislav; see Stanislaus
Stanton; see Stanley
Starla; see Stella
Starling; see Stella
Stella; see Estelle
Steve; see Stephen
Stockton; see Stockley
Suki; see Susan
Sutcliff; see Sutherland
Sutton; see Sutherland
Suzette; see Susan
Swayze; see Swain
Sybilline; see Sibyl
Sydell; see Sidney

Talia; see Natalie
Tally; see Natalie
Tamika; see Tamara
Tamsin; see Thomasa,
  Tavis
Tarrant; see Terrell
Taryn; see Tara
Tasha; see Anastasia
Tatiana; see Tanya
Tavie; see Octavius
Ted; see Edmund,
  Edward
Teddy; see Edmund
Tegan; see Teague
Tennis; see Dennis
Terrell; see Thurlow
Tessa; see Theresa
Thea; see Althea
Theda; see Theodora
Theophania; see
  Theodora
Thorbert; see Thor
Thornley; see Thorne
Thornton; see Thorne
Thurman; see Thurlow
Thurston; see Thurlow
Tibalt; see Theobald
Ticia; see Letitia
Tila; see Mathilda
Tilly; see Mathilda
Tina; see Martina
Tish; see Letitia
Tito; see Robert
Tomlin; see Tomkin
Tony; see Anthony
Tori; see Victoria
Toria; see Victoria
Tova; see Tobias
Tracy; see Theresa
Tricia; see Patricia
Trixie; see Beatrice
Trudy; see Gertrude
Tuckman; see Tucker
Tyna; see Tyne
Tynan; see Tye
Tyron; see Tyrone

Ualtar; see Walter
Uberto; see Hubert
Ugo; see Hugh
Uilliam; see William
Uillioc; see Ulysses
Ulfred; see Ulric
Unice; see Eunice
Upshaw; see Upton

Valina; see Valentine
Vanna; see Vanessa
Vanora; see Vanessa
Vartan; see Varden
Vasily; see William
Verin; see Vera
Verna; see Vernon
Verne; see Vernon
Vibiana; see Vivian
Vidal; see Vida
Vilhelm; see William
Vilhelmina; see
  Wilhelmina
Vilma; see Wilhelmina
Vinnie; see Vincent
Vinson; see Vincent
Vittorio; see Victor
Viveca; see Vivian
Vladislav; see Vladimir

Wadsworth; see Wade
Wagner; see Wayne
Wainwright; see Wayne

Wakeman; see
  Wakefield
Walcott; see Alcott
Walfred; see Waldo
Wallach; see Wallace
Waller; see Walton
Ward; see Howard
Warfield; see Ward
Warton; see Ward
Warwick; see Ward
Watkins; see Watson
Watson; see Walter
Welby; see Wells
Weldon; see Wells
Welford; see Wells
Welton; see Wells
Wendeline; see Wanda
Wharton; see Wheaton
Whitey; see Whit
Whitfield; see Whit
Whitney; see Whit
Wilfred; see William
Wilkie; see William
Wilma; see
  Wilhelmina
Wilson; see William
Wilton; see William
Windsor; see Winslow
Winifred; see Frieda
Witton; see Witt
Wolcott; see Wolfgang
Woodruff; see Woodrow
Wyeth; see Wyatt
Wynton; see Winslow

Xaviera; see Xavier

Yael; see Yale
Yakov; see Jacob
Yedidiyah; see Jedediah
Yesus; see Jesus
Yetta; see Yedda
Yirmeyah; see Jeremiah
Yitzchak; see Isaac
Ymelda; see Imelda
Ynes; see Agnes
Ynez; see Agnes
Yohel; see Joel
Yolanda; see Violet
Yonas; see Jonas
Yorick; see York
Yoseph; see Joseph
Yseult; see Isolda
Yvette; see Yves
Yvonne; see Yves

Zach; see Isaac
Zane; see John
Zarah; see Sarah
Zelda; see Griselda
Zenina; see Zenobia
Zerlinda; see Zara
Ziggy; see Sigmund
Zilvia; see Sylvia
Zoranna; see Zora
Zorina; see Zora
Zsa Zsa; see Susan